DUAL DIASPORA

McGill-Queen's Azrieli Institute of Israel Studies Series

Books in the McGill-Queen's Azrieli Institute of Israel Studies Series reflect the disciplinary and methodological diversity that characterizes the field of Israel studies. Accordingly, the editorial board welcomes proposals for books that report on original research from all areas of scholarly inquiry related to the study of modern Israel, including fine arts, history, literature, translation studies, sociology, political science, law, religious studies, and beyond. The series, which is committed to academic excellence, encompasses comparative works that situate Israel in broader international and cross-national frameworks and works that apply a critical lens.

1 Fictions of Gender
Women, Femininity, and the Zionist Imagination
Orian Zakai

2 Settler-Indigeneity in the West Bank
Edited by Rachel Z. Feldman and Ian McGonigle

3 Created in the Image?
Holocaust Perpetrators in Israeli Fiction
Or Rogovin

4 Dual Diaspora
Post-Soviet Culture in Search of Israeli Identity
Alex Moshkin

DUAL DIASPORA

Post-Soviet Culture in Search of Israeli Identity

ALEX MOSHKIN

McGill-Queen's University Press
Montreal & Kingston • London • Chicago

ISBN 978-0-2280-2455-2 (paper)
ISBN 978-0-2280-2538-2 (ePDF)
ISBN 978-0-2280-2539-9 (ePUB)

Legal deposit third quarter 2025
Bibliothèque et Archives nationales du Québec

Printed in Canada on acid-free paper that is 100% ancient-forest-free, containing 100% sustainable, recycled fibre, and processed chlorine-free.

This book has been published with the help of a grant from the Federation for the Humanities and Social Sciences, through the Awards to Scholarly Publications Program, using funds provided by the Social Sciences and Humanities Research Council of Canada.

Funded by the Government of Canada | Financé par le gouvernement du Canada | Canada

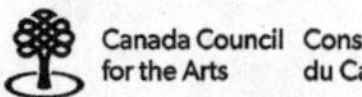

We acknowledge the support of the Canada Council for the Arts.
Nous remercions le Conseil des arts du Canada de son soutien.

McGill-Queen's University Press in Montreal is on land which long served as a site of meeting and exchange amongst Indigenous Peoples, including the Haudenosaunee and Anishinabeg nations. In Kingston it is situated on the territory of the Haudenosaunee and Anishinaabek. We acknowledge and thank the diverse Indigenous Peoples whose footsteps have marked these territories on which peoples of the world now gather.

Library and Archives Canada Cataloguing in Publication

Title: Dual diaspora : post-soviet culture in search of Israeli identity / Alex Moshkin.
Names: Moshkin, Alex, author.
Description: Series statement: McGill-Queen's Azrieli Institute of Israel Studies series ; 4 | Includes bibliographical references and index.
Identifiers: Canadiana (print) 20250139936 | Canadiana (ebook) 20250140039 | ISBN 9780228024552 (paper) | ISBN 9780228025399 (EPUB) | ISBN 9780228025382 (PDF)
Subjects: LCSH: Jews, Russian—Israel—Ethnic identity. | LCSH: Jews, Russian—Israel—Intellectual life. | LCSH: Jews, Russian—Israel—Social life and customs. | LCSH: Immigrants—Israel. | LCSH: Russia (Federation)—Emigration and immigration. | LCSH: Israel—Emigration and immigration.
Classification: LCC DS113.8.R87 M67 2025 | DDC 305.892/4047—dc23

This book was designed and typeset by studio oneonone in Minion 11/14.
Copyediting by Alicia Hibbert.

McGill-Queen's University Press
Suite 1720, 1010 Sherbrooke St West, Montreal, QC, H3A 2R7

Authorized safety representative in the EU: Mare Nostrum Group BV, Mauritskade 21D, 1091 GC Amsterdam, the Netherlands, gpsr@mare-nostrum.co.uk

Contents

Figures

Acknowledgments

As I prepare to release this book into the world, I find myself reflecting on the journey that brought it to life. Writing this book has been a journey of its own – an odyssey through the labyrinths of academic bureaucracy, filled with existential crises and the occasional footnote-induced meltdown. Along the way, I've been fortunate to have the support and guidance of incredible friends, colleagues, and mentors who helped steer me through the chaos.

First and foremost, I want to express my deepest gratitude to Kevin M.F. Platt, the quintessential academic Stakhanovite, who tirelessly dedicated countless hours to unravelling my tangled ideas and shaping this book into a coherent whole. Without his guidance, this work might have ended up as a collection of scattered musings on the relative merits of potato varieties in Eastern Europe. Looking back, I realize there were many other lessons I should have picked up from him as well – like how to barbecue fish, bake a mulberry galette, and mix a killer cocktail.

I am also deeply thankful to Benjamin Nathans and Ann Komaromi for their invaluable guidance during my PhD at Penn and postdoc at UofT. Ben's encyclopedic knowledge of East European and Jewish cultures was as boundless as the Siberian steppes, and his suggestion to structure the book thematically proved to be a real game-changer. Ann's support throughout my job market journey felt like having a personal career coach, even if my interview skills sometimes left hiring committees more puzzled than impressed. Our regular conversations not only enriched this book but also helped keep me sane during the pandemic.

To the many scholars who generously offered their advice, feedback, and the occasional reality check: your contributions have been invaluable. Special thanks to Sasha Senderovich and Miriam Finkelstein for plotting the revolution with me, even if our grand schemes didn't exactly set the world ablaze. I'm also grateful to Ilya Vinitsky, Maggie Levantovskaya, Mikhail Krutikov, Olga Gershenson, Rossen Djagalov, Amelia Glaser, Anna Shternshis, Karolina Krasuska, Timothy Corrigan, Anna Prashizky, Stephanie Sandler, Eliot Borenstein, and Kathryn Hellerstein for being generous interlocutors and producing such inspiring scholarship.

A special thanks to Larissa Remennick, who not only provided incisive feedback but also took the time to discuss my work during my visits to Israel. And to STAB (School of Theory and Activism) in Bishkek, thank you for adopting me as a fellow during my stay in Kyrgyzstan. The fellowship, "Queer Theory, Science Fiction, and Contemporary Art," was a delightful cocktail of intellectual rigour and creative thinking, and drinking it significantly enriched this book. Lastly, I'm grateful to the Frankel Institute at the University of Michigan and the Frankel Institute fellows (Adriana X. Jacobs, Maya Barzilai, Jeffrey Veidlinger, Naomi Seidman, Anita Norich, Roni Mazal, Anna Elena Torres, Joshua Miller, and others) for making it possible to pay rent during the Covid apocalypse, and for giving me the much-needed space to balance academic work and parental responsibilities.

I'm deeply grateful to the intellectual community I'm now fortunate to simply call friends, who generously shared their knowledge, time, and camaraderie while I was writing this book. The lively conversations we had, whether on campus or over a beer, were the lifeblood of this work. A special shoutout to my comrades-in-arms: Pavel Khazanov, Julia Kolchinsky Dasbach, Alison Howard, Joe Liew, Maya Vinokour, Dragana Obradovic, Georgy Mamedov, Wojciech Tworek, Bradley Gorski, Iuliia Skubytska, Sonia Gollance, Olga Breininger-Umetayeva, Brett Winestock, and many others. I'm also deeply thankful to my wonderful colleagues at Koç: Nazmi Ağıl, C. Ceyhun Arslan, Meliz Ergin, Şima İmşir, Sooyong Kim, Mehmet Fatih Uslu, and Mert Bahadir Reisoğlu. Working with you was a real pleasure, and I look forward to meeting you at Kav on my next visit. Special thanks to Verena Hutter, who helped me wage the war against definite and indefinite articles in the manuscript.

I should also thank Erdoğan for his stellar mismanagement of the country's economy, which gave me the final push out of academia. A hearty thanks to Scott Snelleman and Ruth Taylor, who fished me out and whisked me away to Luxembourg – the last stop on my academic journey and probably of my cosmopolitan rootlessness. Although teaching at an international school has its challenges, the support of my outstanding colleagues in Michel Lucius's English department, as well as the school at large, has made it infinitely more manageable.

I am also deeply grateful to my sister, Julia Salant, and my parents, Olga and Sergei Moshkin, for their unconditional love and support. Your brave decision to immigrate to Israel after the collapse of the Soviet Union, and later to Canada in the early 2000s, is the reason this book exists in its present form.

Finally, to Luiza Moshkin, the true hero of this story. Without your love, patience, and gentle reminders that life is more than academia, I wouldn't have made it to the finish line. You and Adam make coming home the best part of every day.

DUAL DIASPORA

Figure 0.1
Zoya Cherkassky-Nnadi, *New Victims*, 2016,
oil on linen, 140 × 230 cm.

INTRODUCTION

Russian-Speaking Jews in Israel

An Establishing Shot

In 2016, Israeli artist Zoya Cherkassky-Nnadi unveiled a large-scale painting, *New Victims*, that visually recalls her family's first moments in Israel in 1991. At first glance, this autobiographical painting resembles a typical Zionist snapshot from Israeli and Western newspapers of the Cold War era (or shortly thereafter), depicting the triumphal arrival of Soviet Jews to their ancestral homeland. In this sense, this is an updated version of the prototypical image of Jewish migrants and pilgrims disembarking from boats and kissing the Holy Land, or a modern retelling of the Exodus story, in which Jews escape from turmoil in the diaspora and find refuge in the land of their ancestors. The oversaturation of Israel's national ideology on the canvas, expressed in the visual dominance of blue and white (Israel's national colours), the patriotically painted EL AL plane, and the cheerful immigration official handing out pocket-size Israeli flags to the newcomers, further underscores the Zionist framing of the moment. These concerted ideological gestures all convey the same message to the newcomers – that they have arrived home.

However, there are cracks in such a simplistic nationalist interpretation of the painting. We may notice, for instance, the stony and world-weary expressions of the adults, visibly apprehensive about the Promised Land that awaits at the end of the airstair. Or the heavy winter clothes of the newcomers, fit for harsh Soviet winters but utterly useless in Israel's Mediterranean climate. Indeed, the immigrants' hefty jackets and winter hats clash with the palm trees in the background and the short sleeves of the immigration official, establishing a stark contrast between the immigrants and their new environment. With these moments of dramatic irony, Cherkassky-Nnadi undercuts a straightforward Israeli narrative of *aliyah* that portrays immigration to Israel as a clear-cut homecoming.[1] Instead, the painting draws attention to bewilderment, hesitation, and dissonance between expectation and reality. "Is this really our new home," the stunned newcomers might be thinking, "or have we just become doubly alienated?" From the foresight of the future, the title of the painting *New Victims* adjudicates this question by reifying the future not yet known – a future of mistreatment, marginalization, and broken dreams. Ultimately, instead of presenting immigration to Israel as a story of homecoming and reunification, the title of the painting, *New Victims*, implies it is a cyclical narrative of victimization and struggle.

On the pages of this book, I follow this population, both real and imagined, as they step off the airplane, place the souvenir flag in their pocket, and leave the air-conditioned space of the Ben Gurion Airport to discover the brave new world of Israeli reality – the intense heat, unfamiliar language, unstable military situation, and the cut-throat logic of market capitalism. The book pays particular attention to the thorny encounter of the newcomers with Israeli society, aptly represented by the encroaching figure of the immigration official who hails the newcomers, in a gesture of Althusserian interpellation, into a ready-made identification by handing them an Israeli flag, the symbol of the country's national identity.[2] How will the newcomers respond to this encounter with Israeli ideology? Will they eagerly shed their old skins along with their heavy Soviet winter clothes and reinvent themselves as "full-fledged" Jews and Israelis? Or, fed up with compulsory ideology in their old country, will they tacitly rebel by throwing the Israeli flag in the nearest garbage bin at Ben Gurion Airport? Furthermore, how might gender, class, and age play a role in shaping their responses? Focusing primarily on works of literature, film, and visual art, the following chapters will chart the diverse journeys of Soviet-born immigrants as they rebuild their lives in Israel, beginning with their arrival in the late 1980s and concluding in the present day with the recent influx of immigrants from Ukraine and Russia, who have sought refuge from war in Ukraine and political crackdowns in Russia only to find themselves caught in the fallout of the war in Gaza.

Russophone-Jewish Culture in Motion: On the Eve of the Soviet Collapse

With the opening of Soviet borders in 1989 and the eventual collapse of the USSR in 1991, the situation of Russophone people and culture changed dramatically. When Soviet citizens emigrated during the Cold War, they knew that they were leaving permanently, never to return. They could not retain apartments or passports and were only allowed to take one small suitcase apiece for their personal belongings. For those who departed the USSR from 1960 to 1988, emigration was often experienced as a form of death – an ultimate separation from one's friends and family, native land, and the Russian tongue. The blow fell heaviest on writers, for whom departure resulted in a formidable barrier between them and their readers in the form of patrolled borders, Soviet censorship, and the tense East-West geopolitical rivalry of the Cold War. As a result, Soviet émigré authors found themselves not only in geographic but also in linguistic exile. Even Vladimir Nabokov, one of the only émigré writers to successfully switch from Russian to English, was deeply marked by this predicament. "My private tragedy," he writes, "is that I had to abandon my natural language, my natural idiom, my rich, infinitely rich and docile Russian tongue, for a second-rate brand of English."[3] Joseph Brodsky, a Nobel laureate exiled from the Soviet Union to the United States, similarly envisions an émigré writer "as a dog or a man, hurtled into outer space in a capsule."[4] Brodsky goes on to reveal that this capsule represents the writer's mother tongue, which "gravitates not earthward but outward in space."[5] These melancholic statements, delivered in perfect English by highly accomplished writers, magnify the challenging plight of most Russophone émigré writers who, unlike Nabokov or Brodsky, were unable to transition to English, German, or Hebrew as languages of their literary expression and therefore lived in relative obscurity within their host countries after immigration.[6]

However, it is important to emphasize that not all émigré writers were aligned in sensibility with Nabokov and Brodsky's exilic pessimism. Many of them, particularly those of Jewish origin who settled in Israel in the 1970s and 1980s, professed no attachment to the Soviet Union as a motherland. This stance is effectively captured by the Hebrew-language slogan used during the Cold War–era campaign advocating for the emigration rights of Soviet Jewry: "Mother Russia: I wish we were orphans" (*ima russiya: hal'vai hayinu yetomim*). In contrast to prominent émigré writers like Ivan Bunin, Nabokov, and Brodsky, who made their homes in Europe and North America, Jewish authors who moved from the USSR to Israel actively challenged the core notions of the Russian émigré narrative. They rejected the idea of Russia as a lost homeland and all other places as sites of disorienting diaspora. Instead, they embraced a Jewish/Zionist metanarrative that presents Jewish migration to Israel as a "homecoming," while portraying life elsewhere in a "lachrymose" key as miserable, dangerous, and threatening death and destruction.[7] Through this shift, Soviet-Jewish émigré writers introduced a fresh perspective in global Russophone literature, placing Israel at its centre and turning away from all other territories as peripheral and insignificant.

In his 1991 lecture, "Russophone Literature in Israel," poet Mikhail Gendelev addressed the distinctiveness of Russophone literature in Israel by highlighting the contrast between Russian and Jewish diasporic narratives. "In contrast to the Russian emigration, which is in exile," Gendelev writes, "we are located in our homeland, and this is our main distinction. Our literature is created without orientation toward Russian realities and a Russian reader; conversely, it addresses Russophone-Israeli readers who live in the realities of a different culture. We describe Israeli reality, drawing from our Israeli or Jewish experience, using a language in which (due to a variety of circumstances) we are more proficient, and knowing that we are being read."[8] Gendelev's manifesto-like lecture, delivered in Jerusalem at the time of the dissolution of the Soviet Union and the opening of borders, grapples with the question of the future of Russophone-Israeli literature and identity, made particularly pressing by the influx of Soviet Jews to Israel after 1989. With a distinctive sense of triumph and a healthy dose of chutzpah, Gendelev boldly asserts that the Soviet Union's "Jewish Question" has finally been solved. All the obstacles that Jews faced in the USSR – the inability to practice Judaism, create Jewish culture, and choose where to live – had been rendered obsolete by the crumbling of the Iron Curtain and the newfound freedom to move to Israel. Gendelev concludes by emphasizing the indigenous status of Russophone authors in Israel, highlighting their Jewishness/Israeliness, thereby foregrounding their majoritarian – as opposed to minoritarian/immigrant – status within the country.

In line with Gendelev's conceptions, the one million Russian-speaking Jews who arrived in Israel after 1989, many of whom had previously faced discrimination, antisemitism, and even Gulag imprisonment, believed they were coming home. They were certain of their Jewish identity, a fact officially inscribed in their Soviet passports and one their Soviet neighbours never let them forget.[9] These migrants expected a grand reunion with their Jewish brethren, with the Cold War Soviet Jewry movement slogan "Let My People Go!" echoing in their ears and images before their eyes from the idyllic brochures of the Jewish Agency representatives that showed the bright future that ostensibly awaited them in the Middle East. Regrettably, the reunion never happened. Instead, the newcomers discovered that the triumphant rhetoric of "homecoming" conceals a simple fact that *aliyah* to Israel is not much different from migration to any other place. They still had to learn how to navigate a new country and an unfamiliar language – and to wade through poverty, unemployment, loneliness, and culture shock. On top of this, their heightened expectations magnified their sense of disillusionment, depriving them of the myth they had cherished – the myth of belonging.

The newcomers were not the only ones left disappointed. *Sabras* (native-born Israelis), writes literary scholar Elana Gomel, who were raised on the novels of Tolstoy and Dostoyevsky, expected the newcomers to be like the characters in *Anna Karenina* and *The Brothers Karamazov*, possessing a "mysterious Russian soul" and "emotional identification with the persecuted and the oppressed."[10] Instead, they found "hardened, cynical, arrogant people whose empathy extended no further than tribal loyalty."[11] Similarly, Larissa Remennick admits that the 1990s newcomers were not "the 'historic gift' of one million Zionist Jews" that Israel has hoped to receive.[12] Contrary to national mythologies, this new wave of immigrants profoundly differed from the ideologically motivated migrants of the 1970s from the USSR, who chose Israel out of Zionist convictions and not for lack of other options.[13] Rather, the 1990s arrivals were predominantly driven by push factors – the crumbling of the Soviet economy, the collapse of the USSR, the rise of popular antisemitism, the Chernobyl nuclear disaster – and by the reality that Israel was the only option available to them, after the United States and Canada closed their doors.[14]

Consequently, many newcomers landed in Israel without much knowledge of Jewish history, culture, and religion. After a century of both voluntary and enforced acculturation in the USSR, Russophone newcomers met a formidable barrier to recognition as Jews in the host society. Many *sabras* were shocked to learn that over 300,000 newcomers were deemed non-Jewish by Israel's religious authorities.[15] Others were dismayed by the newcomers' habit of celebrating Novyi God (New Year's Eve, in Russian), a secular Soviet holiday embraced by Jews, Christians, Muslims, and atheists, but which appeared suspiciously similar to Christmas in the eyes of the Hebrew speakers.[16] Many others were outraged by the proliferation of stores selling non-kosher products that mushroomed in towns with a substantial Soviet-born population. These factors collectively led to a negative perception among the wider Israeli populace of post-Soviet immigrants as inauthentic Jews who, it was imagined, had falsified their identity for immigration purposes. As a result, the "Jewishness" of Russian-speaking émigrés was regularly subject to doubt and scrutiny, fating this population to remain forever suspended between two diasporic conditions. One of Larisa Fialkova's respondents succinctly captures this dilemma: "In Russia I was a Jew, now in Israel I became a Russian."[17]

The frequent misfire of the diasporic return to Israel by Russian-speaking Jews during the 1990s and 2000s became a moment of crystallization of their "dual" identity. Members of this community realized that being a Jew and a Soviet Jew were, in some ways, cognate categories, yet in other ways completely distinct. Reflecting the complexity and variability of this situation, *Dual Diaspora: Post-Soviet Culture in Search of Israeli Identity* refocuses the question of post-Soviet Jewish culture and identity by steering clear of simplistic explanatory mechanisms that conceive "Russianness" and "Jewishness" as unchanging categories across time, space, and people. Instead, I argue that in the context of social pressure and hostility toward a community that ultimately little resembled the inspiring portraits of Soviet-Jewish dissidents (individuals who opposed the Soviet government, often at personal risk) and refuseniks (Jewish individuals denied exit visas by Soviet authorities) that circulated in the West and Israel during the 1970s and 1980s, Israel's Russophone cultural producers created literature, cinema, and visual art as a way to re-accentuate the Jewish component of their ostensibly "diasporic" identities and as a mechanism to frame their complex cultural legacies in the new Israeli reality. Discovering that Israeli society had no place for them, or that they did not fit in the place that had been prepared for them, Russophone émigrés in the 1990s and 2000s created their own niche using one of the only means available: cultural productions.

The book captures diverse cultural responses to the challenging process of migration and the difficulty of finding one's footing in a new society. Some, like the writer Alexander Goldshtein, adopted a defensive stance against the local population, portraying them in an orientalist key as inferior and uncultured, effectively building a wall separating "Russian Street" from the rest of Israel. Others, like the renowned refusenik Natan Sharansky, embraced the project of retroactively adopting a Jewish identity in the Israeli sense by aligning his complex past and identity in the Soviet Union with the dominant narrative of Jewish diasporic experience within Israeli society, as depicted in his books. Still others, such as the bestselling writer Dina Rubina, challenged the prevalent perception of the Russophone community in Israel as insufficiently Jewish by infusing her fictional world with elements of Judaism and Jewish religious discourse, along with nationalist politics. Finally, artist Zoya Cherkassky-Nnadi, who represents a younger generation of Russophone Israelis, embraced a cosmopolitan subject position that eschewed a fixed connection to territory and cultural boundedness as a way of breaking loose from both Israel's and Russia's national modes of identification and from the constraints of local and national politics.

Dual Diaspora

The situation of Russian-speaking Jews in Israel, suspended between two contrasting narratives of diaspora, is *sui generis*. On the one hand, as a linguistically and culturally Russified population, this community is part of the global Russophone diaspora, formed through numerous waves of emigration from the USSR.[18] Participants in this conception of cultural geography place Russia at the core of global Russian-language culture, relegating all other regions to a secondary status as sites of emigration. On the other hand, post-Soviet Jewish migration to Israel has also been seen as part of the "ingathering of the Jewish exiles" (*kibbutz galuyot*) in the Land of Israel – symbolizing the end of their dispersion in the Jewish diaspora.[19] Following Zionist spatial and temporal divisions, this viewpoint aligns post-Soviet migration with the prototypical return of the Jewish people to their ancestral home. Here, Israel assumes the role of the epicentre of the Jewish world, rendering all other territories marginal and insignificant.

The presence of these conflicting meanings and identifications for the same trajectory of ex-Soviet Jewish émigrés points to the existence of multiple centres in the affective geography of this population. This unique situation of "dual diaspora" has fundamental implications that extend beyond the fields of Russian and Jewish Studies. If, as argued by Rogers Brubaker, the clear-cut opposition of "exile" and "homeland" constitutes a foundation for most theories of diaspora, the simultaneous emotional attachments of Russophone Jews to their various "home" and "host" nations indicate a breakdown of the logic of diaspora.[20] Instead of being bound to just one place, Russian-speaking Jews and their cultural production chart multiple paths of belonging, displacement, and homecoming that transcend the centre-periphery binary.

From a methodological standpoint, the case of ex-Soviet Israelis is illuminating because it exposes the inadequacies of what André Levy wryly calls the "solar system model" of diaspora theories, where diasporic communities are imagined as "satellites circulating around their cherished 'mother/father sun' throughout history."[21] The problem with this conceptualization is that it affords individuals only a single cultural/national identity and presumes as axiomatic the assignment of "homeland" and "diaspora." Embracing James Clifford's call to prioritize "routes" over "roots" and Jahan Ramazani's plea to "transnationalize" the study of literature, my book navigates the simultaneous, conflicting, and overlapping emotional attachments of post-Soviet Jews to Israel and sites within the former USSR in order to describe the cultural production of a "dual diaspora," grappling with the uneasy interplay of nostalgia, belonging, and alienation in works that defy conventional diasporic binaries.[22] The fluid coordinates of "dual diaspora" transcend the rigid logic of nationalism, which perceives the nation as "the basic axiom of identity and belonging," and instead create room for nuanced expressions of cultural and national self-fashioning and manoeuvrable identity.[23]

The opening scene of *I vozvraschaetsia veter* (*And the Wind Returns*, 1991), an autobiographical essay film by Soviet-born Israeli director Mikhail Kalik, aptly captures the ambivalence inherent in the concept of "dual diaspora."[24] This film, produced in the same year Gendelev delivered his lecture in Jerusalem, presents a conflicted vision of Soviet-Jewish history and identity. Its opening sequence shows the Ben Gurion Airport in Israel, where a shaky, hand-held camera frames the Soviet-born filmmaker's departure to Moscow after eighteen years in Jerusalem. How are we to understand this scene? Is the filmmaker coming back to his homeland – the land of his birth, youth, and creative energy? Or, alternatively, is this a triumphant journey of a proud Israeli returning to make a cautionary film about the oppression of Jews in the USSR? And what is the significance of the shaky camera: does it tremble from anticipation, dread, or simply the decrepitude of the filmmaker's advanced age? Instead of yielding a conclusive interpretation, *The Wind* presents a simultaneous blend of nostalgia and resentment, belonging and displacement, loss and triumph, capturing what the Israeli poet Leah Goldberg famously calls "the heartache of two homelands" and what I term the condition of dual diaspora.

Cultural Identity

The dual diaspora is not limited to the cultural production of post-Soviet Jews in Israel. It also runs through the vestibules of their identities. Two scholarly approaches dominate the scholarship on the cultural identity and social experience of Russian-speaking Jews. First, there are scholars – mostly working in Jewish studies – who ascribe a lamentable insufficiency of authentic Jewish identity to post-Soviet Jews. These scholars characterize the USSR as the graveyard of Jewish cultural life and tradition and portray Soviet and post-Soviet Jews as a community in decline – an ostracized, deracinated, and assimilated population that, in the course of the Soviet century, lost the authentic Jewish culture of its ancestors. Zvi Gitelman is a prominent advocate of this perspective, arguing that the identity of Soviet and post-Soviet Jews became "thin" and "disaggregated" because, over the course of the Soviet century, it was not grounded in Jewish languages, religious practices, and Jewish customs.[25] Building on Gitelman's research, Judith Kornblatt demonstrates how a "biological" understanding of Jewishness allowed some Jews from the USSR to convert to Orthodox Christianity without feeling that they were forsaking their Jewishness and leaving the tribe.[26] In a reflexive mode, Kornblatt argues that the central paradox of her study is that the majority of Soviet Jews who have undergone conversion felt "*more*, not less Jewish after their Baptism."[27] Lastly, Yaacov Ro'i asserts that even migration to Israel was unable to transform Soviet prodigal sons and daughters back into full-fledged Jews.[28] He concludes: "While the substance of Soviet Jewish thin culture has inevitably changed with immigration to Israel, many of its social and conceptual features have remained the same."[29] Despite distinctions among these scholars, all three operate within a single paradigm, illustrating how, as a community, Soviet Jews were progressively divorced from a presumed authentic Jewishness.

On the other hand, there are scholars – mostly active in Slavic Studies – who marshal a diametrically opposed vision of Soviet and post-Soviet Jewry. Their body of work, which places the question of a variable Jewish identity at the centre of scholarly inquiry, emerges as a counterweight to the paradigm of "thin" and "disaggregated" identity. In the introduction to the *Anthology of Jewish-Russian Literature*, for instance, Maxim Shrayer frames his project as a form of recovery of "Jewish themes" and a re-reading of Jewish-Russian literary works that at first glance contain "only superficially Jewish references."[30] Similarly, Marat Grinberg's recent monograph, *The Soviet Jewish Bookshelf*, argues that the bedrock of Soviet-Jewish identity should not be sought in religious practices, Jewish languages, or Jewish customs. Instead, it can be more readily discovered, quite literally, on their bookshelf. "As Jewish readers," Grinberg writes, "Soviet Jews operated both within the official culture and cautiously, and at times combatively, outside and against it, maintaining a distinct a priori sense of their Jewish difference and subjectivity: ethnic and nationalist, cultural and existential, reinforced and imbued with meaningful content through what and how they read."[31] Finally, Maya Balakirsky Katz's research draws attention to how animation artists in the USSR employed Aesopian techniques to express their unique Jewish identities, smuggling them into their cartoons under the watchful eyes of the censors.[32] Ultimately, the common thread that runs through this research is that the Jewish identity of Russian-speaking Jews was not disaggregated or lost during the Soviet era. Rather, their sense of Jewish difference was encoded in innovative ways within literature and culture, offering a means to evade the punitive gaze of Soviet censorship and waves of discrimination.

Dual Diaspora pushes back both against a surface reading of Russian-speaking Jews as devoid of traditional, historical, and religious "content," and against contrasting claims that this community sustained resilient ties to Jewish history and culture throughout the Soviet era. Ultimately, the book repudiates the constraining "either-or" framework that reifies Russophone and Jewish cultures and identities into rigid, mutually exclusive entities engaged in a zero-sum contest. As Sasha Senderovich rightly notes, "the assumed opposition between 'Russian' as a linguistic medium and literary tradition and 'Jewish' as an enduring ethno-religious identity category" reduces Russian-Jewish literature and identity to a "complicated, continuous balancing act," forever locked in a master-slave struggle for dominance and survival.[33] Instead, this book demonstrates that Russophone-Jewish culture is a dynamic entity, greater than the sum of its parts, a relentless hybrid that, like all human culture, continuously reinvents itself through the fusion of past and present. The categorical differentiation between Russophone and Jewish cultural worlds accounts poorly not only for contemporary Russophone-Israeli Jews in all their multiplicity of self-fashioning, but also for the Soviet reality from which they emerged, where intermarriage and cultural hybridity were common practices and Jewishness coexisted with Russification, Soviet-style modernization and assimilation.[34]

A longue durée perspective can help explain how the cross-pollination of Russian and Jewish cultural worlds came into being. As shown by a number of scholars, Russian culture and higher education were the main mechanisms for social and geographic mobility for Jews both in the Russian Empire and the Soviet Union.[35] Yuri Slezkine describes the overlap between higher education and Russian-Jewish identity as conversion to the "Pushkin faith," while Julia Lerner calls this an "ethnic script" that determines the trajectory of Jewish history in the former USSR.[36] Regardless of terminology used, these scholars emphasize how investing in education and embracing Russian and world culture has been a distinct (minoritarian) strategy of Jewish advancement over the last two centuries. For many Jews – particularly those who migrated from the Pale of Settlement (the territory in Imperial Russia where Jews were legally required to reside) to the urban centres of the Russian Empire, thereby increasing their chances of surviving World War II and the Holocaust – Jewish identity came to be expressed in a manner aligned with the prevailing social conventions of the empire. This manifested through active assimilation into Russian and European culture and a reduced emphasis on Jewish rituals, languages, or religious practices. These dynamics fostered a symbiotic relationship between Russian and Jewish cultural worlds, where being Jewish meant a deep familiarity with Pushkin's works, membership in the intelligentsia, participation in Soviet chess clubs, etc., yet also harboured a fraught connection to one's heritage, often marked by a sense of alienation from the rituals, prayers, and language traditionally associated with Jewish identity.[37]

This configuration became especially pertinent after immigration to Israel, when acculturated Soviet Jews realized that their identity did not conform to the dominant definition of Jewishness in their new social environment. The irony is that Soviet-born Jews became alienated from their Jewishness not only in the USSR but also in Israel. Back in the Soviet Union, many Jews had come to view Russian and world culture as a foundation of Jewishness – as the essence of being for "people of the book." However, upon arriving in Israel, generations nurtured on Pushkin and Tolstoy suddenly confronted the need to recalibrate, if not entirely discard, this concept of Jewishness. In either scenario, this group of highly educated people was called on to reject the cultural riches that they thought comprised their identity, their sacred goods, and that which made them Jewish in the first place.

How did this group of highly educated individuals and proud members of the intelligentsia respond? As we will see, they created an impressive range of cultural works that sought to rearticulate the boundaries of cultural and national belonging and to forge new communal identities in sync with both Israeli society and their Soviet-Russian legacies. In a sense, this "hydraulic" account of political expression – tapping into culture as a means of expression of political ideas and energies because no other outlet is available – has been a cornerstone of Russian intelligentsia life and Russian-language literature and culture since the 1800s. This brings us back to the paradox of the *Dual Diaspora*. On the one hand, post-Soviet immigrants forged literary and visual works to find their footing in their new society and to emphasize their belonging to the Jewish-Israeli majority. On the other hand, the form and shape of this cultural production suggest that the newcomers constructed their Jewish/Israeli identities with the cultural tools available to them as members of the Soviet intelligentsia, bringing into view in a new way the "dual" nature of Russophone-Jewish cultural identities.

Life in Israel

Since 1989, around one million ex-Soviet Jews have made Israel their home, increasing the nation's Jewish population by a remarkable 20 per cent. This surge builds upon the significant influx of 165,000 émigrés from the Soviet Union who arrived during the 1970s and 1980s. Today, it is nearly impossible to imagine Israeli culture and society without the contribution of "the Russians" (*ha-rusim*), as they are commonly known in Israel, even though only one-third of former Soviet Jewish immigrants came to Israel from Russia proper – another third arrived from Ukraine, and the rest from Belarus and other republics. The Russian language can be heard everywhere – on public transportation, on beaches, in synagogues, and even in parliament – becoming Israel's unofficial third language, after Hebrew and Arabic (which was demoted in 2019 and is no longer an official language of Israel). Notably, ex-Soviet software engineers played a pivotal role in the meteoric rise of the hi-tech industry in Israel during the 1990s and 2000s. Coaches and athletes with distinct Russian accents are securing the lion's share of Israel's gold, silver, and bronze medals in the Olympic Games. In the realm of culture, writers and artists originating from the USSR are shaping Israel's Hebrew-language literature, cinema, theatre, visual art, and music. In short, this massive wave of migration has profoundly transformed the country's social, cultural, economic, and political landscapes, as the title of a book by the journalist Lili Galili and politician Roman Bronfman – *The Million That Changed the Middle East* (2013) – attests.[38]

In addition to shaping the Israeli mainstream, post-Soviet immigrants have been instrumental in "diasporizing" Israel by demanding recognition of their distinct linguistic, cultural, and religious diversity. In contrast to previous waves of Jewish migration, post-Soviet Jews were the first group to proudly refuse to throw themselves into Israel's infamous "melting pot," which expected them (as the violent metaphor goes) to melt away difference in order to become fully integrated Israelis.[39] To borrow Nelly Gutina's wry words: "As one enters into the national home, it is customary to leave one's baggage by the door or, better yet, in the trash heap. Rejection of one's previous language, culture, and identification has been prerequisite for joining the Israeli mainstream … When we arrived in Israel the country was already built yet, in our opinion, it was in desperate need of reconstruction [*perestroika*]."[40] Driven by initial disappointment with Israeli culture and society and a desire to preserve their distinct cultural identity, these newcomers went on to forge an alternative cultural and social infrastructure in the Soviet image (or perhaps, the Israeli post-Soviet image), consisting of Russian-language bookstores, publishing houses, newspapers, theatres, ethnic restaurants, external educational initiatives, non-kosher markets, television channels, and even the establishment of a Union of Russophone Writers of Israel. These cultural and social institutions became important platforms for the expression of shared identities among Russophone Jews.

Finally, Russophone Israelis achieved success not only within or in parallel to the Israeli mainstream, but also beyond the borders of the country. The collapse of the USSR brought new opportunities to extraterritorial Russian-language writers, filmmakers, and artists. Through virtual connectivity, integrated book markets, and the mechanisms of global capitalism, Russophone writers in Israel were, through a twist of technological destiny, able to reach millions of potential readers, confidently transcending national boundaries that had been virtually impenetrable just a few years earlier. The case of Dina Rubina illustrates this. Despite being one of Russia's bestselling and most renowned authors, whose books have been published in editions of hundreds of thousands of copies, she lives in relative obscurity among the Hebrew-speaking population of Israel, and her novels remain untranslated into Hebrew. How do we square this circle? In his analysis of Rubina's first bestseller, *Here Comes the Messiah!*, Kevin M.F. Platt argues that it is precisely her "distant" location in Israel and the colourful – and often orientalist – content of her fiction that cemented her success and reputation both in Russia and across the Russophone world. How? By effectively leveraging her "extraterritoriality" as a resource within the globalizing Russophone cultural sphere, the book immerses its readers in "an ethnographic journey through Israel's mosaic of eastern peculiarities."[41] The forces of globalization and literary worldmaking enabled Rubina to sustain her career as a writer and forge transnational connections spanning Russia, Israel, and the world, all while residing in her segregated home of Ma'aleh Adumim in a West Bank settlement.[42]

The case of Rubina notwithstanding, the overarching narrative of mobility, whether within or outside Israel, falls short of accurately portraying the experiences of the majority of post-Soviet cultural producers in Israel. For every successful writer and artist, including the bestselling Dina Rubina, the cosmopolitan Linor Goralik, and the trailblazing Zoya Cherkassky-Nnadi, who managed to accumulate economic and cultural capital in Russia and the West, there are hundreds of unsuccessful ones, who self-publish their works and are left with stacks of unsold hard copies in their homes, peddling or gifting their books to friends and neighbours or, more recently, selling them online, often for a merely symbolic fee. In light of this, Olga Gershenson and David Shneer's observation that "post Soviet Jews, who often maintain multiple passports, multiple homes, and multiple languages, make us re-think the meaning of homeland and diaspora" is only partially accurate.[43] While these theorists identify the major contrast between post-Soviet era and the earlier Cold War period, the transnational reality of economic and social mobility perhaps applies to a lesser degree to Israel's Soviet-born cultural producers.

The case of Ilya Bokshtein is illustrative. Bokshtein, a mystical experimental poet, immigrated to Israel from Moscow in 1972 after serving five years in the Gulag. In Israel, he lived the life of a recluse, publishing little and writing in a pre-Gutenberg form that defied mechanical reproduction. The only book that appeared in his lifetime, *Glints of the Wave* (1986), was "a facsimile reproduction of almost three hundred fifty pages of Bokshtein's handwritten texts illuminated with his drawings": doodling, diagrams, mystical ciphers, and figures.[44] Despite being recognized as one of Israel's most innovative Russian-language writers, he lived a life of poverty and struggle in a public-housing complex in Jaffa until his death in 1999. After his death, Adia Mendelson-Maoz writes, "Relatives sought legal permission to enter his apartment and save his archive, aware of the many literary treasures he left behind, but after a few months of legal procedures they discovered that the Amidar housing authority had evacuated the apartment and thrown out its contents."[45] His relatives attempted to salvage his unpublished poems and prose but, regardless of the famous adage from *The Master and Margarita* that "manuscripts don't burn," they were forced to conclude that manuscripts can certainly be lost in the garbage. This episode is a rich allegory, highlighting both the disregard of Hebrew speakers for Russian-language culture in Israel and the precarious circumstances of many Soviet-born writers and artists.

This incident also illustrates the sad reality that the majority of Israel's Russian-language cultural producers are not in possession of multiple homes in Tel Aviv and Moscow. Some, like Bokshtein, lack any home at all. In fact, poverty, unstable living conditions, and socio-professional downgrading became the leitmotifs of Russophone literature and culture in Israel, as popularized in cinematic works like Arik Kaplun's *Yana's Friends* (1999) and Evgeny Ruman's *Golden Voices* (2019), literary works like Goldshtein's *Aspects of Spiritual Matrimony* and Alex Rif's *Silly Girl of the Regime*, and Cherkassky-Nnadi's art series *Pravda*. These works serve as a necessary corrective to the 2019 media campaign that was mounted in Israel as the country marked the thirtieth anniversary of the "Russian" *aliyah* with a celebratory portrayal of Russian speakers as a model minority, under the banner of the phrase "ha'aliyah achi tova she-hayta lanu" ("the best migration wave we ever had"). This slogan warrants closer scrutiny, not only because it unabashedly celebrates the Soviet *aliyah* at the expense of other immigrant groups, such as Mizrahim and Ethiopians, revealing its orientalist underpinnings, but also because it sweeps under the rug the difficulties and struggles faced by many Soviet immigrants. When viewed in their entirety, the literature, cinema, and visual art of Russian-speaking Jews in Israel offer a nuanced understanding of this community's journey in the country and the hardships many have faced (and continue to face) in their efforts to integrate into Israeli society while preserving their cultural identity.

Looking back at the journey of this community from the moment depicted in Cherkassky-Nnadi's painting, it is clear that the encounter with Israel has brought profound shifts in cultural identities. Most notably, after three decades in Israel, Russian speakers have experienced a significant increase in religious beliefs and practices. While an overwhelming majority identified as non-religious or atheist upon arrival in Israel,[46] recent research shows that in the present, over two-thirds of Russian-speaking Israelis consider themselves to be religious and increasingly affiliate with religious institutions (predominantly with Judaism, while a tiny minority identifies with Christianity or Islam).[47] Furthermore, post-Soviet Israeli cultural producers are gradually embracing Hebrew as their language of choice in cultural expression and literary creation, particularly as concerns the younger generation. If earlier generations of writers and intellectuals perceived the Hebrew language and culture as unsophisticated and provincial, favouring Russian for its association with high culture and world literature, a new wave of artists is generating literary and cinematic works in Hebrew and is involved in projects of cultural translation, aiming to introduce Soviet-Russian cultural heritage to a Hebrew-speaking audience. Finally, the younger generations are shifting their focus away from the Soviet-Jewish past and are beginning to explore their own challenging social and historical experiences in Israel – an aspect largely unaddressed in the creative works of earlier generations.

Dual Diaspora: An Overview

Bringing together scholarship on Russian-Jewish cultural identity with an account of Israeli culture and society at the turn of the twenty-first century, *Dual Diaspora* reveals how the idiosyncrasies of Jewish identification in the USSR were instrumental in triggering the overflow of cultural production by post-Soviet Jewish immigrants after their relocation to Israel. The fundamental claim of this volume is that contemporary Russophone literature and visual art in Israel cannot be understood outside of the social engineering of Jewish life that unfolded throughout the Soviet era, and that much of the cultural production of this population attempts to position their unique post-Soviet Jewish identities in the matrix of Israeli society. Each chapter focuses on a separate subject that occupies a privileged place in contemporary Russophone literature and culture in Israel – Soviet-Jewish history, Jewish religious life, conceptions and practices of cosmopolitanism, and the difficult encounter with Israeli society. These subjects are important because they correspond to possible paths of integration of the Russian-speaking community to Israel and function as distinct wellsprings of identity that seek to transform post-Soviet "otherness" into Israeli belonging.

Chapter 1, "From Dissent to Counterculture: Soviet-Jewish History and Memory in Israel," focuses on accounts of Soviet-Jewish history, which occupy a prominent position in contemporary Russophone culture in Israel. It examines how retroactive engagement with the Soviet-Jewish past has allowed Russian-language authors and filmmakers in Israel to articulate their Jewishness in a manner that is legible to both Israeli and Western audiences – in earlier decades, by situating their history and memory within the broader history of Jewish victimhood, and, in more recent years, by departing from this preexisting narrative. The chapter begins with consideration of Natan Sharansky's autobiographical work, *Fear No Evil* (1988), and Mikhail Kalik's film *And the Wind Returns* (1991), within the larger contexts of their creation and reception, demonstrating how ex-Soviet Israeli cultural producers constructed their vision of Jewish identity to resonate with anti-Soviet political discourse during the Cold War. The chapter then turns to the more recent writing of Alice Bialsky and Alexander Barash during the first two decades of the twenty-first century – showing how they reconsider the late Soviet period from the retrospective vantage of the twenty-first century in an attempt to articulate a less harsh and more tolerant characterization of the Soviet-Jewish experience. In a departure from the older generation's mode of history and memory, the authors emphasize the reciprocity of the Soviet and Jewish worlds in the 1980s by focusing on the cross-pollination of lifestyles in underground artistic circles and on thrilling, and ultimately benign, run-ins with the police. The chapter illustrates a complete transformation in the way ex-Soviet Jewish authors have thought about their past, from historical narratives galvanized by Soviet discrimination to narratives that apprehend the Soviet-Jewish experience through nostalgia and wistfulness.

Chapter 2, "'Excuse Me, Are You Jewish?': The Newfound Religiosity of Post-Soviet Jews in Israel," turns to the subject of religion. It both situates the religious revival among Russian-speaking Jews within larger movements of religious awakening (Jewish, Christian, and Muslim) in the post-Soviet space, and places this interest in religion and spirituality in the local Israeli context. The chapter argues that Russian speakers' rising interest in Judaism is more than a natural rediscovery of roots by Jewish prodigal sons and daughters or an antidote to the near-complete disappearance of religious practice among Jews in the Soviet Union. Instead, it connects this phenomenon to the negative perception of Russian-speaking immigrants among the local population and the media in Israel, which apprehended them as inadequate Jews who do not measure up to authentic Jewish standards because of their atheism, appetite for pork, and indifference to organized religion. Bearing in mind this context of social hostility, some forms of reinvestment in religion by post-Soviet Israelis may be seen as a conscious effort to make themselves "kosher" for local and global consumption. The chapter examines in depth two case studies. Pini Tavger's feature film *More Than I Deserve* (2021) suggests that a turn toward religion among post-Soviet Jews in Israel is often influenced by close proximity to, and mimicry of, their religious-nationalist neighbours on the fringes of Israel. Similarly, Dina Rubina's bestselling novel, *Here Comes the Messiah!* (1995), illustrates that the investment in religiosity by post-Soviet Jews might also be politically motivated, an attempt to assert their belonging to the Jewish majority in Israel at the expense of non-Jewish groups within the country, especially Palestinians.

Chapter 3, "Orientalist Cosmopolitanism: Encounters with the Other in Israel," investigates visions of geography in the literary works of Alexander Goldshtein and the visual art of Zoya Cherkassky-Nnadi, especially as they pertain to the negotiation between local Israeli reality and global contexts. Through an examination of Goldshtein's semi-autobiographical novel set in Israel, *Aspects of Spiritual Matrimony* (2001), the chapter considers how the geographies of Europe, Africa, the Middle East, and the Mediterranean are mobilized to express the author's alienation from – and dissatisfaction with – Israel. This is both indicative of the author's estrangement from Israel and an attempt to escape both Russian and Israeli hegemonic cultural frames and allegiances. Additionally, the chapter reads Goldshtein's mission to "Europeanize" Israel as a form of cultural imperialism that echoes the not-too-distant history of Ashkenazi domination of Mizrahi populations in Israel. The chapter compares Goldshtein's works to Zoya Cherkassky-Nnadi's art series *Pravda* (2012–19) and *Africa-Israel* (2013–18). *Pravda* addresses two intertwined moments in the history of Russian-speaking Jews: life in the Soviet Union before immigration, and the precarious reality in Israel that followed. By placing these histories in dialogue, the chapter shows how Cherkassky-Nnadi's laudatory attitude toward the Soviet past is related to the suffering, humiliation, and rapid downward social mobility that many Soviet-born Jews experienced in Israel after immigration. The chapter then turns to examine select artworks from Cherkassky-Nnadi's series *Africa-Israel*, considering how her sympathetic representation of African asylum seekers in Israel challenges dominant stereotypes and aims to transform the perception of this vulnerable population from dangerous to harmless.

Chapter 4, "Artists of the 1.5 Generation: From Post-Soviet Nostalgia to the 2022 War in Ukraine," examines contemporary Hebrew-language poetry by female poets of the "1.5 generation" – comprising those who were born in the (former) Soviet Union and immigrated to Israel during the 1990s, when they were in their teens. The chapter considers politically engaged works by Alex Rif and Rita Kogan, which present an unflinching account of the traumatic experiences of Russian-speaking women in Israel that is not commonly represented in Israeli literature and culture. Rif, who immigrated to Israel when she was five, focuses on bullying at school, professional downgrading at work, and the intergenerational conflict between parents and children. Kogan, who arrived in Israel at age fifteen, examines the challenges women experience in immigration, including verbal abuse, ethnic and gender stereotyping, and sexual violence at work and in the public sphere. Through artistic rendering and valorization of this community's specific experiences, Rif and Kogan are finding new ways to reconstruct their fragmented post-Soviet Israeli cultural identities in defiance of the patriarchal, monocultural, melting-pot conceptions of Israeli society. The chapter concludes by examining the role and limits of nostalgia in Cherkassky-Nnadi's art series *Soviet Childhood*, particularly in the aftermath of Russia's war in Ukraine.

The conclusion, "The Future of Russophone Culture in Israel," closes the study by considering the future of Russophone-Israeli literature and culture. Major writers and intellectuals in Israel have anticipated the eventual end of Russophone cultural creativity in the Middle East. I push against these claims. Post-Soviet Israeli culture has not dissolved in Israel's cultural melting pot. Rather, the opposite has taken place – it has entered the mainstream of Israeli society and has been successfully transferred to the next generation, albeit having undergone a certain cultural evolution. Not only have members of this population transformed all spheres of social life in Israel – from arts and culture, to politics, technology, and the economy – but they have also set down roots and transformed themselves in the process. They have both become "Israelis" and managed to reclaim their cultural heritage as post-Soviet Jews, demonstrating that acculturation and assimilation are a dynamic, two-way street.

CHAPTER 1

From Dissent to Counterculture

Soviet-Jewish History and Memory in Israel

The Diasporic Condition

On 30 October 2007, Beit Hatfutsoth – the Museum of the Jewish People in Tel Aviv unveiled an impressive multimedia exhibition, *Jews of Struggle: The Jewish National Movement in the USSR, 1967–1989*. The title of the exhibit, *Jews of Struggle*, plays on Elie Wiesel's pioneering book *The Jews of Silence* (1966), which portrayed the Jewish community in the USSR as prodigal sons and daughters who had lost their grandparents' authentic Jewish culture and identity during the Soviet experiment in the twentieth century.[1] In sharp contrast to Wiesel's defeatist portrayal, *Jews of Struggle* presents a counternarrative of Jewish history and identity in the USSR. The exhibition presents Israel's transformative victory in the Six-Day War in 1967 as the turning point that reignited Jewish self-identification, transforming the hitherto "silent" community into a reborn, proud, and re-nationalized collective, a powerful adversary of the Soviet regime, and fervent champions of human rights.

In the introduction to the exhibition's catalogue, the renowned Soviet-Jewish refusenik Natan (Anatoli) Sharansky (b. 1948), who endured nine years in Soviet prisons, declares: "Our personal exodus from the darkness of communist totalitarianism towards the light of the Jewish state is a modern-day retelling of the centuries-old diasporic history of the struggle of the Jewish people against tyranny and in search of freedom."[2] He adds that, similar to Jews in ancient times, "the heroic struggle for freedom of Soviet Jews is deeply instructive: it shows how people's strength, united as one, is able – despite the overwhelming odds to the contrary – to change the path of history."[3] This passage has significant relevance for this chapter because it foregrounds the dominant representation of Jewish history and identity in the USSR, where the Jewish struggle for freedom is depicted as both an escape from the USSR (a historical equivalent of the biblical Egypt) and a return to Israel (cast as the homeland of the Jewish people). Using the biblical narrative of ancient Israelites in Egypt as the prototype of Jewish history, Sharansky recasts the entire twentieth-century Soviet-Jewish experience as a uniform progression from "the darkness of communist totalitarianism" toward "the light of the Jewish state." In so doing, he links the historical memory of Jews in the USSR to Israel's ideological metanarrative of *aliyah*, aiming to create space in Israel's historical consciousness for ex-Soviet immigrants.

Instead of taking Sharansky's triumphant (and somewhat oversimplified) characterization of the Soviet-Jewish past at face value, the chapter adopts a different approach. It examines how and why the narrative of Jewish history in the USSR came to be transformed in the literary and visual works of Soviet-born authors and filmmakers in Israel from the 1980s onwards. Instead of viewing Jewish history as eternal and cyclical, the chapter explores how these artists' retrospective engagement with the Soviet-Jewish past has allowed them to articulate their Jewishness in a manner that is legible to both Israeli and Western audiences – in earlier decades, by framing their history and memory within the broader context of Jewish victimhood, and, in more recent years, by moving away from this established narrative. Ultimately, the chapter reveals a significant shift in the perspectives of post-Soviet Jewish authors regarding their history. It highlights a gradual transformation from historical narratives formed around accounts of Soviet oppression to narratives that now view the Soviet-Jewish past with nostalgia and longing. This shift reflects a generational divide in how Soviet-Jewish history is represented.

The Creation of the Refusenik Identity: Sharansky and Kalik

In his analysis of the literary portrayal of Soviet Jews in American literature, Sasha Senderovich illustrates how, in the cultural imagination of many Western Jews, the dominant image of the "prisoner of Zion" – a figure symbolizing courage and sacrifice in the face of privation and imprisonment, culminating in the fulfillment of the Zionist dream with emigration to Israel – was shaped by the global campaign to "save" Soviet Jewry during the Cold War.[4] Burdened by their failure to save Europe's Jews during the Holocaust, American Jews, as Senderovich explains, embarked on a mission to liberate the "Soviet Jew," who was constructed as similarly in need of rescuing. As part of this rescue, the American Jews would civilize the "Soviet Jews" in their own image and thus redeem themselves and their shortcomings as a community during the Holocaust.[5] While Senderovich's research convincingly demonstrates how Soviet dissidents were "tempered" in the American imagination as heroic fighters for freedom or tragic victims of the ruthless communist regime, he is less concerned with the specific role that Soviet-Jewish dissidents and refuseniks themselves played in shaping this perception.

Indeed, despite Senderovich's discussion of Natan Sharansky and his impact on the literary works of Gary Shteyngart and David Bezmozgis,[6] his analysis overlooks Sharansky's own highly influential narrative of his life experiences behind the Iron Curtain, *Fear No Evil*.[7] As Jonathan Bolton reminds us with respect to Czechoslovak dissidents, these individuals were "writing people … for whom the written word [was] the primary – and often the only – political medium they command[ed]."[8] Therefore, it would be prudent to recognize the significant literary legacy they created through memoirs, autobiographies, and philosophical treatises, produced both during their time in the Soviet Union and after their emigration to Israel, North America, and Europe.[9]

In the writings of refusenik authors in Israel, two themes predominate – victimhood and resilience. The profound emphasis on these themes can be observed already in the titles of their books – from Alexander Voronel's *Trembling of Jewish Woes* to Yuli Kosharovsky's *We Are Jews Again* and Sharansky's *Fear No Evil*. Produced during the last phase of the Cold War, these narratives formulate a collective Jewish identity that is radically separated from Soviet history, society, and culture. For the purposes of the present analysis, Natan Sharansky's *Fear No Evil* (1988) and Mikhail Kalik's film *And the Wind Returns* (1991) (*I vozvraschaetsia veter*; hereafter, *The Wind*) serve as prime examples of the regime of Soviet-Jewish history and memory, insofar as they grapple with the complexities of Jewish experience in the years leading to the Soviet Union's collapse. Produced in 1988 and 1991 respectively, these works emerged at a particular historical moment, when the Soviet world had finally opened up to global intercourse, and the question of Soviet-Jewish history and memory has emerged as one of particular importance in the USSR, Israel, and in the West. They ask: Who will narrate the Soviet-Jewish past, and how? Should consciousness of the Jewish past in the USSR be aimed at the preservation of the Soviet-Jewish community, or should it facilitate their hasty emigration to Israel and the United States? What would be the relationship, without the Iron Curtain, between ex-Soviet Jewish immigrants to Israel and the remaining Jews in the USSR? Where do Soviet Jews belong geographically: in the USSR or in Israel? In an attempt to provide answers to these questions, *Fear No Evil* and *The Wind* articulate the intricacies of the Soviet-Jewish experience in the twentieth century and offer a bleak prognosis concerning the future of Jews in the USSR.

Fear No Evil is based on the life story of Natan Sharansky – the prominent Soviet-Jewish dissident and refusenik whose 1977 incarceration sparked global rallies demanding his release. This memoir – first published in English by the prominent Random House press in 1988 and then translated into nine other languages, including Hebrew and Russian – chronicles Sharansky's battle against the Soviet authorities.[10] The narrative recounts Sharansky's life as a privileged Soviet citizen and as a refusenik before his arrest in 1977 as well as his life afterwards, marked by a gruelling incarceration at Lefortovo Prison in Moscow, a show trial in 1978, and the following nine years in the Soviet prison and Gulag system, where the author was subject to prolonged solitary confinement, force-feeding, psychological torment, extreme cold, meagre sustenance, and demanding physical labour. The book became an important touchstone for subsequent memoirs about life behind the Iron Curtain and crystallized the larger cultural imaginary of Jewish experience in the USSR for Western and Israeli audiences.

The vision of history presented in this memoir is encapsulated in Sharansky's account of his defiant closing statement in court in 1978, reflecting resilience and a profound commitment to his cause despite the personal costs. Sharansky's words reveal an unwavering sense of purpose and historical consciousness that transcends his immediate circumstances:

> Five years ago, I applied for an exit visa to emigrate from the USSR to Israel. Today I am further than ever from my goal. This would seem to be a cause for regret, but that is not the case. These five years were the best of my life. I am happy that I have been able to live them honestly and at peace with my conscience … I feel part of a marvelous historical process – the process of the national revival of Soviet Jewry and its return to the homeland, to Israel … And today, when I am further than ever from my dream, from my people, and from my Avital, and when many difficult years of prisons and camps lie ahead of me, I say to my wife and to my people, *Leshana haba'a b'Yerushalayim* [Next year in Jerusalem].[11]

This statement – synecdochic in function, where a part stands for a larger whole – portrays Sharansky as a martyr of the Jewish people, ready to endure any punishment, extreme cold, or harsh labour for his firm commitment to his cause. Not unlike other refusenik memoirs, Sharansky attributes his newfound "inner freedom" to the moment he applied for an exit visa, openly seeking permission to leave the Soviet Union and emigrate to Israel.[12] Notably, Sharansky intertwines his political struggle against the Soviet apparatus with the rediscovery of his long-forgotten Jewish identity and his activism for the rights of Jews in the USSR.[13] Consequently, he views his personal struggle in politics as emblematic of the collective journey of Soviet Jews, who have embarked on "a marvelous historical process – the process of the national revival of Soviet Jewry and its return to the homeland, to Israel."[14] At the conclusion of his statement, Sharansky ceases to speak in the state-supported Russian language and proudly proclaims in Hebrew, like a true Zionist – "*Leshana haba'a b'Yerushalayim*" (Next year in Jerusalem).[15] The invocation of "Next year in Jerusalem" encapsulates a timeless hope and a staunch belief in the ultimate realization of these goals, reflecting both personal and collective dimensions of his vision of history.

The passage primarily focuses on Sharansky's spirited Jewish identity and his commitment to this heritage, but it may not accurately capture his younger self's reality.[16] In his memoir, Sharansky admits that during his first two decades of life, he had little connection to Judaism. He grew up in a secular household in Soviet Ukraine, where Jewish culture and identity were downplayed and discouraged, and his parents did not provide him with any Jewish education or exposure to religious practices. Despite this, the theme of Jewishness takes centre stage in his narrative, from the book's title – a quote from the Torah – to the memoir's closing pages, where Sharansky makes *aliyah* and reunites with his spouse in Jerusalem. This idea of a "recovered identity," prevalent in refusenik memoirs, is especially striking. Here, as in many other such cases, this was an identity the author never previously inhabited. Sharansky's evocation of a "recovered identity" might be seen as an effort to tap into the established triumphalist vision of a refusenik identity prevalent in the West and Israel (that Senderovich identifies in his article) with the goal of re-accentuating the Jewish component of the authors' "diasporic" past. Given the book's original publication in the United States and its primary intended audiences of American and European Jews, this explanation is particularly fitting.

Despite Sharansky's rudimentary knowledge of Jewish culture during the years of his biography that he narrates, the book is steeped in Jewish history, culture, and religion. Jewish holidays, including Hanukkah, Passover, and Yom Kippur, figure prominently in the narrative. One particularly memorable scene recounts how Sharansky celebrated Hanukkah in a Soviet prison.[17] He begins by setting the scene: the holiday of Hanukkah is approaching, and Sharansky is the only Jew in prison. After explaining that Hanukkah symbolizes national freedom and a return to one's culture despite forced assimilation, however, Sharansky's friends in what he refers to as "our kibbutz" agreed to celebrate the holiday with him.[18] They even crafted a wooden menorah for him, decorated it, and found some candles. On the sixth night of Hanukkah, the guards confiscate his makeshift menorah and candles, leading him to declare a hunger strike in protest. Hoping to end the strike before a Moscow commission arrives, the prison commander, Major Osin, invites Sharansky to his office. Sharansky requests the return of his menorah, but Osin is unable to back down in front of the regiment. In a clever move, Sharansky proposes a compromise: he asks Osin to let him celebrate Hanukkah right there and then in the office, with the confiscated menorah. Osin agrees, and the menorah reappears on the table. Sharansky relishes in describing each step of the celebration, and how he tricked Osin: "I arranged the candles and went to the coat rack for my hat, explaining to Osin that during the prayer you must stand with your head covered and at the end say 'Amen.'"[19] The major followed suit, so Sharansky proceeded to light the candles, reciting his idiosyncratic prayer in Hebrew: "Blessed are You, God, for allowing me to rejoice on this day of Hanukkah, the holiday of our liberation, the holiday of our return to the way of our fathers. Blessed are You, God, for allowing me to light these candles. May you allow me to light the Hanukkah candles many times in your city, Jerusalem, with my wife, Avital, and my family and friends."[20] Inspired by Osin's unexpected cooperation, Sharansky adds in Hebrew: "And may the day come when all our enemies, who today are planning our destruction, will stand before us and hear our prayers and say 'Amen.'"[21] To which Osin echoes back, "Amen."[22] Filled with joy, Sharansky returns to the barracks, where he celebrates the end of Hanukkah with his fellow prisoners and recounts what transpired with Osin. "Naturally, I told them about Osin's 'conversion,'" he concludes, "and it soon became the talk of the camp. I realized that revenge was inevitable, but I also knew they had plenty of other reasons to punish me."[23]

This passage highlights how Jewish tradition enabled Sharansky to forge connections with his fellow prisoners and the Jewish people more generally, while simultaneously functioning as a wedge between him and the Soviet regime. The prisoners' immediate desire to celebrate Hanukkah with Sharansky suggests that, following Marina Tsvetayeva's famous dictum that in the confines of the Soviet Union "all poets are Jews,"[24] all prisoners in the Soviet Union were (metaphorically) Jews as well. The biblical narrative of Hanukkah becomes the framing device by which Sharansky and other prisoners comprehend their present situation in the Soviet Union. Moreover, Hanukkah holds symbolic weight because it parallels Sharansky's situation with that of the ancient Maccabees. Indeed, Hanukkah celebrates how a small group of faithful Jews, the Maccabees, rebelled against demands to accept a foreign culture and beliefs, overpowered one of the strongest armies in the world, and reclaimed the Holy Temple in Jerusalem. This reminds Jews worldwide that Jewish history involves a series of violent demands to assimilate and abandon their faith. The heroism of the Maccabees seems to inspire Sharansky, setting him on a head-to-head collision with the prison commander. Ultimately, the trickster-like protagonist outsmarts the dull-witted Osin and even tricks him into cursing the Soviet regime. Both heroic narratives – ancient and modern – conclude with a miraculous resolution and the victory of the downtrodden over the mighty masters. However, Sharansky's account omits the fact that the Hanukkah story and the Maccabean Revolt were also a struggle against Hellenized Jews. While the Zionist narrative portrays it as a successful struggle of the Jewish nation against an external enemy who forbade them from living a Jewish life in their homeland, the Maccabees' main opponents were other Jews who had adopted Hellenistic culture and customs. By externalizing the enemy and omitting the intra-Jewish conflict it also involved, Sharansky's rejigged Hanukkah perfectly fits his narrative of one man's victory over a ruthless foreign enemy and neatly aligns with Zionist ideology.

One may observe a similar allegorical characterization of the historical situation of Jews in the USSR in most literary and cinematic works by Jewish refuseniks. One such example is Mikhail Kalik's cinematic memoir, *The Wind* (1991), which closely mirrors Sharansky's portrayal of Soviet-Jewish history. Structurally, the two works are quite different. While Sharansky's *Fear No Evil* presents a straightforward narrative of one man's defiance against a totalitarian state that captivates the audience through humour, clear-cut morality, and unwavering courage, Kalik's *The Wind* is a non-linear art film that deliberately challenges viewers with its artful complexity, encouraging deep and prolonged contemplation. *The Wind* is a deeply personal and introspective exploration of the filmmaker's life and the tumultuous historical events that shaped Soviet Jewish identity. Set against the backdrop of Stalinist repression and societal antisemitism, the film weaves together chronicle-documentary footage with fragments from Kalik's previous works. It chronicles Kalik's own experiences, from his childhood during World War II to his adult reflections on Stalin's purges and the struggles of Soviet Jews. Through a blend of autobiography, archival footage, and historical critique, Kalik confronts themes of memory, trauma, and cultural identity, offering a poetic meditation on his artistic journey and the enduring impact of Soviet history on Jewish consciousness.

Despite their divergent styles, *Fear No Evil* and *The Wind* share a profound engagement with the Soviet past, particularly in their exploration of Soviet-Jewish history. Both works embrace what Salo W. Baron terms a "lachrymose conception of Jewish history," portraying Jewish experience as a series of catastrophes and persecutions.[25] Both narratives are driven by a desire to confront the personal and collective trauma endured by Soviet Jews, often overlooked in official Soviet history. Therefore, they include references to the 1930s purges, the brutal Gulag system, the murder of Solomon Mikhoels, and numerous arrests, suicides, and imprisonments. Since footage of the Gulag is rare, Kalik reconstructs his own experience in the Gulag as part of this buried history. To accomplish this, Kalik meticulously rebuilt a haunting Gulag set from the blueprints stored in his memory, eerily populating it with guards, dogs, and harrowing violence. Ultimately, each narrative arc concludes with the protagonist's decision to emigrate to Israel, underscoring the profound rupture between the Jewish and Soviet worlds over the course of the twentieth century.

The collective history that emerges from the literary and cinematic works of Sharansky, Kalik, and their peers can be attributed to the interplay of two parallel historical processes. On the one hand, the historical labour of *The Wind* and *Fear No Evil* can be seen as an attempt to recover previously inaccessible and silenced histories of Jews in the USSR during a time of broad reconsideration of the basic facts and significance of the twentieth century in the Soviet Union. Therefore, the direct focus of these works on prison camps, purges, police brutality, artistic and political censorship, and ethnic discrimination and persecution reflects the internal situation in the Soviet Union in the second part of the 1980s, when widespread discussions and revelations concerning the social, economic, and political state of Soviet society and previously suppressed elements of the historical record were taking place publicly as a result of Mikhail Gorbachev's policy of glasnost (openness).

However, this analysis overlooks the broader geopolitical context in which both *Fear No Evil* and *The Wind* were created. *The Wind* was the outcome of an official invitation to Kalik – an Israeli director and citizen of seventeen years – by Moscow's Gorky Film Studios to travel to the Soviet Union and undertake a project of his choosing. Similarly, *Fear No Evil* was made possible by Sharansky's book contract with Random House following his arrival in Israel. The book's editing, carried out by William Novak, a renowned ghostwriter for biographies of prominent figures such as First Lady Nancy Reagan, Lee Iacocca, and Magic Johnson, contributed to shaping the narrative for Western audiences. These "production histories" illuminate the transnational nature of the culture industry during the Cold War era, showcasing the flow of capital, culture, and ideas across the Iron Curtain, the Western Bloc, and Israel. Responding to Western fascination with life in the USSR at a time when fast-moving social transformations had vaulted

Soviet events to the top of the headlines, historical accounts by Sharansky, Kalik, and other dissidents and refuseniks, produced after their emigration, sought to provide Israeli and Western audiences with a rare glimpse into the Orwellian dystopia hidden behind the Iron Curtain. In doing so, they participated in the global economy of Cold War cultural discourse.

The uncompromisingly binary portrayal of the Jewish experience in the USSR as falling into the categories of heroic Jewish fighters or passive victims of the totalitarian state is perhaps the main historical drawback of this literary and cinematic corpus. By weaving their individual biographies into narratives of collective Jewish history, Kalik and Sharansky present historical portraits of political and cultural elites in the large cities that obfuscate the experiences of the majority of Soviet Jews. This approach overlooks the intricate and reciprocal nature of Jewish-Soviet relations and overstates the anti-Soviet or Zionist orientation of most Soviet Jews. In reality, the majority of Soviet Jews were not dissidents and refuseniks, nor did they participate in studying Hebrew or Torah in illegal gatherings.

Casting all Soviet Jews as perpetual outsiders, political non-conformists, and passive victims of the regime not only overlooks the significant professional, cultural, and political achievements of the broader Jewish community,[26] but also fails to account for Kalik's own remarkable professional journey from admission to the prestigious All-Union State Institute of Cinematography, VGIK, to becoming a prominent cinematic figure in the Soviet Union and Sharansky's impressive educational and professional development as a Soviet scientist after graduating from the esteemed Moscow Institute of Physics and Technology. The focus on solely negative aspects of Soviet-Jewish life and experience in *Fear No Evil* and *The Wind* perpetuates a Zionist master narrative that imagines Jewish life in Europe as inevitably leading to either Hitler's or Stalin's camps and presents Israel as the only escape route from these dangers. This oversimplification ignores the complex realities of Jewish life in the USSR and reduces the multifaceted experiences of Soviet Jews to a singular narrative.

Ultimately, *The Wind* and *Fear No Evil* leverage the Israeli discourse of "homecoming" in the interest of legibility for both Israeli and American audiences – two nation-states actively advocating for the emigration rights of Soviet Jews.[27] Spatially, the organizational logic of both memoirs revolves around the Zionist master narrative, finding stability and safety for Jews only in the geography of Israel. In *The Wind,* Kalik embarks on a harrowing return journey to the USSR, delving into Soviet history, and the narrative concludes with an aerial shot implying Kalik's departure for Israel. Similarly, *Fear No Evil* begins with Sharansky's arrest and incarceration in the Soviet Union and ends at Berlin's Glienicke Bridge – an intensely guarded passage from the Soviet Bloc to the American sector of West Berlin – in a spy exchange operation that grants Sharansky his freedom. The memoir concludes with a joyful reunion between Sharansky and his wife, Avital, in the Old City of Jerusalem. Geographically and ideologically, both narratives culminate in a triumphant passage to Israel, earned through a courageous struggle against inhumane Soviet authorities. Against all odds, the protagonists arrive home and symbolically reunite with what they perceive as their people and their country, defying the challenges they faced. Both works conclude with a profound sense of belonging, familiarity, and resolution as the emigrants encounter Jerusalem and the State of Israel for the first time, signifying the culmination of their journey.

The portrayal of a "happily ever after" in Israel in these works does not always align with the actual experiences of Soviet Jews after emigration. Similar to romantic comedies and fairy tales, *The Wind* and *Fear No Evil* conclude with an idealized happy ending, presenting the audience with a fantasy rather than acknowledging the complex and bittersweet post-migration reality. In the context of the Cold War's zero-sum logic, both America and Israel sought to depict Soviet Jewry as a downtrodden community in need of "saving." Sharansky and Kalik's works served this purpose, aligning with the inspirational narrative desired by these nations. However, the actual experiences of Soviet Jews encompass much more complexity beyond the simplified portrayal found in these works. As Anna Shternshis reminds us, "It was only upon arrival in the US that [Soviet Jews] learned that American Jews had narrativized [their lives] in the Soviet Union as a story of oppression and persecution, and had cast themselves as the liberating heroes."[28] In reality, "most Jews who left the Soviet Union had lived there quite comfortably – though they were not wealthy by Western standards, they were by no means poor – so it was altogether easier to publicly adopt a narrative of 'fleeing antisemitism' than to impart the complicated calculus that went into assessing their opportunities." In other words, the neat and oversimplified narrative of oppression obscures the complex and multifaceted reality experienced by most Soviet Jews, resulting in dissonance and ambivalence that cuts across both parts of their divided Soviet-Jewish identity.

This dissonance is most clearly visible in the affective structure of *The Wind*. Despite its devotion to the Israeli narrative of homecoming, the film is permeated with nostalgia and a relentless sense of loss and dual alienation. These motifs are articulated most clearly in an early scene in which Kalik reunites with his old friends and colleagues at a restaurant in Moscow after eighteen years of separation. It is a heartfelt portrayal of Soviet hospitality and one of the film's most touching moments. The returning director is dumbstruck by the emotions that overwhelm him. Through first-person point-of-view camera work, Kalik captures a picturesque scene of Russian *zastol'ye* (a festive meal or banquet): the table is overflowing with traditional Soviet food, *Sovetskoe* champagne is poured into frosty crystal glasses, and one of the guests plays guitar and sings a rendition of David Samoilov's poem "One Day" (1981), in classic Russian bardic manner:

> One day, I will visit you,
> One day, one day …
> When I feel victory,
> When I find a new path.[29]

The singing continues with these evocative lines:

> One day I will find you
> Confused, as always.
> One day you and I will fade together
> Into the years of my past.[30]

Through this song, the filmmaker aptly navigates the complexities of the Soviet-Israeli experience. In this moment of his narrative, Kalik refuses to choose between Soviet culture and the Land of Israel, instead presenting a simultaneous experience of nostalgia and resentment, belonging and homelessness, triumph and loss. This duality captures the essence of the dual diasporic condition faced by the Soviet-Israeli population, reflecting their intricate and often contradictory emotions.

Ultimately, the bardic song reveals the pathos of Kalik's dual alienation. Its addressee is not a woman; it is the Soviet Union. After eighteen years of exile, Kalik returns to the place of his lost childhood and artistic vitality to reclaim his history, identity, and sense of self. Simultaneously, the song articulates the pain of separation and the deep connection he still feels with his past. Notably, the director frames his return in a heroic key. He returns to the Soviet Union on his own terms: "When I feel victory / When I find a new path."[31] Yet his triumphant composure conceals as much as it reveals. The bard deliberately omits, between the two stanzas performed in the film, one stanza from Samoilov's poem:

> One day I will see you,
> One day, one day …
> And I will come to hate my life,
> And in tears, I will drop on your bosom.[32]

These words, had they been performed, would have challenged the Zionist ethos of repatriation by expressing longing for the Soviet past. This act of self-censorship sheds light on the operations of Zionist ideology and the symbolic violence it inflicts on the filmmaker. This palimpsest reveals the tragic impossibility of articulating a coherent Soviet-Jewish-Israeli identity within the orthogonal structures of Israeli and Soviet ideological and cultural projects before the dissolution of the Soviet Union and the end of the Cold War. Although Sharansky's narrative ends on a triumphant note with his release from the Soviet prison, joyful reunion with his wife, and a congratulatory call from American president Ronald Reagan, the book also highlights an inherent antagonism between the Jewish and Soviet worlds. Released in 1989 and 1991 during the USSR's collapse, *Fear No Evil* and *The Wind* symbolically mark the end of the first phase of Soviet-Israeli literature and cinema characterized by identity dissonance and a lachrymose conception of Soviet-Jewish history.

The Last Soviet-Jewish Generation in Israel: Bialsky and Barash

With the collapse of the Soviet Union and the end of the Cold War, the cultural significance, prestige, and ideological value of dissident and refusenik narratives fell into sharp decline. Importantly, the ideological motivation of Jewish diaspora and Zionism no longer served as the driving force behind the mass migration of post-Soviet Jews to Israel.[33] Unlike the ideologically motivated emigration flows of the 1970s – emigrants who, according to Larissa Remennick, "espoused Zionism and had moved to Israel because they wanted to live in the Jewish State" – the immigrants of the 1990s relocated to Israel largely in response to the economic, political, and social chaos that had swept through Russia, Ukraine, and the former USSR.[34] This newer generation of emigrants harboured less bitterness and resentment toward their country of birth. In contrast to the complete dismissal of Soviet history, culture, and identity by members of the 1970s wave, many of whom chose to trade their "diasporic" Slavic names for Hebrew ones, adopted Hebrew as the primary language for their families and children, and deliberately rejected anything perceived as Soviet, Russian, or communist, the 1990s cohort was disposed to leverage their knowledge of the Russian language, culture, and history to their own advantage, both in Israel and within the broader Jewish and Russophone diasporas.[35]

As a result, the previously entrenched understanding of the USSR as a totalitarian state, with a focus on terror, ideology, and the KGB, and the adulatory representation of Soviet-Jewish history, featuring heroic struggles of dissidents and refuseniks, loosened their hold on the narratives of ex-Soviet writers in Israel during the 1990s, especially among those who did not partake in dissent. After fifteen years in Israel, the new generation of authors began to shift away from a Manichean and morally laden view of the Soviet Union and world politics and instead focused on the inner and uneven dynamics and distribution of the Soviet-Jewish experience across the twentieth century. The first cohort of writers to challenge the lachrymose account of Soviet-Jewish history included individuals who belonged to the "last Soviet generation," to borrow Yurchak's terminology in *Everything Was Forever, Until It Was No More*.[36] In Yurchak's study, the last Soviet generation refers to individuals who were born in the 1960s and 1970s, came of age in the late Soviet era, and were in their twenties and thirties when the Soviet Union ceased to exist. Not guided by first-hand experience of extensive persecution and repression, the last Soviet generation in Israel extensively modified the historical narrative proposed by Sharansky and Kalik. In their writings, the dissident narrative – which often implied a homology between Stalin and Hitler, communism and fascism, and the Soviet Union and Nazi Germany – was thoroughly revised.

It is important to emphasize that for Yurchak, the last Soviet generation is not a descriptive or sociological category that purports to capture some essential or representative characteristic of the late Soviet identity. Instead, this is conceptual portraiture that applies solely to individuals who embraced a particular set of practices and de-territorial subject positions that were both "inside and outside of the rhetorical field of [official Soviet] discourse, neither simply in support nor simply in opposition."[37] These individuals did not directly confront the regime like the dissidents, nor did they fully pledge allegiance as card-carrying party members. Instead, they engaged in autonomous cultural and social practices that ran parallel to authoritative state discourse and official social structures. Uninterested in politics or state ideology, they developed a remarkable ability to navigate state institutions and find a measure of freedom and autonomy within them to pursue private interests, such as reading and discussing literature, listening to rock music, and organizing vibrant and alcohol-infused dance parties (*diskoteki* and *tusovki*). As Yurchak points out, members of the last Soviet generation "actively engaged in creating various new pursuits, identities, and forms of living that were enabled by authoritative discourse, but not necessarily defined by it."[38]

When the Jewish echelons of this "generation of janitors and night watchmen,"[39] to borrow Boris Grebenshchikov's description of the last Soviet generation, made their way to Israel during the 1990s and began documenting their life experiences in the first decade of the twenty-first century, their personal accounts of Soviet-Jewish history differed significantly from those of their parents' generation, the dissidents and refuseniks. The main point of departure for the Israeli members of the last Soviet generation, such as Alexander Barash (b. 1960), David Dector (b. 1961), Alice Bialsky (b. 1968), Dmitry Deitch (b. 1969), and Alexander Ilichevsky (b. 1970), was their strategic avoidance of narratives of Jewish victimhood, heroism, and the renaissance of Soviet-Jewish identity.[40] Unlike the dissident model, which often depicted Soviet-Jewish history as a struggle between Jews and the totalitarian Soviet state, the members of the last Soviet generation tended to emphasize the reciprocity of the Soviet and Jewish worlds during the 1980s and downplay the importance of their Jewishness for shaping their lives.

I take Alice Bialsky's semi-autobiographical novel, *The Crown Is Not Heavy*[41] (in Russian; *We Saw the Night*[42] in Hebrew translation), and Alexander Barash's poeticized memoirs, *Happy Childhood*[43] and *A Time of One's Own*,[44] as representative works reflecting the historical experiences of the last Soviet-Jewish generation in Israel. These autobiographical texts are uninterested in victimhood as a mode of discourse because it categorically separates Jews from other social groups in the USSR and excludes them from the fabric of everyday Soviet life. While these narratives do acknowledge instances of institutional and popular antisemitism in the USSR, they focus more on other aspects of historical experiences. Specifically, their retrospective retelling of life under Brezhnev and Gorbachev emphasizes a sense of excitement, openness, and a burning desire for autonomy. Consequently, the historical accounts of the last Soviet generation are punctuated by nostalgia for pre-immigration lives and the enchantment of growing up in the late 1970s and 1980s. After nearly two decades in Israel, this nostalgic view of the Soviet past reveals how the long-term stay in Israel could lead to a selective blindness to the challenges faced by Jews in the Soviet era. Focusing largely on the countercultural activities of the younger generation of Soviet Jews, these writers describe a unique generational experience that is less burdened by overt forms of prejudice and persecution than that of previous generations.

Bialsky's *The Crown Is Not Heavy* and Barash's *A Time of One's Own* offer a particular nostalgic interpretation of the late Soviet era, characteristic of the last Soviet generation. These semi-autobiographical coming-of-age *Künstlerromane* delve into the authors' artistic development during the late Soviet period, marked by the gradual erosion of Brezhnev-era orthodoxies and the emergence of an uneven sense of freedom, which was officially recognized and co-opted by Gorbachev's transformative policies in the late 1980s. The cultural changes depicted in these works reflect the societal shifts that accompanied the introduction of policies such as *glasnost* and *perestroika* (restructuring), which sought to reform and liberalize the Soviet system. Focusing on the flourishing of rock music, book clubs, religious circles, underground art, youth culture, sexual revolution, and poetic and narcotic experimentations, and featuring a large cast of renowned cultural figures (Viktor Tsoi, Boris Grebenshchikov, Petr Mamonov, Dmitrii Prigov, Timur Kibirov, and Lev Rubinstein), *The Crown Is Not Heavy* and *A Time of One's Own* evoke the grand excitement of living in Moscow during the 1980s and being part of the underground artistic circles that brought together like-minded painters, poets, musicians, students, clergymen, and actors. As fictional works about the past, they critique official modes of history writing and fill in the gaps left by official historical accounts.

Alice Bialsky's *The Crown Is Not Heavy*, published in Russian in 2012 and translated into Hebrew in 2014, follows the coming-of-age journey of Alisa Blank, an eighteen-year-old Jewish girl from an intelligentsia family. The novel is set in the transformative year of 1988 in Moscow. In this time of radical change, Alisa abandons her university studies to become a rock-and-roll journalist. The story revolves around her unrequited love for Gromov, who represents the epitome of cool for Alisa. He is a few years older, publishes the underground rock *samizdat* journal *Gonzo*, an homage to Hunter S. Thompson, and, like his idol, enthusiastically engages in illegal activities, such as organizing underground music festivals and daringly breaking into construction sites to indulge in revelry with fellow punk musicians.[45] Gromov guides Alisa through Moscow's underground culture, introducing her (and the reader) to illegal punk concerts, drugs, sex, petty crime, experimental art, and thrilling run-ins with the police.

Alexander Barash's poetic memoir *A Time of One's Own* is set in the same historical period, retroactively recounting and analyzing the author's pre-emigration years in Moscow during the 1980s. Combining autobiographical prose, theoretical writing, and poetic texts, *A Time of One's Own* reproduces the late Soviet epoch at a time of great cultural, social, and political changes in the era of Gorbachev's *glasnost* and *perestroika*. Like Bialsky, Barash uses his involvement in the underground scene during the 1980s to anchor a recognizable Soviet historical narrative of *perestroika*. In each chapter, he focuses on different subcultures in Moscow. In the chapter "Literary Salons," for instance, Barash recounts his early initiation into the world of underground literary clubs, where he discovers a unique synergy between Jewish dissent and Christian Orthodox revival. In the chapter "Epsilon Salon," the author describes his experience as a coeditor of the *samizdat* publication *Epsilon Salon*, where early writings by Dimitry Prigov, Lev Rubinstein, and Vladimir Sorokin were published. Finally, the chapters "Rock" and "Megapolis" focus on Barash's diverse involvements in Moscow's secret rock scene, which included hosting an underground concert performed by Boris Grebenshchikov – a trailblazing Soviet rock musician and, coincidentally, Alisa Blank's idol – in Barash's own apartment, and founding the underground rock band Megapolis, for which Barash served as the main lyricist.

Because of these thematic similarities, *The Crown Is Not Heavy* and *A Time of One's Own* present strikingly similar theories and conceptions of late Soviet parallel culture. At the start of Bialsky's novel, Gromov and Alisa attend an underground punk festival organized by Gromov. Along the way, the self-styled *enfant terrible* passionately shares his theory of counterculture, which he adapts from the writings of Mikhail Bakhtin, popular among hip and edgy late Soviet intellectual circles. He categorizes the rock music movement in Russia during the late 1980s into three streams. The first stream is "pop music" – many rock bands transitioned to pop music under governmental pressure, with Kino being a prime example. The second stream is "liberal music," musicians who "finally got to see their hour of glory and rushed to battle against the degenerate Soviet mentality. They say that they do it to kill the Soviet monster, but I say that they do it to replace it."[46] He adds that their ultimate goal is personal comfort. Finally, the third stream is "authentic counterculture," a movement that exists parallel to the Soviet apparatus, not competing with it but remaining at the margins. Gromov argues that true counterculture does not seek to compete with or overthrow the Soviet regime but rather exists in a parallel, alternative space, content to stay "at the bottom of the bottle." Similarly, in *A Time of One's Own*, Barash explores what he calls an "anthropological" portrait of his generation. At first, he claims that his generation cultivates "detachment" (*otstranennost'*)"[47] but quickly retracts his assertion: "On second thought – detachment from what? Rather, it is immersion in … one's obsessions: literature, cinema, art … In this universe – within this autonomous, humane, and artistic space – we were self-sufficient, not 'detached.'"[48] He brings this thought to a conclusion when he states: "Even protest and despair are foreign to the person of the 'new wave' [*cheloveku 'novoi volnyi'*] – not alien, but simply distant. One can understand these emotions, but never identify with them."[49]

Both novels illustrate a late Soviet parallel culture that rejects mainstream Soviet life and values. Instead of direct opposition, this culture creates an alternative space where individuals can immerse themselves in personal and artistic pursuits, maintaining a sense of self-sufficiency and detachment from the oppressive regime. What is striking about these conceptions of the late Soviet parallel culture is their anti-bourgeois and anti-political spirit. In Bialsky's text, Gromov critiques the "liberal" character of some rock musicians who seek "a life of comfort for themselves" – in contrast to the authentic counterculture he and his fellow Siberian punk musicians ostensibly represent. Similarly, Barash's account highlights the importance of avoiding politics and dissent for the "pure" countercultural individual, contrasting it with the stances of cynical party members and "outdated" dissidents. Ultimately, both Bialsky and Barash – along with Yurchak – emphatically divide the whole spectrum of Soviet society into three distinct groups – indoctrinated communists, outdated dissidents/liberals, and the autonomous younger generation – and clearly identify with and favour the last one.

Addressing the structural flaw in Yurchak's theoretical division of Soviet society and social experience into such neat categories, Kevin M.F. Platt and Benjamin Nathans argue that Yurchak's framework, while insightful, oversimplifies the complex dynamics of late Soviet society. They propose that while Yurchak's analysis does move away from categorizing Soviet culture through recourse to binary oppositions ("official and unofficial, coercive and resistant, mendacious and truth-seeking"), it still remains to some extent reductive. Specifically, they argue that Yurchak merely replaces one dichotomy with another. Instead of presenting party activists and dissidents as distinct, Yurchak portrays them as mirror images of one another, "sharing 'the same rhetorical devices,' both pathologically obsessed with the literal truth/falsehood of official discourse, and jointly serving as the 'other' against which 'normal' people defined themselves."[50] Instead, Platt and Nathans propose a more extensive genealogy of what they term the "imaginary private sphere" that connects the generation of dissidents and their political tactics of dissent (drafting petitions, collecting signatures, demonstrating, and disseminating illegal texts via *samizdat*) with the tactics of the last Soviet generation and their pursuit of autonomous, extra-political activities such as listening to rock music or attending literary and religious *kruzhki* (social clubs). Ultimately, Platt and Nathans suggest that examining the continuity between the dissidents and the last Soviet generation, rather than pitting them against each other, reveals a potential misrecognition of the political implications of being a nonconformist in late Soviet society by Yurchak and, by extension, Barash and Bialsky. When Barash casually states that "one can understand [the dissidents], but never identify with them," he draws a clear line between the "hip" members of his generation and the "outdated" dissidents.[51] However, this claim is disingenuous if we consider it in the context of the Soviet Union's desire to control all areas of cultural, social, and political life. In such a context, Barash's project of charting out an autonomous space free of politics for the members of his generation is paradoxically an overtly political gesture that emphatically links them to the dissident movement.[52]

Despite this genealogical tie, Barash and Bialsky's autobiographical novels present a fundamentally different account of the Soviet-Jewish experience in the 1970s and 1980s from the one proposed by Sharansky and Kalik. The post-Stalinist social contract, which had established a direct link between ideological loyalty and material rewards and an increased sphere for private activity, played a crucial role in shaping this difference. Under this arrangement, specific actions, like publicly criticizing the Soviet government in the Western press, faced severe punishments, while other practices, such as buying Wrangler jeans on the black market or attending punk concerts, generally had fewer repercussions. The historical experiences of figures like Natan Sharansky, Mikhail Kalik, and Igor Guberman, who endured years in the Gulag, stand in stark contrast to the experiences of the younger generation of writers like Alice Bialsky and Alexander Barash. Because of this fundamental difference, the autobiographical narratives of the last Soviet generation can portray the Soviet Union as a playground for coming-of-age narratives and as a twilight source of inspiration that fuels the protagonists' creativity, restless existence, and desire for autonomy and independence. Nevertheless, the continued central place of the state in *The Crown Is Not Heavy* and *A Time of One's Own* betrays the fact that underneath their protagonists' deterritorialized cultural and social practices (like those described by Yurchak) lies a highly centralized, top-down model of Soviet society against which these activities and practices are directed. To put it differently, Bialsky and Barash's protagonists' aspiration to exist *vnye* (in Yurchak's terms, a privileged subject position that is simultaneously inside and outside of the authoritative discourse)[53] is not merely a philosophical choice, as Yurchak suggests, but something that must be earned through struggle.

This interplay between the politics of identity of the last Soviet generation and the official Soviet state is evident at the very start of Bialsky's book, where Alisa describes the importance of cultivating a distinct rock 'n' roll image to assert identity. "The look was everything," she says, "black leather jacket, skinny black jeans, tall army boots all laced up, messy punk hair and black sunglasses at any time of the year were the indispensable uniform for any self-respecting rocker."[54] "My biggest pride was black motorcycle goggles from the time of World War II," she adds. "When I wore them in public, covered in black leather, with dark hair protruding in all directions, people dispersed to all sides ... No one argued with me – not even the controller on the subway or cleaning ladies in the department stores. Everyone just let me be."[55] Alisa's appearance and deliberate self-fashioning to be *vnye* (Russian for "outside" or "beyond") social conventions become an act of resistance against the conformist expectations and norms of Soviet state and society. Embracing the vibrant rock subculture of the late 1980s, she adopts punk fashion and a DIY style to express her opposition to the collectivist ethos of Soviet society. The autonomy of being *vnye* in art, dress, and everyday behaviour, which Yurchak describes as a strategy to mark out an area of activity free of politics and economic rationality, is shown in Bialsky's narrative to carry significant political implications in a society where the state seeks to control all areas of cultural, social, and political life – including clothing. The book demonstrates how individuals with long hair and unconventional clothes often faced scrutiny and even physical assault from the police. Recycling fashion and reshuffling history, Alisa uses her "individuality" as a weapon to keep people off. However, by doing so, she also inadvertently places herself in opposition to the Soviet state and becomes a magnet to the watchful eye of the police (*militsiia*).

This scene also illustrates how Alisa's de-territorialized subject position ostensibly places her outside of history – both Soviet and Jewish. The history of World War II, for instance, crystallized in the trunk of grandmother Sofa where Alisa finds the black motorcycle goggles, demonstrates the uncertain relationship between the last Soviet-Jewish generation (to which Alisa belongs) and that of her grandparents, the Red Army veterans. For Alisa, the various trophies that Grandfather Matvei had brought from war are seen as mere material signs devoid of historical content. Alisa has an uncomplicated relationship even to the World War II goggles, which once belonged to a Nazi soldier – they do not conjure up the trauma of the Holocaust, the history of the Great Patriotic War, or trigger a visceral response to the site of suffering and mourning. Instead, Alisa views them as a superficial mark of her individuality, which ultimately positions her outside of both Soviet and Jewish societies and their special relationships to World War II and the Holocaust. Being *vnye*, at least for Alisa, is not simply a mindset but the result of various alienating strategies that have little to do with the past and everything to do with the present. As a result, the history of

World War II is turned into kitsch and may be consumed as a signifier without a referent.

In both *The Crown Is Not Heavy* and *A Time of One's Own*, the prevailing political landscape is that of the police state, characterized by social vigilance, intolerance of individuality, and administrative control through coercion and intimidation. Bialsky illustrates this dynamic in the relationship between punk subculture and official Soviet culture. "At the entrance of Gorbushka rock club in Moscow gathered the punks," she writes. "They were truly hardcore: colorful mohawks, tattoos, piercings. All this at the heart of Soviet Russia … where everyone who wears torn jeans and has a Mohawk hairstyle gets immediately seized by the police, taken to the station, and mercilessly beaten and thrown in jail."[56] However, Alisa's depiction of a clear division between the police and society, and between official and unofficial culture, might be historically inaccurate in the context of 1988, a period of explosion of suppressed historical narratives, literary works, and censored films. Even the surge in underground punk and rock music, as described in the autobiographical texts of Bialsky and Barash, was an outcome of systemic changes resulting from Gorbachev's reforms. In this light, the notion of being *vnye* presented by these authors may have been an alternative system of coordinates that emerged from within the Soviet system itself or, perhaps, an epiphenomenon of its eventual collapse. Bialsky and Barash's claim to have opted out of the totalitarian model of Soviet society could also be seen as a strategic move to assert individual agency, presenting oneself as a force that disrupted the course of Soviet history rather than merely the product of someone else's policies. In this, we see the problems associated with claiming a "deterritorialized" position retrospectively, after history itself has both passed judgment on the Soviet Union and rendered the struggle against it passé.

Moreover, the clear-cut differentiation of punk and Soviet identities in these texts is perhaps too simplistic. Throughout the narrative, Alisa cultivates her countercultural appearance, supported by wacky clothes, army boots, a leather coat with Gagarin and Lenin pins on it, torn stockings and fishnets, a semi-shaved head, and a pair of the Nazi goggles. Yet when confronted by the police, Alisa tells us, and "asked to see my papers, I took off my [World War II] goggles, handed them my internal passport and spoke to them with the voice of an educated girl from a respectable family. They always let me go."[57] This chameleon-like ability to adapt suggests that the boundaries between punk and Soviet identities are more fluid and transient, challenging the notion of a rigidly divided totalitarian model with Manichean oppositions. Alisa's successful code-switching with the police demonstrates that having the right credentials can render the state's social vigilance relatively harmless and that the interplay between punk subculture and Soviet society is more nuanced than simple rebellion against the system.

Additionally, Bialsky's, Barash's, and even Yurchak's texts can be read within the nexus of contemporary interest in the relationship between history, trauma, and nostalgia in the post-Soviet context.[58] Post-Soviet nostalgia – an intensely cathected affective relationship to the "lost" Soviet past – was widespread in the 1990s and 2000s across former Soviet territories and populations. The collapse of the USSR led many to believe that history had come to a halt, demanding a complete evaluation of a past that had been sapped of its ideological underpinnings.[59] Nostalgia, in this context, presented the hope that the lost past might be recoverable, but this longing was supercharged by the knowledge of its irrevocable disappearance. While we may think that nostalgia is a subjective construction, Olga Shevchenko and Maya Nadkarni argue that nostalgia is shaped by various institutionalized forces, including economic interests, political agendas, and social institutions.[60] In other words, while Soviet nostalgia in Russia eventually intertwined with the dominant patriotic narrative of history promoted by the Putin administration, in Israel, it largely served as a coping mechanism, particularly for those facing the challenges of immigrant life, expressing a paradoxical combination of yearning and animosity towards the Soviet era.[61]

Nostalgia for the experience of growing up during Gorbachev's time, with its ideals of freedom, the West, and democracy, is deeply ingrained in the coming-of-age narratives of the last Soviet generation, such as the works by Barash and Bialsky. Still, their vision of Soviet-Jewish history is, once again, quite limited. Unlike the emphasis on a national *Bildungsroman* in dissident writings, which highlights the revival of religious and national consciousness among Soviet Jews, the last Soviet-Jewish generation places the individual at the forefront of its historical vision. As Yurchak argued, the *vnye* position is not about high politics or challenging the regime; rather, it is a survival tactic in the face of competing hegemonic forces and authoritarian discourses.

However, the history of the last Soviet generation also intertwines with the history of the Soviet-Jewish elites: children of well-to-do parents and members of the intelligentsia from the urban centres who inherited their parents' social and symbolic capital, as well as their legacy of other-thinking and non-conformity. This is precisely what distinguishes the coming-of-age narratives of Israel's last Soviet generation from the traditional European *Bildungsroman*, where protagonists typically mature and conform to societal norms. Instead of maturation and integration into the dominant Soviet culture, Barash's *A Time of One's Own* concludes, like Sharansky's and Kalik's narratives, with the protagonist's emigration to Israel. Similarly, Bialsky's novel ends with the protagonist escaping from Soviet authorities. Toward the end of the story, Alisa, heartbroken after her final breakup with Gromov, wanders through her favourite Moscow neighbourhood and accidentally finds herself in a psychiatric asylum. Unimpressed by Alisa's countercultural appearance and poetic-philosophical answers referencing Mandelstam and existentialism, the Soviet therapist contemplates locking her up. As the therapist leaves the room to get help, the book concludes with Alisa's escape from the psychiatric clinic.

Sitting on a window ledge before taking a daring leap to freedom, Alisa considers: "The escape from the Soviet government through the window – this probably passes down among us, 'Balkans,' [code word for Jews] in blood. This whole thing reminded me of my grandfather Matvei who had also escaped from the NKVD through the window [during the Great Terror]."[62] She jumps out of the window and disappears into the streets of Moscow. It is significant that in this final scene, Alisa acknowledges a genealogy of Jewish non-conformism that starts with her grandfather Matvei during the Great Terror, invokes the late Soviet phenomenon of dissidents held in psychiatric clinics and treated with psychoactive drugs due to their non-conformist behaviour, and ends with youth rebellion against Soviet norms and institutions. Dissent becomes the framing device that connects the different generations of Soviet-Jewish history, from her grandfather to herself. At the end of both *A Time of One's Own* and *The Crown Is Not Heavy*, the protagonists reconcile their deterritorialized practices with the legacy of dissent – Barash's protagonist through emigration, Alisa by actively resisting Soviet authority.

Conclusion

The literary and cinematic works of these two generations of writers and filmmakers are closely intertwined with the narrative of Israeli history. Natan Sharansky's *Fear No Evil* and Mikhail Kalik's *And the Wind Returns* inscribe the attempts by Russian-speaking Jews to embrace the Zionist project of identity-building in the context of the Cold War, the collapsing Soviet Union, and the new reality in Israel. Sharansky was able to glean financial and professional rewards from his fame – his books sold millions of copies and were translated into dozens of languages. Professionally Sharansky managed to climb to the top of Israel's occupational ladder, serving at the ministerial level in the Israeli government for ten years. He is a past chair of the Jewish Agency and a current chair for the Institute for the Study of Global Antisemitism and Policy (ISGAP). Upon his arrival to Israel, Kalik was treated like a celebrity. He was visited by famous writers, filmmakers, and politicians, was given an apartment in Tel Aviv, and received favourable news coverage in the Israeli media. His first Israeli film, *Three and One* (1974), was personally subsidized by Pinchas Sapir, Israel's minister of finance. The film's failure at the box office, however, resulted in the alienation of Israel's cultural elites and ended with Kalik's (first) retirement from commercial cinema (he continued making documentary films). The filmmaker was consigned to obscurity not only in the USSR, where his films were banned, but also in Israel, where his films were largely ignored.

After the collapse of the USSR and the normalization of Israel's relations with post-Soviet countries, a notable shift occurred among younger generations of Russian-speaking Jews such as Alexander Barash and Alice Bialsky. This generation of writers and cultural producers began to turn away from the lachrymose conception of the Soviet-Jewish past as formulated by Sharansky and Kalik, instead adopting a more positive view of their Soviet-Jewish history and heritage. In their first-person accounts, instead of dwelling on the hardships of the USSR, they depicted their experiences in the Soviet Union as an exciting time, marked by thrilling run-ins with the police, enthusiastic engagement with underground art and music, and alternative lifestyles that blossomed during the transformative era of perestroika and the crumbling of the Soviet world. Having lived in Israel for almost two decades, their wistful memory of the Soviet past reflects their lengthy sojourn in Israel and a selective forgetting of the difficulties of the

Soviet era for Jews. This larger project of historical revisionism of the Soviet past would predominate in Israel until Russia's invasion of Ukraine in 2022, as explored in chapter 4 of this book. The invasion brought a new reality that shattered any lingering nostalgia for the Soviet era. Younger generations of authors who had viewed the Soviet past through a lens of excitement and transformation were forced to confront the darker aspects of this history. The ongoing conflict highlighted the oppressive and violent elements of the Soviet regime that had been glossed over, leading these writers to reassess their earlier perspectives.

CHAPTER 2

"Excuse Me, Are You Jewish?"

The Newfound Religiosity of Post-Soviet Jews in Israel

The Sausage *Aliyah*

In 2012, Zoya Cherkassky-Nnadi created a small-scale drawing titled *Kashrut Check*, which measures 14 by 17 cm and was made using pencils and markers on paper. The artwork depicted an Orthodox rabbi conducting a home visit to a young family from the USSR who were undergoing conversion to Judaism. The subject took hold of the artist, leading her to revisit it a year later. This time, she reimagined the work on a larger scale, using tempera on linen, resulting in a piece twice the size of the original and rich in intricate details. In 2016, Cherkassky-Nnadi returned to this painting one last time, producing a monumental oil painting measuring 120 by 150 cm, which she named *Rabbi's Deliquium*. Figure 2.1 shows the latest version of the artwork.

What is depicted in the painting? During the process of *giyur* (Hebrew for "conversion to Judaism") in Israel, there comes a stage where the individual undergoing conversion receives an unexpected visit from a rabbi. This visit is part of the conversion process mandated by state rabbinic authorities in Israel, whose purpose is to ensure that the person converting is adhering to the regulations and traditions of Judaism, including maintaining a kosher kitchen. Cherkassky-Nnadi depicts this exact moment, taking us *in medias res*, as a young family from the former USSR is taken aback by an unexpected visit from a rabbi. At first glance, everything seems to align

Figure 2.1
Zoya Cherkassky-Nnadi, *Rabbi's Deliquium*, 2016, oil on linen, 120 × 150 cm.

with proper kosher practices. The couple is dressed modestly, the man wearing a kippah and the woman's hair hidden behind a scarf. The table is set with Sabbath candles, a kiddush cup, and a prayer book, all prepared for the Sabbath rituals. They even go the extra mile by placing a kippah on a baby, although traditionally this is done at a later age. An Israeli flag is visible at the upper centre of the painting, adorning the gift calendar from Leumi Bank (Hebrew for "national"). Overall, the couple's religious devotion appears in synch with Israel's nationalism.

Despite the "kosher" appearance of their home, seemingly in line with religious guidelines, the visiting rabbi remains unconvinced. He decides to dig deeper by inspecting their refrigerator. To his horror, he discovers a large pig snout staring back at him, directly contradicting the couple's purported adherence to Jewish dietary laws. Of course, the pig's snout symbolizes more than just pork; it serves as a representation of the post-Soviet immigrant community in a broader sense. Among Hebrew speakers, immigrants from the USSR were frequently referred to as "aliyat naknik" (sausage *aliyah*). This term not only hints at the material rather than ideological motivations behind post-Soviet Jewish immigration, but also suggests the community's penchant for pork, thereby implying a lack of genuine connection to Judaism.

Despite the absurd and comic nature of the painting, the situation is profoundly serious. As Amitai Mendelsohn explains, in the Soviet Union, "Jewishness was considered to be passed down through the male line, whereas according to halakha (Jewish religious law), which is what counts in Israel, only a Jewish mother could confer Jewish identity for her offspring."[1] Through conversion, the couple depicted in the painting, like many other immigrants from the USSR who found themselves unrecognized as Jews in Israel, sought to achieve greater integration into Israeli society, enhance their civic and economic prospects, and obtain access to rights and benefits reserved for Jewish citizens only. The presence of a pig's snout in their refrigerator could potentially undermine all the efforts and aspirations of the young family, putting their social standing in jeopardy. Looking back at the faces of the couple, we can detect traces of sadness, anxiety, and fear. Even the newborn seems to grasp the gravity of the situation. At the mercy of the rabbi, who holds the sole authority to grant them status as Jews in Israel, the couple anxiously awaits their fate, uncertain of the price they will need to pay for the disparity between their Jewish identity and their dietary practices.

Taking the painting as a point of departure, this chapter examines Israeli literature and cinema of post-Soviet Jews and argues that the growing interest in Judaism among ex-Soviet Jews is more than a natural rediscovery of roots or an antidote to the near-complete disappearance of religious practice among Jews in the Soviet Union. Instead, the chapter connects this newly sparked interest in faith to three factors: 1) negative perception of Russian-speaking immigrants among the local population and the media in Israel, which apprehend them as inadequate Jews who do not measure up to authentic Jewish standards because of their atheism, appetite for pork, and indifference to organized religion; 2) demographic settlement patterns of ex-Soviet Jews in the Israeli periphery, primarily populated by religious

Zionists and Mizrahi Jews; 3) a conscious strategy to tap into religion as a way to frame themselves as part of the Jewish majority in Israel, often at the expense of non-Jewish groups.

The chapter examines two case studies: Pini Tavger's film *More Than I Deserve* (2021) and Dina Rubina's bestselling novel *Here Comes the Messiah!* (1995). Tavger's film indicates that post-Soviet Jews are often drawn toward religion by proximity to, and mimicry of, their religious-nationalist neighbours on the fringes of Israel. In other words, post-Soviet Jews use religion as a means to assimilate and counter the stereotype that they are inadequate Jews who do not meet "authentic" Jewish standards. This tendency is especially visible in areas with a more traditional and religious population. Rubina's novel, set in a West Bank settlement, suggests that the resurgence of religion in Israel's Russophone literature is used to reaffirm a sense of belonging for Soviet-born Jews among the Jewish majority in Israel, especially among religious Zionists, and to contrast them with non-Jewish demographics, particularly Palestinians. This differential identity politics held specific implications for the political commitments of ex-Soviet Jews. I will demonstrate this through my analysis of Rubina's works, which consistently conflate Jewish religion with nationalist politics by casting Palestinians as dangerous terrorists and framing the Land of Israel as inherently sacred and exclusively Jewish.

Ex-Soviet Jews and Religion

Most Jewish studies scholars from Israel and North America have found Soviet and post-Soviet Jews wanting in their knowledge of Jewish traditions, cultural heritage, and practices. Zvi Gitelman uses negative terms such as "thin culture," "symbolic ethnicity," and "disaggregated identity" to describe the cultural and religious affiliation of Soviet Jews.[2] According to Gitelman, during the twentieth century, Soviet-Jewish identity came to be emptied of its traditional, historical, and religious content, and as such Soviet Jews came to define themselves in predominantly ethnic and secular terms.[3] The existence of two different Russian words to designate a Jewish person – an ethnic one, *evrei*, and a religious one, *iudei* – indicates the uncoupling of Judaism and Jewishness in the cultural and religious identities of Soviet-born Jews.

Gitelman's claims align with empirical evidence. Surveys conducted by Gitelman, Chervyakov, and Shapiro, which involved over 3,000 Jews from Russia and Ukraine in 1992 and 1997, demonstrated that the vast majority of Russian and Ukrainian Jews did not associate religious practice with being Jewish. When asked about the criteria for being considered "a genuine Jew," responses emphasizing ethnic pride, defending Jewish honour, not concealing Jewish identity, and remembering the Holocaust accounted for over 70 per cent. Conversely, responses involving religious observance, such as belief in God, marrying within the faith, understanding Judaism's basics, circumcising sons, adhering to *kashrut* dietary laws, observing the Sabbath, and attending synagogue, were significantly underrepresented, garnering only about 6 per cent. These findings underscore the limited role of religious practice and traditional customs in shaping the identity of Russian and Ukrainian Jews in the post-Soviet era. Reflecting on this, Fran Markowitz concludes that "when Soviet Jews think about what makes them Jewish, they arrive at one certain criterion – being born a Jew."[4]

In her foundational work, *Doubly Chosen: Jewish Identity, the Soviet Intelligentsia, and the Russian Orthodox Church*, Judith Kornblatt shows how a biological understanding of Jewishness allowed her Soviet-Jewish respondents to convert to Orthodox Christianity without feeling as if they were rejecting their Jewishness and leaving the tribe. Surprisingly, a considerable portion of Russian and Ukrainian Jews – about 60 per cent – did not view conversion to Christianity as negating their Jewish identity, reflecting a clear separation of ethnic and religious components of their Soviet-Jewish identities.[5] Paradoxically, Kornblatt found that a majority of Soviet Jews who converted to Christianity felt "*more*, not less Jewish after their Baptism."[6] This phenomenon challenges prevailing paradigms that view assimilation, intermarriage, and conversion as threats to Jewish identity, indicating that individuals can fortify their Jewish identity even after such transformations.

A common thread among these studies is the shared conclusion that Soviet Jews have progressively distanced themselves from religion, Judaism, and what is considered "authentic" Jewish culture. Gitelman attributes this trend to the fading foundation in Jewish languages, active religious engagement, and traditional customs. When the religiosity of Soviet-born Jews is finally given the spotlight, as in Kornblatt's study, it is Christianity, not Judaism, that takes centre stage. Other studies, such as Sonja Luehrmann's

Secularism: Soviet Style, emphasize factors like governmental suppression of religion, the Soviet promotion of scientific atheism, and the resulting religious void within Soviet society.[7] Ultimately, these studies arrive at a similar consensus – that the Soviet Jewish community has become increasingly disconnected from Judaism.

When we examine the religiosity of post-Soviet Jews after their relocation to Israel, however, an unexpected and intriguing narrative unfolds. Israeli scholars such as Julia Lerner, Larissa Remennick, and Nelly Elias have meticulously documented a significant rise in religious knowledge, active involvement, and observance within the ex-Soviet Jewish community in Israel over the past three decades. In contrast to Gitelman's findings from 1992 and 1997, the comprehensive survey conducted by Remennick and Prashizky in 2012, encompassing 507 former Soviet emigrants in Israel, indicated that religious and traditional observance of ex-Soviet Jews had grown to four times the amount registered in Gitelman's surveys.[8] Remarkably, a shift occurred from 75 per cent of post-Soviet Jews self-identifying as atheists in Israel in 1993 to only 30 per cent declaring themselves as atheists by 2012.[9] This transformation is particularly striking given the ideological secularity of the Israeli state (albeit not fully realized in practice) and the historical hostility to religion among Zionists and early state leaders. While these findings effectively illustrate the changing patterns of religiosity and identity within the post-Soviet Jewish community in Israel, they, frustratingly, do not fully explain the underlying reasons driving these transformations.

To answer this question, let us return to Cherkassky-Nnadi's painting. In a sense, the artwork captures the intense suspicion of Israeli religious authorities toward post-Soviet immigrants, subjecting their (Jewish) identities to careful scrutiny. Granted, this suspicion arose through the newcomers' limited understanding of Judaism, Jewish culture, and Israeli society, as indicated by Gitelman and others. Although not explicitly stated by Remennick and Prashizky, their conclusion that the increased religious engagement among post-Soviet Jews reflects "social conformism rather than expressions of their newly discovered Judaic piety" is especially poignant.[10] In the new social environment, where post-Soviet immigrants were often seen as "pork eaters," embracing religion had diverse motivations. For some, it was a means of assimilating into Israeli societal norms; others used religion to establish their position within the Israeli Jewish majority; still others were driven by strong right-wing politics that aligned with the religious Zionists’ worldview.[11] These multifaceted factors highlight the complex interplay between personal decisions and the larger social context in shaping the religious commitment of post-Soviet Jews in Israel.

Religious Mimicry in the Israeli Periphery: Pini Tavger’s *More Than I Deserve*

The director Pini Tavger was born in 1978 to immigrants from Russia and Ukraine who settled in Israel in the 1970s and was raised in a Russian-speaking household. Tavger’s cultural background plays a significant role in shaping his art. During his studies in the Film and Television Department at Tel Aviv University, he directed two short films about the ex-Soviet community in Israel: *Weitzman Street 10* (2006) and *Pinchas* (2008). Both films garnered acclaim at various film festivals, received important awards, and were screened on television in Israel and Europe. *Weitzman Street 10* is an absurdist depiction of a family of newly arrived former USSR immigrants, who are (literally, but also symbolically) searching for their home on Weitzman Street against the backdrop of shelling of Tel Aviv during the first Gulf War. The second film, inspired by Tavger’s own life, centres on Pinchas, a young immigrant boy from the USSR, who lives with his mother, who prioritizes her own needs over his. In the midst of this challenging environment, Pinchas forms a meaningful connection with a neighbour, an Orthodox Jew from a Mizrahi family, who gradually introduces Pinchas to religion.

Unlike most cultural producers from the USSR, Tavger has gained widespread popularity in Israel. After his studies at Tel Aviv University, he hosted the Israeli version of the American reality show *Beauty and the Geek*, a role he fulfilled for three seasons. This marked the beginning of his acting career, during which he achieved nationwide fame. He starred in the extremely popular musical telenovela *Hashir shelanu*, alongside renowned singer and actress Ninet Tayeb. He went from portraying the traumatized kibbutznik boy in the critically acclaimed *Sweet Mud* (2006) to depicting ultra-Orthodox Jews and a gay drag artist leading a dual life in *More Than a Heartbeat* (2012). In addition to acting, Tavger is also actively involved in theatre and creates his own original music – mostly rock and pop. Recently, he released his debut album *Hakol roed* (*Everything Trembles*, 2019).

After a career as an actor and musician, Tavger returned to directing with his debut feature film, *More Than I Deserve*, adapted from his earlier short film *Pinchas*. The film follows Ukrainian immigrant Pinchas, a young boy living with his mother, Tamara. Tamara, engaged in an affair with a married man and working night shifts, struggles to be present for Pinchas, leaving him mostly alone. The plot takes off when Pinchas overhears that boys from his school are taking free bar mitzvah lessons from Shimon, an ultra-Orthodox man and his neighbour. Against his mother's will, Pinchas signs up for these lessons, and Shimon becomes a father figure for the youth. As the movie unfolds, Tamara recognizes Shimon's positive impact on her son. Shimon and Tamara's friendship evolves into romance, considerably complicating their lives. Everyone opposes this union – Shimon's parents, the rabbis who advocate for a traditional match, and even Pinchas, who is initially unsure how to respond. Succumbing to peer pressure, Shimon breaks up with Tamara, and her life falls back into disarray. Pinchas is left to help his mother piece her life back together.

Although the film is not strictly autobiographical, Tavger drew on his personal experiences when creating the story. As he notes in an interview:

> Like Pinchas, my parents divorced when I was a kid, and I was raised by a single mother. I yearned for the presence of a father figure, and I met a neighbor, a Chabadnik, who sparked my interest in religion and told me about the significance of my name, that Pinchas was considered a hero … I was jealous that he had a large, warm Mizrahi family, and I enjoyed the sense of unity when they attended synagogue together. I made the decision to become observant – for two weeks, I wore a kippah on my head. I was only six years old, and it worried my mother a little; she said, "When you're 13, you can decide whether you want to be observant."[12]

In this quote, Tavger explains why Pinchas the character, Pini the director, and many Russian-speaking immigrants chose to turn to religion after arriving in Israel. The previous section ended with a question: "Why do post-Soviet Jews become religious?" The movie provides insight into the appeal of religion for post-Soviet Jews, stranded in a new country, including the allure of a vibrant Jewish community, the sense of belonging through communal aspects of religion, and its potential to heal personal and family wounds.

The opening sequence of the film depicts thirteen-year-old Pinchas returning home from school. His mother is asleep amid a near-empty fridge, dirty dishes, scattered beer bottles, and unopened moving boxes piled up on the floor. The scene shifts to a concrete soccer field where Pinchas sits, his back to us, watching neighbourhood kids play soccer. Amid their laughter and excitement, the camera focuses on Pinchas's solemn expression. He waits eagerly to join the game but is overlooked, as another boy is chosen instead. Pinchas exclaims, "But I was here first." However, the world of thirteen-year-old boys is not fair, leaving him sidelined. The scene then cuts back to Pinchas's home, where his now-awake mother, draped in a towel, cooks him ham sausage and eggs with one hand, cigarette in the other. Once again, a passive-aggressive tracking shot reveals empty beer bottles, unopened moving boxes, a messy kitchen, and the poverty and neglect that surround them.

Through this opening sequence, the director highlights the isolation and alienation experienced by the titular character. In the unnamed periphery town, he stands apart from the broader Israeli society. He has no friends, the neighbourhood kids do not want to play with him, and he is relegated to the sidelines of the society he yearns to belong to. While everyone is having fun, he is brooding and melancholy. This outsider status, the film suggests, is linked to his post-Soviet background. The food that he eats – pork – acts as a symbol of the boy's otherness, and a mechanism for creating social boundaries within Israeli society. It remains unclear whether the boy is aware of kashrut laws and whether he chooses to eat ham sausage out of ignorance, indifference, or due to a lack of alternative options, given the family's limited financial means.

The narrative picks up pace when Pinchas learns that the boys he is eager to become friends with receive free Bar Mitzvah lessons from Shimon, an ultra-Orthodox man living in the neighbourhood. But why does Pinchas develop a religious interest? In the film, we see that Pinchas follows Chabadnik Shimon not because it is a natural reconnection to his roots as a Soviet-born prodigal son but mainly because other children are doing it, and he wants to blend in. In other words, it was an attempt to counteract his feelings of isolation and being an outsider, and to find a community. In a world where his single mother struggles to support herself and her teenage son and is unable – or perhaps unwilling – to provide the emotional connection he yearns for, joining other kids to study for his bar mitzvah offers him the support, community, and nurturing environment he lacks at the start of the movie.

While feelings of community and a sense of belonging are major motivations to join religious organizations, Tavger further underscores his point by juxtaposing the two homes Pinchas experiences – Mizrahi and "Russian." The somewhat stereotypical Mizrahi home radiates warmth with its close-knit family, religion, traditions, and plentiful food – all the things Pinchas desires. In contrast, the "Russian" home is depicted as dark, alienating, lonely, overtly sexual, unwelcoming, and notably precarious. It contains empty beer bottles, unopened moving boxes, cigarette smoke, an empty fridge, and windows that are rarely opened. This environment captures a broken family, shattered dreams, and unstable circumstances. Shimon's world of religion starkly contrasts with Pinchas's immigrant situation, and this is why the prospects of religion so attract Pinchas – it offers an escape from his bleak reality and a way to undo his "Russianness" and become more Jewish. It is significant that in their first conversation, Shimon explains to Pinchas the meaning of his name by recounting the story of the biblical Pinchas, who killed the Israelite prince Zimri and a foreign princess with a spear during their sexual act. With this parable about the dangers of assimilation, Shimon effectively "Judaizes" the pork-eating Pinchas by incorporating him into the collective Jewish history and the fold with the Jewish people.

Not only does Pinchas catch the religious "bug" after his encounter with Shimon, but so does Tamara. While religion becomes a means for Pinchas to join a community of boys his age and find a fatherly figure in Shimon, for Tamara, a physical relation with Shimon, and by extension a spiritual relation with God, can be seen as an attempt to build a functional family home that could replace her broken "Russian" one. Tamara's religious awakening is more practical than spiritual. Her disposal of "contaminated" dishes and utensils is not driven by a concern for religious laws, but rather by her desire to cook for Shimon and present herself as "pure" to the man she is interested in. Similarly, her first experience in the mikveh (ritual bath) is not about religion, God, or spirituality. It is about her determination to change her life, win Shimon's affection, and appear more "purified" according to Shimon's stringent Jewish standards, which do not align with her overt "Russianness." Ultimately, just as Pinchas wears a kippah to shed his "Russian" identity, Tamara immerses herself in the mikveh for the same reason – to distance herself from her "Soviet" background.

Another significant factor for Pinchas's growing religiosity is the film's setting in the Israeli periphery. Vicki Idzinsky's study, "Becoming Israeli, Becoming Mizrahi?," proposes that to comprehend the social dynamics of the ex-Soviet community in Israel, we need to pay more attention to the remote towns on the edge of Israeli geography where they settled.[13] The mass arrival of ex-Soviet Jews to Israel during the 1990s resulted in an unprecedented housing shortage, inflation, and widespread unemployment. In just one year, rent prices tripled, pushing the housing market to its limit, especially in major cities like Tel Aviv, Jerusalem, and Haifa. These conditions forced many newcomers to the working-class outskirts of Israel's geography, where rent was more affordable due to government incentives and subsidies. In these areas, Russian speakers crossed paths with Mizrahi Jews, whom the state had forced to settle there in the 1950s. Recognizing this prehistory is crucial because in these shared spaces, ex-Soviet newcomers, particularly the younger generation, learned what it meant to be Israeli from their largely Mizrahi and religious neighbours, adopting their ideas, customs, and religious identities.

The religiosity of both Pinchas and Tamara in the movie can be seen as a form of identification with, and mimicry of, their religious Mizrahi neighbour Shimon. The film repeatedly portrays Pinchas's and Tamara's religiosity as performative and inauthentic gestures. Throughout the movie, they are not depicted as holding genuine beliefs in God or having a profound understanding of religious practices. This is emphasized in both the short and extended versions of the film. For instance, Tamara requires step-by-step instruction on what to do during the mikveh (ritual bath) or a Shabbat dinner, while Pinchas struggles with reciting prayers in the synagogue. Another example of religious performativity occurs in the short version of the film when Pinchas crafts a kippah and tallit from a comic book since he lacks these items. However, this performativity does not diminish the sincerity of their efforts to genuinely experience religion. Wearing a comic book kippah, sneaking into a synagogue uninvited, and studying for bar mitzvah reflect Pinchas's genuine desire to assimilate as an Israeli because, in the low-income area where he lives, religion is the primary way of being Israeli that Pinchas knows of. Ultimately, Pinchas's story reveals how post-Soviet Jews endeavoured to "translate" themselves into authentic Israelis by embracing the cultural and religious toolkit of Mizrahi Jews they encountered in Israel's periphery.[14] In a sense, this strategy of assimilation repeats the history of Jews from Arab countries who migrated to Israel in the 1950s. In his book *The Arab Jew: A Postcolonial Reading of Nationalism, Religion, and Ethnicity*, Shenhav demonstrates that for many Mizrahi Jews, adopting religious Zionist identities was a strategy for assimilation and survival in Israeli society.[15] "I argue," Shenhav writes, "that the Arab Jews had no choice but to be 'religious' in order to have a voice in Zionist discourse."[16] This adoption and adaptation were driven by the desire for acceptance and upward mobility in a society that marginalized them based on their ethnic and cultural background, which was perceived as too Arab and, therefore, threatening and incompatible with the Zionist foundation of the State of Israel.[17] By aligning with the dominant religious Zionist ideology, Arab Jews sought to mitigate social and economic disadvantages, often at the expense of their Arab cultural heritage. Thus, post-Soviet immigrants' emphasis on religiosity to assert Jewish identity in response to marginalization is not just a typological similarity with Mizrahi Jews but a specific tradition of "rite of passage" for marginalized immigrant Jewish communities in Israel, including Sephardic, Mizrahi, and Ethiopian Jews, on their path toward acceptance and integration in the country.

As the film draws to a close, the clash between religion and Pinchas's Russianness becomes increasingly evident, revealing their inability to coexist. Faith requires the obliteration of his post-Soviet identity, symbolically embodied by his mother. When Shimon leaves Tamara to marry his Orthodox *shiduch* (match), she regresses into self-destructive behaviour stereotypically associated with "Russian" women – excessive drinking, going out, and sexual affairs. One day, as Pinchas returns home from school, he hears his mother's sexual encounter with her married ex-partner, Yossi. Like the biblical Pinchas, the boy wields a modern-day "spear," in this case, a kitchen knife, barges into his mother's room, raises the knife overhead, and, muttering a prayer, directs it against the sinner, Yossi, inflicting a deep cut on his arm but failing to replicate the biblical Pinchas's double slaying.

How can we interpret this psychoanalytical, primordial, biblical drama? Does it imply that to be fully connected to Judaism, one must symbolically kill one's mother, relinquish post-Soviet mentality, and sever all ties with one's diasporic origin? Or, alternatively, does it underscore the complexity of identity negotiation in any transformative journey, especially one that juggles both religious awakening and immigration? In the last scene, Pinchas stands at a crossroads. He can either proceed with his bar mitzvah or return home and care for his intoxicated mother. Returning home, he tends to her as she vomits, assuming a parental role and lying that his bar mitzvah went well. This scene shifts familial roles – the boy cooks, irons, and nurtures. He embraces a parent-like role, emblematic of immigrant dynamics where children assume parental responsibilities due to their faster assimilation into the country's language and culture. She remains the infantile adolescent, indulging in partying and drinking, while he is left to piece together the shattered fragments of their family. As he returns to the dark "Russian" home, turning his back on religion and his bar mitzvah ceremony, he has learned critical lessons from his experiences. In the last scene, after she finishes emptying her bowels, Pinchas and Tamara are sprawled out on the floor, surrounded by poverty and dilapidation.

The juxtaposition of religious books on one side and the toilet on the other is telling, symbolizing the disillusionment and abandonment of religion in the face of harsh realities faced by newcomers. The sacredness of

Figure 2.2
Pini Tavger, *More Than I Deserve* (2021): Pinchas (played by Micha Prudovsky) and Tamara (played by Ana Dubrovitzki) are left helpless by the harsh reality at the film's end.

religious texts, traditionally associated with purity, spiritual guidance, and hope, is placed in direct opposition to the profane and abject environment of the toilet, a space associated with waste and filth. This powerful imagery underscores the dissonance between the promise of a better life through religious devotion and the actual lived experience of marginalization and hardship. Ultimately, the film can be interpreted as a condemnation of the Orthodox religious community's hostility toward outsiders, exemplified by how Pinchas and Tamara are lured into believing in a better life, only to be rejected yet again. This rejection underscores the exclusionary practices within certain religious communities toward immigrants from the USSR, who are viewed as impure and in need of complete religious transformation to be accepted. Pinchas's decision to abandon religion is a poignant commentary on the failures of the religious communities to embrace and support the Russophone *olim*. However, it is important to note that not all immigrants from the USSR followed the same path as Pinchas, as the rest of the chapter will illustrate.

From Soviet Goyim to Religious Zionists: Dina Rubina's *Here Comes the Messiah!*

Dina Rubina is a renowned contemporary Russian-language writer, whose books are popular among Russophone audiences in Russia, Israel, Europe, and North America. She was born and raised in Tashkent, where her Jewish family was evacuated during World War II. To pursue a literary career, Rubina first moved to Moscow in 1984. When Gorbachev legalized emigration in 1989, the author and her family uprooted themselves a second time, settling in the large West Bank settlement of Ma'ale Adumim, near Jerusalem, in 1990. In Israel, she wrote her first and perhaps most renowned novel, *Vot idet mashiah!* (*Here Comes the Messiah*!). Published in 1996 in Russian (and translated into English in 2000 but not into Hebrew), the novel offers a humorous sketch of the everyday life of ex-Soviet Jewish émigrés in the West Bank, Jerusalem, and Tel Aviv. The subject of cultural and religious identities of this community is depicted through a diverse cast of vibrant characters that populate the pages of *Messiah*. Among them are self-proclaimed messiahs and zealots: Mustafa, a holy fool of Mizrahi extraction, who wanders back and forth between Jerusalem and Tel Aviv, asking for alms and singing "Here Comes the Messiah";[18] Angel-of-Paradise, the Russian Diaspora Spiritual Center's director, who clinically dies at the start of the novel but later returns to life;[19] and a tattooed, half-naked, religious lunatic with supernatural strength arriving, like a Messiah, in South Tel Aviv on Yom Kippur, claiming he was sent by God to the Children of Israel to unite the "recalcitrant tribes."[20]

Critically, *Messiah* is often analyzed as part of transnational Russophone and Jewish literature. Mikhail Krutikov considers the novel in the context of contemporary Russophone Jewish writing in Russia, Israel, and Germany, and interprets it as a narrative of disillusionment. "Among the shattered dreams [that the novel depicts]," he writes, "are the comfort of homecoming, the security of the state, and the sense of purpose of Zionism."[21] Similarly, Maggie Levantovskaya looks at how Rubina's novel complicates notions of settledness, nationalism, and Zionism and instead advocates for mobility that unsettles the link between people and territory.[22] However, their analysis of the global positioning of *Messiah* and its subversion of Israel's homecoming narrative overlooks the novel's palpable right-wing and Zionist elements. As a result, the transnational reading of the novel detaches it from its local ideological context. This section will highlight the proper cultural and political context for interpreting the novel: mid-1990s Israel in general and the settlements in particular.

The novel can be seen as a response to Zvi Gitelman's view on the "thin" identity of post-Soviet Jews and their perception as "non-kosher" in Israel. From the first pages, *Messiah* presents a confident performance of Jewishness with deep ties to Judaism and rich in Jewish history, culture, and religious allusions. The novel starts with an epigraph from the Jewish philosopher Maimonides – "I believe with perfect faith in the coming of the Messiah, and, though he tarry, I will wait daily for his coming,"[23] asserting that centuries have not weakened this belief. The novel then establishes a uniquely Jewish chronotope, marking the date as "kaf zain in the month of Adar, five thousand seven hundred fifty-five" (27 February 1996) and describing an Israeli reality, mentioning an incident involving Hezbollah guerillas and Israeli soldiers patrolling the Lebanese border.[24] These references place the reader in a distinct Jewish temporality rooted in Jewish geography and spirituality. In addition, the use of *nashi soldatyi*, "our soldiers," for Israeli soldiers emphasizes ex-Soviet Jews' belonging within Israeli society, in contrast to other works portraying newcomers as culturally conflicted outsiders.

The novel is constructed in an episodic manner, with many loose threads, and follows two protagonists. The first is Ziama, an intellectual who, like Rubina herself, moved from Moscow to a West Bank settlement. She boasts of her quick absorption process, which rekindles her dormant Jewish identity. She masters Hebrew, starts to keep Jewish dietary laws, and lives in accordance with *halakha*. The second protagonist is writer N., a successful and sarcastic writer who also lives in the ex-Soviet enclave on the West Bank, near Ziama's settlement of Neve-Ephraim. Her world is more culturally Russian, with limited religious expressions. N. is writing a novel about Russian speakers in Israel, with Ziama as her protagonist. The novel alternates between Ziama's and writer N.'s points of view. As the novel progresses, it becomes increasingly unclear whether Ziama is a figment of writer N.'s imagination or an actual person inspiring the character. The two protagonists' narratives converge only at the end of the novel, when they meet in a Jerusalem restaurant on Yom Kippur, and writer N.'s good-for-nothing son Shmulik unintentionally shoots Ziama while trying to stop a Palestinian planning a terrorist attack. The novel concludes in heaven, where Ziama reunites with her beloved grandfather and learns that he is the Messiah. Redemption ensues.

Critics have commented on the difference between writer N. and Ziama. Mikhail Krutikov suggests that the two protagonists reflect the two parts of the author's own split identity: Ziama, "a convinced Zionist [who] comes to live in a community of settlers on the West Bank," and writer N., "who struggles with the problems of immigrant life in Israel."[25] Kevin M.F. Platt views them as representing different immigration experiences: Ziama embodies assimilation, and writer N. reflects segregation.[26] Maggie Levantovskaya considers them polar opposites, with writer N. using Ziama as a projection of her desire for return migration.[27] All three view Ziama as an idealized Zionist poster child, contrasting sharply with the "real" struggles of ex-Soviet immigrants who face doubts and hardships. If Ziama symbolizes a triumphant homecoming, then writer N. – alongside other Russophone characters in the novel – represents a failure to integrate into Israeli society.

While writer N. is often used to illustrate broader arguments about the social alienation of post-Soviet Jews in Israel, these interpretations, though reflective of the social reality of the Russophone community in Israel, do not align with the novel's underlying Zionist logic. For instance, let us look at a key scene that recounts writer N.'s flashback to her arrival at Ben Gurion Airport in Israel. In this scene, the narrator immerses us in writer N.'s thoughts as she observes armed Israeli soldiers around her. "She suddenly felt such an endless orphanhood, homelessness, deprivation, and a nauseating terror," the narrator notes. "She understood that it was the same from birth to death – she was doomed to being escorted by automatic weapons; and it didn't matter – whether to the execution pit, or whether to save her life. Everything was finished, everything perished, and there was nowhere to return to; return was impossible."[28] Indeed, it is possible to read this scene as undermining Israel's ideological claim to be the natural and exclusive homeland of the Jewish people, where Jews are safe. Writer N.'s visceral reaction to the presence of armed soldiers at Ben Gurion Airport reflects a profound sense of alienation and existential dread, suggesting that for her, the promised refuge in Israel is fraught with fear and uncertainty rather than security and belonging. The parallel between immigration to Israel and the execution pits of the Holocaust is especially jarring, particularly when read against Israel's self-image as a refuge for Jews worldwide.

At the same time, the image of automatic weapons does not solely evoke fear – it also implies security and protection, particularly for writer N. and other Jews in Israel (as opposed to Palestinians). Despite the initial shock at the sight of weapons, and the surprising inability to register that armed soldiers are present in many airports in many countries, writer N. also notes that automatic weapons can also "save her life" – a thought that stands in direct opposition to the image of Jewish helplessness during the Holocaust. This juxtaposition highlights the complex feelings writer N. experiences as an immigrant in Israel, where the presence of armed soldiers can be both unsettling and reassuring (at least to the Jewish population). The importance of automatic weapons and the ability to protect oneself becomes especially clear at the end of the novel, which concludes with an outbreak of Palestinian violence directed at Israeli civilians.

While this scene challenges Israel's homecoming narrative, it is significant that Rubina juxtaposes it with a contrasting scene in a kibbutz that immediately follows the airport encounter, in which the lost Eden is reclaimed. In the twin scene, writer N. enjoys a serene family vacation on a kibbutz in Israel – a swimming pool beneath an open sky, nature all around them, her son blissfully swimming, and her husband photographing every moment. There, writer N. achieves a perfect synergy between herself and her adopted country, resulting in a strong sense of national belonging. As a result of her sojourn, N. experiences a transformative shift in her perception – a veil seems to lift as if a "wet film suddenly began to slip off the surrounding world. Residual droplets rolled down and away, and then there at the corner, the dear sun began cheerily to shine."[29] Writer N.'s spiritual blindness in the USSR contrasts with her newly found sense of clarity and spiritual fulfillment following a year and a half in Israel. Ultimately, what critics describe as N.'s – and the broader ex-Soviet community's – quintessential condition of "rootlessness" is a mere moment of transition that passes fairly quickly. Indeed, the scene on the kibbutz suggests that the mythical and ideological narrative of *aliyah* is not subverted – it might be paused, momentarily adjusted, yet the overall ideological trajectory remains intact. Israel continues to function as the ultimate homeland of the Jewish people and a place where they achieve happiness and fulfillment.

Rubina depicts Ziama's homecoming in even more powerful terms. "She'd already absorbed this country and its population," she writes, reversing the traditional dynamics between immigrants and the host country.[30] Rubina likens Ziama's integration into Israel to the moment a mother sees her child, "brought to [her] breast for its first feeding."[31] This intimate metaphor suggests a biological, familial, and blood relation between Ziama and the Jewish people in Israel. It fundamentally extends the biological understanding of Jewishness from the Soviet context to the Israeli one. After spending more time in Israel, the narrator continues, "partially forgotten little words and flourishes of Grandpa surfaced in [Ziama's] memory: he'd say 'meileh,' when he had 'okay' in mind; would often sigh 'khob rakhmones' and would pronounce the name Jerusalem as 'Yersholoim.'"[32] In other words, a short vacation in the Jewish state catalyzes the return of Ziama's Jewish identity that remained dormant during the Soviet era. Yiddish words begin to return to Ziama, the lost tradition of honouring the Sabbath is resurrected, until ultimately "she began meeting her dead relatives on the streets, in stores, on public transportation" – a clear messianic trope that conflates immigration with redemption.[33] With this scene, Rubina illustrates that the obliterated Jewish identity of ex-Soviet Jews can be quickly recovered in the correct environment.

Both writer N.'s and Ziama's journeys back to Jewish culture eschew any notions of rootlessness or alienation. Instead, both characters are fully grounded in their host country. Their bond with the nation reflects Derrida's concept of "ontopology," where physical bodies and territories intertwine – here, through a connection between Jews and the biblical Land of Israel.[34] Derrida's theory of ontopology (a portmanteau word combining "ontology," the study of being, and "topology," the study of place or space) suggests that one's identity and existence are inherently linked to a specific place, merging the physical and cultural aspects of belonging.[35] However, amid the array of choices and diverse cultural expressions available for her integration into Israel, Ziama does not choose Zionism or nationalism. Instead, she observes: "In those very days, she'd felt herself to be a pebble, inserted with precision into a curve in the pattern of a huge mosaic panel, a tiny single piece gleaned by the hand of the One who'd thought up the entire pattern."[36] The comment perceives God, "the One who'd thought up the entire pattern" of history, to be solely responsible for Ziama's arrival in Israel.[37] The omniscient narrator subscribes to the same (spiritual) logic regarding the Soviet Jewish migration to Israel, stating:

> Here's the way many think: the empire collapsed, and that's the reason its viscera – a human mash – began to throng, flow, pour out of it. A widespread delusion, a substitution of the consequence for the cause. But perhaps the supports ["podporki"] flew out from under that most recent in a long line of great empires for the actual purpose of driving God's flock back to its patch of age-old grazing land, all in accordance with a drafted – not today, oh not today! – plan? The Jewish God is more than a mere impish house spirit ["barabashka"]. Read the Prophets slowly and closely.[38]

In a bold move, the narrator substitutes the *historical* logic of chronology, where the present is understood in relation to the past, with a providential logic that uses God and a future event as primary explanatory mechanisms to account for historical change. Soviet-Jewish immigration to Israel is not attributed to social and political factors like antisemitism, Gorbachev's emigration policy, the Soviet state's collapse, or the 1990 closure of US borders to Soviet Jews. Instead, the narrator – full of chutzpah – asserts that the Soviet Union collapsed to fulfill the messianic plan of gathering Jewish exiles in the Land of Israel. Rubina's reference to the Books of Prophets (Nevi'im) and the divine plan of "driving God's flock back to its patch of age-old grazing land" is not coincidental.[39] Rubina employs biblical imagery of the shepherd (God) and his flock (children of Israel) to suggest that Isaiah's prophecy of exiles gathering (Isaiah 11:11–12) has materialized.

Rubina's religious explanation for the secular phenomenon of Jewish migration to Israel can be better understood in the context of the messianic perspective of religious Zionist thinkers like Rav Abraham Isaac Kook (1865–1935) and Rav Zvi Yehuda Kook (1891–1982). In their religious philosophy, they attempted to reconcile secular Zionism with Orthodox Judaism. When secular Zionism emerged in nineteenth-century Europe, most Orthodox leaders opposed it, seeing it as heretical and opposed to traditional Jewish law. Orthodox rabbis prohibited mass return to Israel, believing that only the Messiah could gather the people. Initiating resettlement was considered sacrilegious, doubting God's power to bring Jews back.

Dissatisfied with what he saw as a paralyzing doctrine that only augmented the miserable situation of Jews in the diaspora, Rav Abraham Isaac Kook (Rav Kook) developed a theological answer to the Orthodox doctrine that infused Zionism with religious and messianic fervour. Instead of viewing the formation of a Jewish state as a disruption of tradition, he saw it as "*at'halta dege'ula*, an active beginning of redemption."[40] In his revolutionary treatise, Rav Kook asserted that both religious and secular Zionism hastens the arrival of the Messiah because "a Jewish nationalist, no matter how secular his intentions, is steeped in the divine spirit."[41] He also insisted that secular Zionists are guided by religious spark (*nitzotz*) in their soul, and it is the "role of religious Zionists … to help them to establish a Jewish state and turn the religious spark in them into a great light."[42] Ultimately, Kook's philosophy helped reconcile Zionism with Judaism and contributed to the spiritualization of the Land of Israel, revitalizing the concept of *eretz yisrael ha shlema* (the Greater Israel) – the notion that the entire biblical territory of Israel, including both the West Bank and Gaza, is the Jewish people's rightful land.

These ideas came to play a crucial role following Israel's victory in the 1967 War when, to borrow the words of Israel's national poet, Natan Alterman, the army "effectively erased the difference between the State of Israel and the Land of Israel."[43] This notion of the spiritual union of Jews and the Land, the belief in the redemptive end of history, and the subordinate status of non-Jews (so-called *goyim*) in Israel became central to the Jewish settlement efforts after 1967 – after Israel occupied the West Bank, Gaza Strip, Golan Heights, Sinai Peninsula, and all of Jerusalem. In 1974, Rav Kook's son, Zvi Yehuda, led the Gush Emunim movement (Hebrew for "bloc of the faithful"), advocating Jewish settlements in newly conquered territories after the Yom Kippur War (1973). He staunchly asserted that the entire Land of Israel – referred to as Greater Israel – was divinely granted to Jews and was not open for sharing. "All this land is ours, absolutely belonging to all of us," he bombastically exclaimed.[44] "It is non-transferable to others, even in part. It is an inheritance to us from our forefathers."[45] Then he added: "Once and for all, it is clear that there are no 'Arab' territories or 'Arab' lands but only the Land of Israel, to which others have come and upon which they have built without our permission."[46] He ominously concluded that settling these lands "is a divine commandment that must be carried out on pain of death."[47] These words gained special significance after the 1995 assassination of Yitzhak Rabin, who pursued a land-for-peace approach in the Israeli-Palestinian conflict, by a university student with strong religious Zionist beliefs.

This context is important because the novel is set in the West Bank settlement, where many ex-Soviet Jews settled due to lower rent prices, encountering religious Zionists professing Rav Kook's ideas. While most scholars link ex-Soviet Jews' religious and political identities to their Soviet past, *Messiah* offers a different way of looking at this phenomenon. Instead, the novel shifts the analytic focus to the interactions between Russian-speaking newcomers and Hebrew-speaking settlers. In the settlement, Rubina shows that post-Soviet Jews embraced "Israeliness" through their religious, nationalist, and right-wing neighbours, adopting their ideas, traditions, and politics. Why did post-Soviet émigrés so quickly and smoothly adopt the settler mindset? Was it because they were a *tabula rasa* ready to be written upon? Or, more persuasively, was it because their pre-existing "Soviet" mentality was already, paradoxically, closely aligned with that of their religious-nationalist neighbours?

Despite the recent arrival of the post-Soviet community in Israel, the narrator and characters are well-versed in settler discourse. Their neighbourhood, known as *Machaneh rusi* (or, the Russian Camp), is steeped in religious allusions and references to the Old Testament and described as the exclusive "center of the earth" and "world's bull's eye."[48] This settlement is also tied to the messianic prophecy, a place where "mountains would part, streams would flow from Jerusalem, and all nations on Earth would gather in the Valley of Jehoshaphat."[49] Rubina not only aligns the topographical coordinates of the Russian Camp with the centre of the universe but also engages in a religious mapping of geography, superimposing spatial coordinates onto the spiritual geography of redemption.

The use of phrases like "our sacred places" and "our Mount of Olives" by various Russophone characters in the novel reflects a primordial – and more importantly, nationalist – connection between people and the land.[50] In these instances, the newcomers naturally root themselves in contested territory beyond the Green Line by invoking the Bible and ancient Jewish history. However, these historical ties are either carefully selected or even brazenly fabricated to politically justify present sovereignty over the land, which is then projected into a future-oriented prophecy predicting the arrival of the Messiah. Glaringly absent in Rubina's depiction, however, is a thorough exploration of the political implications of this territory in the Israeli-Palestinian conflict.[51] Thus, in the novel, religion functions as a guardian of Israel's unified Jewish national identity and as a tool for maintaining political and geographic divisions between Jews and non-Jews.

In contrast to other literary and cinematic works that depict the relations between Russian and Hebrew speakers – especially in Israel's peripheries – in terms of violence, hostility, and competition over limited jobs and resources, Rubina's novel portrays a genuine sense of harmony and camaraderie between them. For instance, Chaim, veteran of Israel's 1948 War and Ziama's Hebrew-speaking friend, drives her daily to work and, at one point, saves Ziama from Palestinian violence. In another scene, Rubina portrays post-Soviet newcomers praying alongside their Hebrew-speaking neighbours, welcoming the holy day in the settlement. As if writing to contradict the image of Russian-speaking Jews as un-kosher atheists, the novel's characters are shown to be just as pious as their Hebrew-speaking neighbours.

The novel also highlights intergenerational camaraderie between ex-Soviets who arrived in Israel in the 1970s and the more recent newcomers (a phenomenon that, according to most accounts, is in fact rather rare).

Chana Cohen, an émigré from the 1970s, volunteers to translate the "information leaflet" for Neve-Ephraim from Hebrew to Russian. A cursory look at the leaflet's content, which includes weapon check times, protests against the "criminal government of the Left," aid for pious and needy families, and warm wishes to emigrant families from the USSR, not only hints at a tight-knit settlement community following the Jewish principle of *tzedakah* (charity) but also showcases Neve-Ephraim's role as an assimilating and socializing agent for the newcomers.[52] Ultimately, the novel expresses, or constructs, a particular synergy between ex-Soviet newcomers (and their distaste for left-wing politics) and the more radical ideological positions of settlers regarding the role of Jews in Israel and Jewish-Palestinian relations.

Remarkably, Rubina's novel, written in 1995–96 and published shortly after Prime Minister Yitzhak Rabin's assassination by a student influenced by radical religious Zionist ideology, portrays the settlement enterprise in a positive manner. Since becoming Israel's prime minister in 1974, Rabin's relationship with chief rabbis of religious communities and West Bank settlements was marked by conflict and hostility. Famously, he called them "ayatollahs" impeding the peace process and referred to settlers as a "Jewish Hamas" and a "cancer in the body of Israeli democracy."[53] When Rabin initiated the Oslo Accord in 1993, which aimed to give Palestinians authority over the West Bank and Gaza, dismantle some Israeli settlements, and transfer occupied territories in exchange for Palestinian commitment to peace and recognizing Israel's right to exist, the religious and nationalist factions within Israeli society were furious.

From 1993 to 1995, religious Zionists engaged in continuous protests, both legal and illegal, in Tel Aviv and outside Rabin's residence. They circulated images showing Rabin in Hitler's or Arafat's uniform. Some rabbis even used the concept of "din rodef" (Hebrew for "the law of the pursuer") to argue that Rabin's plan to cede parts of the biblical Land of Israel to non-Jews justified his assassination on religious grounds.[54] In this context of political and religious incitement, on 4 November 1995, following a large pro-Rabin rally in a central Tel Aviv square, Yigal Amir – an Orthodox Jewish law student at Bar Ilan University – assassinated the prime minister. Later, Amir told the police that the halakhic ruling against Rabin by West Bank rabbis compelled his action.[55]

In this fraught political context, Rubina's portrayal of Neve-Ephraim settlers and rabbis as kind and compassionate individuals ready to help fellow Jews is deeply troubling, especially considering their indirect complicity in the assassination of Rabin. Indeed, *Messiah* stages several scenes of confrontations between the settlers and the left-wing government, and the author's sympathies are unambiguously with the political right. In one such scene, Rubina describes a protest on a Judean hill in the West Bank. Settlers are shown as calm and peaceful, arriving at the scene with "women, children, baby carriages."[56] Rubina personifies the settlers through a young, red-bearded rabbi wearing a traditional blue and white kippah worn by religious Zionists. The rabbi attempts to reason with the policemen and explain their perspective. It turns out that the ancient city of Ai was located right here, the rabbi tells them. For approximately six years, a group of American Jewish archaeologists has been using their hard-earned vacations to conduct excavations. They reside in caravans, and the local settlers provide them with food as long as they continue their digging. "Besides the foundations of several homes and an extremely ancient synagogue," he continues, "they've excavated a mikveh with a mosaic floor, an oil-press with a stone reservoir, a drain for olive oil, and a heavy, blue millstone."[57] This exchange depicts settlers as determined and peaceful individuals who care about what they perceive as their historical homeland. Furthermore, it suggests that their fight for their homeland is not limited to Jewish people in Israel alone; rather, it is shared by Jews across the diaspora. By highlighting American Jewish archaeologists' devoted efforts, Rubina portrays a cross-border unity between American and Israeli Jews. The earth itself becomes a repository of history, concealing evidence that underscores the profound link between Jews and the Land of Israel.

In contrast to Jews who seek love, friendship, and peaceful coexistence, "the Arabs" are portrayed as violent intruders. This portrayal is illustrated through a passage where a red-headed rabbi comments: "Take a look ... The Arabs stole over here at night and pried the millstone loose. It was probably difficult to do, but they don't lack strength. They couldn't carry it away. But if we surrender the hill to them, they'll turn into hash all the monuments of our history that prevent them from proving we were never here."[58] This scene positions Palestinians as a threat to Jewish history, monuments, and lives. While Israelis use history and archaeology to (peacefully) demonstrate the connection between Jews and the Land of Israel, Palestinians resort to violence and falsehoods to deny this connection. Their ulterior goal, Rubina suggests, is to challenge Israel's legitimacy and portray Jews as European colonizers without historical ties.[59] While Rubina might not view Jewish history in Israel/Palestine this way, her portrayal of the rabbi unintentionally reveals his – and the settlers' – territorial ambitions. Toward the end of the scene, readers learn that the religious Zionist rabbi, identified by his knitted kippah, envisions more than just defending the hill where they protest. Looking past it, he tells his Jewish interlocutor: "Listen, what do you call people who spit on their history? All this," he motions his hand toward the hills around him, "is our national property [natsional'noe dostoyanie]."[60] This expansionist gesture mentally and discursively annexes extensive territories held by Palestinians, thereby depicting the rabbi as a colonial agent, ready for conquest, annexation, and settlement. Like earlier waves of Zionist pioneers, when the rabbi scans the landscape, he only sees empty land, disregarding the presence of Palestinians who currently live there.

The novel revisits the trope of empty land on more than one occasion. In one scene, a fourth-year student, Gingik, and his mother, Nachama, are taken on an army helicopter ride so the boy can have a bird's-eye view of Neve-Ephraim. Nachama reflects on the area's past: "Good Lord, I can't believe it. Do you know what was here fifteen years ago? Naked emptiness. Two caravans, a military post … During the Yom Kippur War, my brother was killed here. We slept in a tent. There was no gas, no light. Look how many trees we've planted!"[61] She questions whether the government might abandon their settlement to "the Arabs," highlighting her fear of losing the land they have developed. The pilot, a military man, does not respond. The scene tacitly advocates for Jewish settlement in the West Bank, shifting from religious arguments to emphasizing the labour of Jewish settlers. The concept of "making the desert bloom," once championed by early Zionist pioneers in the 1920s, is now used by modern settlers to validate their claim.[62] By presenting the land as still empty as late as 1973, Rubina avoids acknowledging the displacement of Palestinians due to Jewish expansion. This portrayal transforms settlers from radical figures who terrorize Palestinians into diligent cultivators who pay with blood and toil for their right to live in Israel. It also obscures the Palestinian narrative. The backdrop of an empty desert emphasizes Palestinians' inability to leave a lasting mark on the land, effectively erasing them out of history. Like in the earlier demonstration scene, Rubina indicts the left-wing government's evacuation plans, reflecting a fear that such actions would lead to the land being "desecrated by the Arabs."[63]

While the helicopter pilot remains silent in the face of Nachama's biting questions, the police officers in the protest scene do not. Instead, the novel shows how they are forced, against their will, to use violence to disperse demonstrators. The author powerfully portrays the confrontation, with mounted police roughly pushing protesters down the mountain and officers grabbing a woman by the arms and hauling her along the dirt. Not only does the standoff between defenceless women and children on one side and mounted police on the other clearly evoke sympathy for the settlers, but it also recreates what Chaim Yavin calls an "established ritual" by the government and the settlers: showing the world how difficult it is to evacuate the settlements. This theatre of violence, Yavin suggests, is used to obscure the daily structural violence against Palestinians, including checkpoints, restricted roads, grazing permissions, and settler attacks with military backing.[64] Ultimately, this scene shifts the usual dynamic between Israeli police and settlers. By portraying reluctant officers enforcing anti-Jewish violence under government orders, Rubina indicts the left-wing government (specifically Rabin's) and urges an end to intra-Jewish violence. By highlighting the brutality of the confrontation, she reinforces settlers' sense of being persecuted by both the Israeli government and Palestinians while ignoring a contrasting view of settlers as agents of colonization and violence.

Violence – whether incited by religious conviction or otherwise – plays an important role in the novel, especially toward the end. In addition to instances of intra-Jewish violence, which are comparatively few, violence is predominantly associated with the Palestinians and is linked to the apocalyptical war between Jews and Gentiles that signals the coming of the Messiah.[65] At the start of the last chapter, Ron Katz, a polemical author for Ziama's literary journal, emphasizes this idea. He states: "The Mashiach won't come while these bitches are selling out the country. He won't even show his nose. Oh, for sure, when the Arabs succeed in chasing us onto reservations, he'll show up to knock out some leftist teeth."[66] Katz's comment about the relation of violence and the Messiah not only reveals his anti-leftist stance on land-for-peace deals but also suggests that the persistent Palestinian violence shapes genuine religious faith and messianic hope. To put it differently, he implies that the messianic era will arrive when the conflict between Jews and Palestinians reaches a critical point. For him, this is intertwined with the terrorism following Rabin's Oslo Accord, which fractured Israel's political sphere. Katz views the Messiah as a guardian figure for the Jewish people, akin to a Golem, echoing N.'s double-edged analysis of the automatic weapons at Ben Gurion Airport. Palestinian terror, Katz's words suggest, is responsible for Israel's national trauma while paradoxically hastening Jewish redemption.

The first victim of Palestinian violence in the novel is Chaim Gork, Ziama's close friend with whom she carpools to work. He is killed near Neve-Ephraim, "not far from the mosque."[67] Before his death is reported, we learn that Chaim had once escorted Holocaust survivors to Palestine, standing up against British officials to save survivors from internment in Cyprus. Rubina then reveals that Chaim was shot on his way home, targeted from a minaret near the settlement. This sharp contrast between Chaim's altruism (he is literally aiding the ingathering of exiles and forming a teleological link between the Holocaust and Israel!) and a hidden terrorist using a minaret as a sniper's nest generates sympathy for Chaim and directly links terrorism and Islam. The casual connection between the mosque and the act of terror acts as a dog whistle that reinforces a stereotypical representation of Palestinians as extremist terrorists who must be controlled or eliminated.

In her oeuvre, Rubina frequently depicts Islam through a lens of fear and animosity. For instance, in the short story "White Donkey Waiting for the Savior," the protagonist describes her reaction to the call to prayer (*adhan*) from a mosque in Jerusalem with the following: "A nasal roar invaded my ears and sent a shiver down my spine. It took me a moment to realize it was a regular call to prayer, that ungainly howl I hear every morning at dawn from across the ravine. But here, magnified by powerful speakers, it became a foreboding battle cry."[68] This passage graphically conveys the protagonist's intense discomfort and alienation. The use of phrases like "nasal roar" and "ungainly howl" suggests an animalistic and unpleasant quality to the call to prayer, while "foreboding battle cry" evokes a sense of imminent danger and conflict.[69] Rubina's choice to frame the *adhan* in such hostile terms reflects a broader tendency to depict Islam and its practices as antagonistic and violent. Despite her background in a Muslim-majority country like Uzbekistan, where the call to prayer is a common sound, Rubina uses her characters to project an image of Islam that is steeped in menace and conflict. In another novella, *The Cats of Jerusalem*, Rubina's narrator describes unfinished Palestinian houses without glass windows as "blinded by the sterile hatred of their builders."[70] Indeed, hatred, violence, and repugnance seem to be Rubina's chosen tropes for describing Islam, Palestinians, and even their property.

The lachrymose conception of Jewish history, to borrow Salo W. Baron's phrase, turns into a definitive declaration of the relationship between territory, violence, and agency at the end of the novel. After a night of heavy drinking, Sasha Rabinovich, a Soviet émigré from Neve-Ephraim, goes to mikveh to cleanse himself for Yom Kippur. There, he meets Michael, a French émigré with a heritage tied to Alfred Dreyfus, the famous Jewish officer wrongly accused of treason, symbolizing the challenges of Jewish assimilation in Europe. Michael, whose family remained in France and thrived there, poses a question to Rabinovich: "Do you know how our life in the land of the goyim differs from our life here?"[71] He answers his own question with a stark contrast. On one hand, Michael describes how, despite Jews' deep historical and familial connections to the diaspora land, they will always face rejection and hostility there. He paints a grim picture where the land of the diaspora will eventually turn against Jews, saying, "Dirty stinking kike! Clear off my body!" even as they contribute to and identify with it.[72] This land, according to Michael, will reject and alienate them, leaving them with a sense of unfulfilled spiritual connection and bitterness. But the Land of Israel, Michael continues, will always welcome Jews back with open arms, no matter how long they have been away. He evokes an image of Israel as nurturing and generous, providing a profound and exclusive bond that diaspora lands cannot offer. "That's what this land is – for you. And only for you," Michael concludes.[73] "For others it was stone, unfeeling stone, like a frigid woman. Because one can exile a woman to another's harem, can take her by force – but an aggressor can never expect a sigh of love from her."[74]

With this sexist extended metaphor, Michael presents two intertwined conceptions of Jewish rootedness. On one hand, he imagines diaspora as inevitably linked to alienation, hostility, and antisemitism. Using the historical narrative of Alfred Dreyfus as a paradigm of diasporic Jewish history,

Michael suggests that Jews will always be eternal strangers in the diaspora, regardless of their attempts at assimilation. Michael's words posit a direct connection between indigenous population and territory (at the expense of non-indigenous groups) and imply – in the Zionist key – that the only remedy to the dangers of diaspora is the possession of a homeland – Israel – where Jews can find both safety and a deep-rooted connection. At the same time, the passage challenges the previous notion held by Nachama that territory can be secured through either labour or war. Instead, it presents a mystical vision of an eternal and inalienable homeland, emphasizing an inherent, spiritual connection between people and territory. To bring his point across, Michael anthropomorphizes Israel, framing it as both a caring mother toward its children and as a "frigid woman" toward outsiders. Nonchalantly, Michael deploys the metaphor of a harem – evoking Muslim cultures, of course – to imply the land's domination, imprisonment, and sexual violence by previous "aggressors" who took it "by force."[75] In so doing, Rubina repurposes the imagery of the "rape of the land," previously used to describe Jews' "ravaging" of Germany, to reframe the relationship between Muslims and Israel. According to this portrayal, previous occupants of the land were unable to leave their mark on it or make it love them in return. In contrast, when Jews – the rightful owners – return after two thousand years of exile, the desert transforms into a lush Garden of Eden. This scene, set in a mikveh on Yom Kippur eve, underscores a spiritual and mystical bond between Jews and the Land of Israel.

The novel ends with a protracted Yom Kippur service at two synagogues, Chabad and non-Chabad, where Russian, French, and Hebrew-speaking Jews gather for the reading of *Kol Nidre*. Rubina meticulously describes the moving impact of the cantor's words on the audience, capturing the harmony of the scene. The entire Neve-Ephraim community, regardless of language or country of origin, participates in the ceremony. The narrator then zooms in on the intense conversation between post-Soviet Jews and God. The newcomers beg for forgiveness from the all-powerful deity, and we see how this activity hits a nerve, affecting attendees on a visceral and existential level. Importantly, Rubina juxtaposes the two synagogues to frame the Russian, Hebrew, and French speakers as part of one extended Jewish family. Whereas in Zvi Gitelman's account, the Soviet-born community is divorced from Judaism, and in Larissa Remennick's account, their religiosity is skin-deep and instrumental, *Messiah* presents a different reality where post-Soviet Jews in Israel are devout and pious. In the synagogue in the West Bank settlement, the act of prayer, and the words of the prayer, inspire their belonging to the Jewish people. Rubina concludes the scene with a vision of Jewish unity and cohesion.

Instead of ending the novel on a positive note of unity and spirituality, Rubina concludes with a burst of political violence. In the final pages, a new character enters the novel: Ibtisam Shahada, a "flabby, unattractive young lady of mature age – in the spring she'd hit her twenty-second year"[76] – from a nearby Palestinian village near Hebron. The sharp oxymoronic phrase "young lady of a mature age," in reference to a woman of twenty-two years, constitutes a thinly veiled criticism of patriarchal Muslim society, which pressures women to marry at a young age. Four months before Yom Kippur, Rubina tells us, Shahada becomes pregnant after being seduced by her former teacher, Abd-El-Vakhab. "Her brothers were going to kill her, [and] there was no other way" to avert the disgrace of the family, the narrator adds.[77] The teacher, who does not want to marry Shahada, comes up with a solution: "It'd be better to kill a Jew, they'll take you to prison, you'll give birth and stay there. And your family will have honor."[78] Though hesitant, Shahada reluctantly agrees. By linking the act of terror to the intersection of restrictive Muslim beliefs and patriarchal Palestinian traditions, Rubina undermines the core of the Palestinian political movement.

The scene shifts to a Jerusalem restaurant, where the novel's characters have gathered to celebrate the end of Yom Kippur and break their fast. The novel takes a dark turn as Ibtisam Shahada enters the restaurant. The final scene is presented mainly from the Palestinian character's point of view – the first time this happens in the novel. The window into Palestinian psyche is not intended to humanize or evoke sympathy for Shahada, but rather to intensify our aversion toward her. Before striking, Shahada realizes that the man sitting next to her target "looked like a doctor, the surgeon who'd repaired her father's hernia last spring."[79] As readers, we know that he is in fact the very same man. But this recognition does not stop Shahada. She "squeezed the knife handle with numbed fingers, convulsively yanked up her hand and … began to shriek as if it weren't she plunging the knife into another, but as if it were she being stabbed."[80] Rubina describes the scream as a "totally formless, unendurable, petrified shriek, this endless cry of hatred," tying it to the previously mentioned description of the call to prayer, reinforcing the author's portrayal of Islam as a religion of violence.[81] The name that Rubina chooses for the Palestinian attacker, Shahada, a term linked to the Islamic declaration of faith, further connects Islam and terrorism.

Despite offering a glimpse into Shahada's psyche, Rubina is not interested in understanding her or connecting Israel's military control over the West Bank and Gaza to the phenomenon of suicide bombers. In *Messiah*, there are no separation barriers, checkpoints, roadblocks, home demolitions, detentions, or the everyday challenges of living under Israeli authority. For Rubina, the attempted murder is simply Shahada's way of coping with her Muslim oppression and an escape from the honour killing by her brothers – it is not a political act. In the end, Shahada fails in her mission. She misses Ziama's neck. However, Ziama is killed by a bullet from writer N.'s son, Shmulik, who tries to intervene but misses the terrorist and hits her victim instead. Rubina concludes with sarcasm, noting that Ibtisam Shahada "was saved forever. Her brothers would not kill her. Great Allah, they would not kill her."[82] This scene, along with its portrayal of Islam, starkly contrasts with the depiction of Judaism in an earlier synagogue scene, which conveys brotherhood and peace among participants. Islam, the novel suggests, only yields violence and death.

The novel ends, as the title anticipates, with the arrival of the Messiah. After her death, Ziama is immersed in the spring waters of Jerusalem and becomes one with the city. There she is greeted by her grandfather, who triumphantly declares: "Shake off the dust, get up, mount upon [vossiad'] Yersholoim … unwind the bonds from your neck, captive daughter of Zion."[83] As noted by Roman Katsman, these words echo the famous passage from Isaiah 52[84]:

> Awake, awake,
> Clothe yourself in your strength, O Zion;
> Clothe yourself in your beautiful garments,
> O Jerusalem, the holy city;
> For the uncircumcised and the unclean
> Will no longer come into you.
> Shake yourself from the dust, rise up,
> O captive Jerusalem;
> Loose yourself from the chains around your neck,
> O captive daughter of Zion.[85]

In this scene, Ziama is called upon, much like Isaiah's Jerusalem, to rise from captivity, shake off dust, and free herself from chains. In the biblical context, this passage heralds the redemption of Jerusalem, held captive by foreign forces but destined to be freed. The parallel between Ziama and Jerusalem suggests the novel's theme of redeeming Jerusalem from Palestinian violence through divine intervention. The reader is left with the convergence of God, the Jewish people, and Jerusalem, a recurring motif throughout *Messiah*, also the messianic promise to "his people."[86] Just as God's promise in Isaiah assures that Jerusalem will be protected from "the uncircumcised and defiled," Rubina implores God to uphold this promise in the present moment and save Israelis from Palestinian terrorism.

As Ziama becomes one with the Holy City, she reaches an epiphany. Filled with joy, she asks: "Grandpa, are you the Mashiach?"[87] He replies: "Nu, Mashiach … Hey, mameleh, get up, don't tarry, I'm so happy to see you."[88] The novel closes with a messianic promise, either from God or from the Messiah: "When I arrive, when I show up, eventually, at my stormy home, I will raise her from the dead."[89] The words from the Yom Kippur ceremony of *kaparot* (atonement) suggest Ziama's sacrificial role and her potential to absolve the sins of Israel, granting them the possibility of redemption.[90] This ending ties up the novel's exploration of the link between violence and belonging. At first, writer N. sees automatic weapons as disrupting her sense of belonging to Israel and the Jewish people. The sight of weapons catalyzes her epiphany that Jews are not safe in the world and that Israel is not a safe place for them. As a result, she realizes that *complete* returns are not possible ("there was nowhere to return to; return was impossible") until the Messiah comes and sets everything and everyone in their proper place.[91] However, it is precisely Ziama's violent confrontation with a Palestinian terrorist that earns her place in heaven and a metaphyseal union with the people of Israel and her grandfather. In a dialectical fashion, the novel throws these two things – belonging and automatic weapons – into relief. In her death by a semi-automatic rifle, Ziama becomes a religious martyr and earns her eternal reward. Her death is not portrayed through a socio-political lens as another victim of the Israeli-Palestinian conflict. Rather, it is presented as part of a messianic prophecy, securing her place in heaven. Like a ritual scapegoat, Ziama's Yom Kippur death symbolically atones for the unspecified sins of the Jewish people, enabling redemption. Ultimately, the novel confirms Katz's words that Palestinian violence and hatred will catalyze the messianic age and divine redemption. Politics, at the novel's end, transforms into religion.

In conclusion, the chapter offers a profound analysis of how religious revival among Russian-speaking Jews is entangled with their social and political realities in Israel. This renewed interest in Judaism, far from being a mere return to tradition or a reaction to Soviet secularism, emerges as a strategic response to the marginalization these immigrants face. In tandem, Tavger's and Rubina's works illuminate how religious engagement can serve both as a means of coping with social exclusion and as a tool for asserting belonging within the dominant Jewish majority. *More Than I Deserve* suggests that immigrants may turn toward religion as a way to align themselves with the religious-nationalist sentiments of their Israeli neighbours. In contrast, *Messiah* portrays religious involvement as a political strategy to assert their belonging within the Jewish majority, often at the expense of non-Jewish groups like Palestinians.

CHAPTER 3

Orientalist Cosmopolitanism

Encounters with the Other in Israel

Western and Soviet Cosmopolitanism

Scholars in both Slavic and Jewish studies rarely engage with critical work on cosmopolitanism. This reluctance stems from the peculiar historical usage of the term "rootless cosmopolitan" in the Soviet Union and Nazi Germany and the pejorative association of Jews with a lack of patriotism and parasitism that was used to fuel their persecution in both countries.[1] In the Soviet Union, the term "rootless cosmopolitan" (*bezrodnyi kosmopolit*) emerged in the 1940s and 1950s during Stalin's notorious "anti-cosmopolitan" campaign against Western things in general, and Jews in particular.[2] The term tapped into the xenophobic reservoir of Soviet culture and society, associating Jews with global economic conspiracy, Western spies, and double agents. Because of this historical legacy, most Slavic and Jewish studies scholars avoid using the term due to its tainted history. Recently, there have been efforts to reclaim the term. For example, Maggie Levantovskaya re-appropriates it in her scholarly work, arguing that the phrase captures the essence of rootlessness, mobility, and transnationalism prevalent in post-Soviet Jewish literature in Russia, Israel, and the United States.

Whether one rejects or embraces the term, "rootless cosmopolitanism" is either outright dismissed as official propaganda or hastily celebrated for its progressive connotations in cultural identity construction. What remains excluded, however, is serious engagement with cosmopolitanism both as an intellectual formation and as a historical category of practice for Soviet Jews. This disavowal is all the more surprising if we acknowledge that during the Soviet era, Russian-speaking Jews in urban centres were indeed disproportionately represented among the intelligentsia, and that for many, a strong affinity for "global" (read, "Western") culture was an important marker of identity.[3] In a certain sense, being part of the Soviet intelligentsia meant embodying cosmopolitanism – appreciating world culture, casually quoting Goethe and Pushkin at the kitchen table, and being well-versed in contemporary artistic and social trends in Europe and America despite never having been there. In what follows, I propose to distinguish between cosmopolitanism as a category of political contestation – how political and social actors historically used it in the Soviet context – and cosmopolitanism as a category of analysis, describing how the idea of global identification shapes various cultural, social, and political practices. Separating the two will allow for a more nuanced understanding of the way Russian-speaking Jews aspired to cosmopolitan practice while resisting the cosmopolitan label.

It is important to note that the term "cosmopolitanism" carries different meanings in the Soviet and Western contexts. Traditionally, Western cosmopolitanism is associated with individuals who are (predominantly) male, urban, mobile, educated, wealthy, polyglot, and border crossing. In the Soviet Union, there were two competing versions of cosmopolitanism – official and unofficial. The official was the state-sanctioned project of Soviet Internationalism, which included efforts like Maxim Gorky's World Literature (Mirovaya Literatura) publishing house, the literary journal *International Literature* (*Internatsionalnaya Literatura*), and various translation projects that aimed to translate foreign literature and thereby bring the world to Soviet citizens.[4] All these projects aimed to introduce global literary works to Soviet readers under strict ideological controls, promoting a controlled form of international cultural engagement that aligned with Soviet values. Rossen Djagalov's book *From Internationalism to Postcolonialism: Literature and Cinema between the Second and the Third Worlds* discusses this version of Soviet cosmopolitanism, illustrating how literature and cinema served as bridges between the Second and Third Worlds, promoting solidarity and shared revolutionary ideals.[5]

The other version of cosmopolitanism in the USSR was underground and unofficial, characterized by the extensive circulation of illegally published literature (both local and foreign) in the *samizdat*. Foreign works by authors such as James Joyce, Vladimir Nabokov, and Samuel Beckett were translated into Russian, typed, and then disseminated clandestinely, as they were otherwise inaccessible due to state censorship.[6] For instance, Jose Vergara's *All Future Plunges to the Past: James Joyce in Russian Literature* (2021) delves into this underground literary culture, highlighting how Russian translators and readers engaged with Joyce's complex narratives despite the risks involved.[7] This form of underground cosmopolitanism represented intellectual resistance, where Soviet citizens sought to connect with broader global cultural currents in defiance of official restrictions.

In both the official and underground versions of Soviet cosmopolitanism, however, investment in global culture became a crucial mechanism for understanding the world. In a society where physical travel was heavily restricted and accessible only to a select few, cosmopolitanism manifested through a deep engagement with foreign cultures, becoming a project of cultural affinity rather than physical mobility. These intellectual pursuits allowed Soviet citizens to compensate for the travel restrictions, which particularly affected Jews. Furthermore, within the context of systemic economic shortages in the Soviet Union, cultural capital became an important currency that could enable Soviet citizens to achieve social and geographic mobility, gain access to professional organizations, obtain desired residence permits in major cities (*propiska*), and enjoy preferential access to goods and services.

Since culture became an important mechanism for securing a position in Soviet society, Soviet Jews were particularly eager to seize this opportunity. Even before the Soviet Union, Jews in the Russian Empire relied on high culture and higher education as the main strategies for achieving social and geographic mobility.[8] For instance, Yuri Slezkine characterizes the intersection of higher education and Russian-Jewish identity as conversion to the "Pushkin faith," while Julia Lerner calls this an "ethnic script" that can predict the trajectory of the history of Jews from the USSR.[9] Other scholars – most notably Zvi Gitelman – disagree. They argue that the widespread acculturation of Russian and Soviet Jews was primarily driven by coercion and violence.[10] Gitelman's work, *A Century of Ambivalence*, emphasizes how traditional Jewish culture, history, and religion were coded as atavistic and retrograde expressions that were incompatible with the Soviet vision of a new society. As a result, Jews were compelled to give up their religion, languages, professions, dress codes, and way of life.

Instead of pitting these opposing histories of Jewish participation in the Soviet cosmopolitan project against each other, considering them together offers a more complete understanding of the remarkable social and cultural mobility of Soviet Jews and sheds light on their experiences after immigrating to Israel. In the Soviet Union, Jews internalized the prevailing belief that culture is one of the central criteria that differentiates between people, leading them to expect that they could use their cultural capital to stake a favourable place in Israeli society. Thrust into a new environment with a different system of cultural coordinates, generations of Jews raised on Pushkin and Tolstoy suddenly realized that the Soviet-Jewish cosmopolitan model based on Russian and world culture required some recalibration. In Israel, they felt compelled to give up the cultural baggage that they thought comprised their identity, their sacred goods, and that which made them Jewish in the first place.

In this chapter, I explore how two Soviet-born Israeli artists, Alexander Goldshtein and Zoya Cherkassky-Nnadi, engage with Soviet cosmopolitanism in their literary and visual works in Israel. First, I turn to Goldshtein's semi-autobiographical novel, set in Israel, *Aspects of Spiritual Matrimony* (2001), and consider how the geographies of Europe, Africa, the Middle East, and the Mediterranean are mobilized to express the author's alienation from – and dissatisfaction with – Israel. This is both indicative of the author's estrangement from Israel and constitutes an attempt to escape the rigid force fields of both Russian and Israeli forms of cultural and collective identification. Additionally, I consider how Goldshtein's particular cosmopolitan subject position is much more in line with the Soviet intelligentsia's accumulation of world culture than with the ambivalence toward it more typical of Israeli society as a whole. In his ongoing dialogue with Walter Benjamin, Roman and Greek mythology, the Russian avant-garde, and Egyptian and Chinese history, Goldshtein – in a utopian gesture that expresses both pathos and pain – attempts to transcend Israeli reality by creating an autonomous space (in the Soviet image) where symbolic capital can be converted into prestige and monetary value.

The chapter compares Goldshtein's works to Zoya Cherkassky-Nnadi's art series *Pravda* (2012–19) and *Africa-Israel* (2013–18). The first series focuses on two intertwined moments in the history of Russian-speaking Jews: life in the Soviet Union before immigration and the challenging reality in Israel that followed. By placing these histories in dialogue, the chapter shows how Cherkassky-Nnadi's affectionate attitude toward the Soviet past is related to the hardships, humiliation, and downward social mobility experienced by many Russian speakers in Israel. Unlike Goldshtein, who used cosmopolitanism as a means of escaping the constraints of the Soviet Union and Israel, Cherkassky-Nnadi does the opposite. She deploys cosmopolitanism as a way to illuminate the experiences of minority groups in Israel, both before and after their immigration. The chapter examines select artworks from Cherkassky-Nnadi's *Africa-Israel* series (2013–18), exploring how her compassionate portrayal of refugees in Israel challenges harmful stereotypes of this community as criminals and drug dealers.

Alexander Goldshtein: The Imperial Cosmopolitan

Alexander Goldshtein became cosmopolitan by default. Born in 1957 on the western edge of the Soviet empire in Tallinn, Estonia, he later settled in the culturally diverse city of Baku, Azerbaijan, where he resided for three decades. He immigrated to Israel in 1990, just prior to the collapse of the Soviet Union, during the ethnic violence and mass deportations of Armenians that took place in Baku in the late 1980s and early 1990s. This violent period, notes Mikhail Krutikov, "left a powerful impression on Goldshtein, [making] the problem of cohabitation of Muslims, Christians, and Jews … central to his writing."[11] In his gut-wrenching essay "1990," Goldshtein recalls the horrors of ethnic violence, pogroms, and the mass deportation of Armenians by Azeris. As a member of the Jewish minority, he experienced dread and anguish witnessing these gory scenes, wondering if Jews would be next in line. Goldshtein's later writings frequently revisit the notion of a "clash of civilizations" between Christianity and Islam. In particular, the violent end of the Soviet cosmopolitan project that he witnessed reinforces his skepticism about the viability of cross-cultural relations. The complexities and challenges of multicultural coexistence thus colour his cosmopolitan perspective.

In his brief life, which was cut short by lung cancer at the age of forty-eight, Goldshtein published four books, all of which were written in Russian after his immigration to Israel. These books became the fertile soil for his cosmopolitanism. In Russia, they were celebrated as bold works of cerebral prose, countering the rise of post-Soviet popular literature, and blurring the lines between literature, autobiography, and cultural theory.[12] Indeed, these stylistically hybrid works cover a range of topics, including medieval poetry, Latin American and Asian history, Russian and European avant-garde, Roman and Greek antiquity, and American and European politics. Most of his works straddle the line between fiction and essay, featuring complex narratives that explore themes of identity, exile, and cultural dislocation. Goldshtein embodies the epitome of a Soviet-Jewish ideal *intelligent*. His dedication to culture was so extreme that, even on his deathbed, consumed by lung cancer, breathing with the help of a respiration machine, he nonetheless refused to take morphine to keep his senses sharp and complete his last book, *Quiet Fields* (in which he inscribed, like Timothy Leary, his own death).[13] He died as he put the final full stop on the manuscript, concluding his life and art in the same breath.

Goldshtein's immigration to Israel in 1990 marked a significant turning point in his writing career. His first book, *A Farewell to Narcissus* (*Rasstavanie s Nartsissom*), reflects the author's dedication to Russian literature and world culture. The book is a collection of essays that performs – at times with relish and always with great erudition – a postmortem on the Soviet cultural body. Produced in 1997, at a moment when history (according to Francis Fukayama's influential essay on the end of history) was still thought to have ended, *A Farewell to Narcissus* attempts to make sense of the Soviet cultural legacy by situating it within the framework of world culture. The book's preface formulates Goldshtein's larger ambitions. The book is written at a time of a great loss, the author announces. A major era of Russian literature in the twentieth century – from avant-garde and socialist realism to sots art and conceptualism – has concluded, leaving behind only confusion. This confusion is unlikely to resolve soon, he adds, but analyzing the current crisis and period is not the main aim of this book. "Immersed in the rhetoric of necrological ceremonies, the author would like to perform a thorough memorial rite and only then return to the present and the future, which are now merged into one anyhow."[14] Therefore, this book serves as a wreath, a memorial tribute. Although the dead might claim that the "tomb is a cenotaph, and the body is intact and hidden in a secure place – they are mistaken, they are simply wrong."[15] Clearly influenced by Fukuyama's thesis on the end of history, the passage (and the book as a whole) conflates the Soviet regime with Soviet culture and confidently declares the end of both. However, this perspective now appears outdated, as the legacy of the Soviet Union continues to shape current events, including memory wars, historiographic debate, attempts to either bury Lenin or resurrect Stalin, and different geopolitical conflicts in the post-Soviet region like Russia's ruthless invasion of Ukraine in 2022. Goldshtein's approach to the Soviet past reflects the historical context of his writing, the 1990s, a period marked by a sense of closure and the need to find new narratives for history.[16]

The book sets up an opposition between "narcissistic" Soviet culture and "orphic" European culture, drawing inspiration from Greek mythology.[17] The narcissistic Soviet culture is criticized as self-absorbed, insular, and autocannibalistic, while the European culture – linked to the legendary musician, poet, and prophet Orpheus, who had the ability to enchant all living things and even inanimate objects with his music – is celebrated as heteroglot, authentic, and progressive, betraying the author's cosmopolitan bias toward European culture. Goldshtein's overall attitude toward Soviet history and culture is telling – they become "meaningful" and "intelligible" only in the context of world culture; in themselves, they are considered opaque and not worthy of consideration. That is why *A Farewell to Narcissus* puts Soviet culture in dialogue with the dominant European and American artistic trends, analyzing figures like Sorokin alongside Beckett and Mayakovsky in conjunction with the Marquis de Sade. By doing so, the book heralds a new phase of Russian literature after the USSR's collapse, demonstrating the much-needed transition from Narcissus to Orpheus. The book earned Goldshtein unparalleled recognition, winning him two esteemed literary prizes in Russia – the Minor Booker and Antibooker – propelling him to the forefront of the Russophone literary scene.

Goldshtein's great success as a writer did not diminish his existential melancholia in Israel. In his autobiographical texts and interviews, he frequently laments his inability to secure a job in the academy, persistent poverty, and experience of cultural scarcity as leitmotifs of his life in Israel.[18] However, beneath the persona of the struggling artist that Goldshtein strives to cultivate, it is also possible to reconstruct his life in Israel differently. Indeed, Goldshtein did not find a job in the academy (unsurprising considering that he refused to learn Hebrew during his fifteen years in Israel), but promptly after his arrival in Israel, he found a job as a journalist for the prominent Russophone newspaper *Vesti*. In arts and culture, his achievements are even more impressive. He became a member of the editorial board of the highbrow literary journal *Zerkalo*, co-curated Tel Aviv's avant-garde literary salon *Kryisha*, and engaged in various daring "actionist" performances alongside political activist Alexander Brenner and contemporary painter Alexander Rotenberg.[19] The image of the melancholic artist was so important for Goldshtein because it allowed him to align himself with the tradition of the Russian intelligentsia, positioning him as part of an educated post-Soviet Jewish minority amid what he viewed as a largely backward Israeli populace in need of guidance and enlightenment (the so-called *narod)*.[20]

Most of his writings and interviews reproduce this self-appointed position of cultural superiority. For instance, this is how Goldshtein characterizes his relationship to Israel in the Israeli newspaper *Haaretz*: "When I arrived in Israel, I was disappointed by Israel's Mizrahi character. I thought that the Jewishness I would find there would be the Jewish civilization I was familiar with since childhood ... based on the writings of Franz Kafka and Bruno Schulz."[21]

Goldshtein's statement reveals a clear expectation of cultural continuity that was unmet, highlighting his preference for a European Jewish intellectual tradition over the cultural landscape of Israel. Thrust into a new environment with a different system of cultural coordinates in which a poet, to turn Yevgeny Yevtushenko's famous *bon mot* on its head, is much less than a poet, many Russian-speaking Jews realized with Kurtz's horror that the Soviet cosmopolitan model based on Russian and world culture required some recalibration.[22] In their analysis of post-Soviet Jewish cultural identity, social scientists Lomsky-Feder and Rapoport argue that "individual and collective identities of Russian-speaking Jews are predicated on the interplay between whiteness, cultural capital, and strong sense of solidarity between Jews."[23] In this statement, Goldshtein's strong antipathy toward Israel and its "Mizrahi" character (read: non-white, uncultured, and uncivilized) is a reaction to what he perceives as Israel's un-cosmopolitan devaluation of world culture and a competing model of a Jewishness not aligned with the pillars identified by Lomsky-Feder and Rapoport. Ultimately, Goldshtein's framing of his disappointment implies a contrast between the presumed superiority of Ashkenazi Jewish heritage, linked to European literary giants, and the supposed inferiority of Mizrahi Jewish culture in Israel, thereby revealing Eurocentric and orientalist overtones.

Goldshtein's explorations of Russian and European cultures in *A Farewell to Narcissus* and his polemics on the divide between Russian-speaking and Hebrew-speaking Israelis reveal a bifurcated vision of East and West. According to Mikhail Krutikov's analysis, this intermediary and constantly shifting position between East and West "runs through the core of Goldshtein's thinking and imagination."[24] Yet this is not to say that "East" and "West" in Goldshtein's philosophy hold the same analytical weight and prestige. Throughout his writings, Goldshtein portrays himself as a quintessential (Western) intellectual forced into a lifelong exile in the East – first in Baku and then in Israel. For instance, in his last book *Remember Famagusta*, he articulates his stance toward his surroundings: "Despising the East," he writes, "I spent my whole life in the East."[25] A few pages later he elaborates on this theme, emphasizing the dominance of nationalism in "Eastern" cultures: "In the East, there is no word more powerful than the nation."[26] This assertion underscores Goldshtein's perspective on the East as a place where collective identity and allegiance hold paramount importance, contrasting sharply with his vaunted ideals of Western cosmopolitanism, individualism, and post-national identification.

In Goldshtein's second book, *Aspects of Spiritual Matrimony* (2001), written a decade after his move to Israel, the focus shifts from the Soviet culture and history he left behind to his new experiences in Israel. In a blend of fiction, autobiography, and literary criticism, Goldshtein depicts his everyday life in Israel, marked by apartment shortage, economic instability, and flâneuring in Tel Aviv and Jaffa. In an interview with *Haaretz*, Goldshtein said that he turned his disappointment with Israel's non-Ashkenazi character into literature, referring to this very book. Indeed, the book includes dozens of abrasive and racist remarks against non-European groups, reducing them to verbal caricatures and objectifying them as statues, hookahs, Disney characters, and household objects.

In the chapter "Street Life: Races and Birds," for instance, Goldshtein casually fixates on an African woman sitting across from him on the bus, without noting whether she is a Jewish woman from Ethiopia, a tourist, a temporary resident, or a refugee/asylum seeker. Instead, from a position of threatened superiority and condescension, he describes her with harsh objectification: "The blackie barged in and threw herself on the seat in front of me. She was young and coffee-coloured, with a quarter of milky-mulatto foam, and her buttery mocha torso towering at least three meters high above the ground."[27] His observation of her "pumpkin-shaped breasts," "torso of a giant," and "wooden-log thighs" blends gastronomy, mythology, and ecology, employing defamiliarizing strategies to dehumanize her. She is a food to be consumed, or a physical object to be examined, but not a human being in her own right.[28] This description reduces the woman to mere physical attributes, turning her into a racial stereotype. Goldshtein's language reinforces a colonial gaze, where the woman becomes an object of fascination and exoticism, devoid of humanity and personal narrative. Without flinching, Goldshtein concludes that "she was far from being a human: no fear, no desire, the tranquility of an idol, a cave totem of the cannibals."[29] The comparison to an idol or a totem reinforces the colonial mindset, depicting her as something primitive and exotic. The use of such a derogatory, misogynistic, and racially charged description is deeply troubling, revealing the author's bigoted perspective and exoticism toward individuals of non-European descent.

Goldshtein's persistent focus on poverty, the abject, and what he refers to as the "sad eyes" of the lower classes he encounters in Jaffa and South Tel Aviv has been viewed by sympathetic critics like Ilya Kukulin as reflecting postcolonial sensibility or class solidarity.[30] However, I disagree with this interpretation. Goldshtein's descriptions of the people he encounters – Orthodox and Mizrahi Jews, Palestinians, asylum seekers from Africa, and foreign workers from Asia – are steeped in unsettling exoticism and orientalism. His writing adopts a census-like technique, meticulously formulating, classifying, and sorting these groups into distinct categories. By employing this method, the empire's tool of choice, Goldshtein carves out a purportedly neutral space for himself and fellow ex-Soviet Jewish immigrants in Israel, setting them apart from the various forms of otherness he imposes on everyone else. Yet, this so-called neutrality ultimately reveals his underlying sense of superiority, as evidenced by the fact that he feels entitled to categorize others.

In an ironic twist, the author's cosmopolitan-intellectual perspective, which strove to bridge the gap between Soviet-Russian and Western cultures in his first book (*A Farewell to Narcissus*), transforms into a xenophobic, unreflective, and outright hostile stance toward non-Western cultures and peoples in his second book (*Aspects of Spiritual Matrimony*). The drastic change in the portrayal of Israeli culture and its people provides further evidence for Dmitry Shumsky's findings in his analysis of the Russian-speaking community in Israel. Shumsky's article locates the origins of contemporary orientalism of ex-Soviet Israeli intellectuals in the Russian-Soviet legacy of imperialism in Central Asia, the Caucuses, and the Far East.[31] According to Shumsky, the peculiar imagination and representation of Palestinians and Mizrahi Jews as backward, uncivilized, and threatening serves a specific purpose for post-Soviet émigrés in Israel. It allows them to establish a favourable position for themselves within the Western, Ashkenazi, and European echelons of Israeli society. At the same time, the expressed Islamophobia operates on a global scale, framing Israel, Russia, and the broader Western world as united against a common (Middle) Eastern enemy. This strategic framing enables ex-Soviet intellectuals in Israel to reaffirm their political and cultural ties with their country of origin while asserting the relevance of their cultural toolkit in the current Israeli and global context.

Drawing on Shumsky's research, one can interpret Goldshtein's xenophobic and exoticizing descriptions as a relocation of Soviet-style racism to Israel. Shumsky's theory highlights the fact that the xenophobia exhibited by post-Soviet Jews in Israel, including Goldshtein's writings, is not an isolated, unique, and arbitrary occurrence. Rather, it reflects a broader pattern among the Russian-speaking intelligentsia in Israel and other countries such as the United States, Germany, and Canada.[32] In other words, the Russian-speaking *intelligenty* who indulge in xenophobic and racist slurs are not the exception to the rule but the rule itself.[33] By focusing on Goldshtein's fetishist attachment to various minorities and his overinvestment in the rhetoric of culture, empire, and civilization, it is evident that Goldshtein uses Western culture to produce a sense of superiority for the ex-Soviet Jewish community in Israel and to stake their claim to a distinctive position within the Israeli and post-Soviet cultural fields.[34]

The most evident example of this tendency is in the shockingly blunt chapter "The Invasion," at the start of *Aspects of Spiritual Matrimony*. In this section, Goldshtein refers to Ethiopian Jews as "wrinkled, starved half-baked humans";[35] Thais, Filipinos, and Malay are labelled "dog-eaters";[36]

and Chinese people are referred to as "perverts."[37] Steeped in racism and bigotry, the author concludes the chapter with the following passage, quoted at length so the reader can fully grasp the extent of Goldshtein's prejudice and disdain for others:

> The conclusion is clear: everyone should stay at their place – Romanians in Romania, Filipinos in the Philippines, Thais in Thailand, Malay in Malaysia, and Chinese in China ... Their presence is a malign tumor for Israel. The mixing of races, somewhat permissible in larger nation-states, brings death to Israel, in addition to the death that irrevocably descends on us from the coasts of Jordan and the Arabian deserts ... The Jewish character of the country, which seems like an axiom from the outside, can hardly be proven from within. When I speak of Jews, I'm referring to Ashkenazi Jews, of course ... After two thousand years in Western countries (more European than the Europeans themselves), they returned to Israel, to Canaan's bosom, and were knocked of their feet by the market's bustle, the Levantine laziness, and the unbearable heat ... Instead of sweet and sour meats, stuffed spike-fish, honey cakes, and chopped herring with egg and onion, most Ashkenazim now prefer pita bread filled with stomach-irritating hummus. These traitors adore soccer, drink beer by the gallon, sing Arabic melodies of traders from Yemen and Morocco, and leer after women's bodies ... Philosophy is ridiculed, poetry withered, and no one except the select Russians and a handful of foreigners read on the buses or at the beach. Palm trees – not pages – rustle in the wind. The same eastern wind extinguishes the last embers of Western enlightenment. Our own mothers will soon be unable to distinguish us from the landscape ... The east has enclosed on us like a shroud. The last light of European civilization is leaving the Ashkenazi soul. Do we really need to hasten our death, and by accepting Filipinos, Malay, Thais, and Chinese, prematurely fall into the abyss of the Asiatic night?[38]

This deliberately provocative passage reveals a deeply prejudiced and ethnocentric perspective, laden with cultural elitism and fear of cultural dilution. The call for ethnic and national segregation – "everyone should stay at his place" – reflects the author's belief in rigid boundaries between peoples, implying that cultural and racial mixing within Israel is not just undesirable but catastrophic. Despite the neat division between Mizrahi and Ashkenazi, Arabic and Jewish, and Europe and the Levant, the passage insists on maintaining these binaries as separate and distinct, preserving the elevated term in its supposed purity and unadulterated state. Goldshtein goes further and describes the presence of non-European immigrants as "a malign tumor," suggesting that they threaten the very existence of Israel. His rhetoric intensifies with apocalyptic imagery, portraying race mixing as a force that could bring death to Israel, paralleling it with the military threats from the Jordanian coast and Arabian deserts. This portrayal amplifies his xenophobic view that the purity of Jewish identity, specifically Ashkenazi Jewish identity, is under siege in Israel.

For the Soviet *intelligent*, Western high culture appears to determine social hierarchies. Even Jewishness in this passage is not rooted in religious or biological identity but rather seen as cultural content derived from acquired European learning. This binary logic perpetuates the portrayal of the West as a superior civilization threatened by an irrational and dangerous East. Goldshtein exalts Ashkenazi culture through privileged tropes such as philosophy and poetry, while the East, represented by Mizrahi Jewry, is associated with commerce, laziness, sensuality, intoxication, and death. Similar to Samuel Huntington's theory of the clash of civilizations, Goldshtein's divisive narrative about East and West, and his essentialist view of cultures – ignoring their contested and interdependent nature – arguably fuels the very cultural conflicts he claims to merely describe.

This passage illuminates how an excessive idealization of culture, whether Russian, Western, or global, and unwavering faith in civilization's path can lead to unreflective blindness and symbolic violence against non-European places, cultures, and peoples. It also reveals unexpected parallels between cosmopolitanism and orientalism, two theories that are traditionally viewed as polar opposites. For one, it discloses how cosmopolitanism's fascination with non-European cultures and peoples may inadvertently reify the imperial gaze and the logic of binary relations, echoing Latour's critique of cosmopolitanism as a "war plan disguised as a peace plan."[39] Furthermore, like the colonial paradigm, Goldshtein's discourse on otherness becomes a means of asserting selfhood, mastery, and totality. Ultimately, his writings show that exposure to cultural diversity does not necessarily result in progressive awareness and respect for foreign specificity. In fact, in some cases it leads to just the opposite – a sense of cultural superiority, indifference, and even hostility toward other cultures and peoples.

Some scholars argue that Shumsky's theory misses an opportunity to present post-Soviet Jews in Israel in all of their complexity. For instance, Lomsky-Feder, Rapoport, and Lerner contend that Shumsky's representation of Israel's social dynamics is overly simplistic and dichotomous.[40] Specifically, they argue that Shumsky ignores the linguistic, social, and economic marginality of Russian speakers in Israel, as well as the hostility they face from the dominant Israeli society. From this perspective, Goldshtein's portrayal of Palestinians, Mizrahi Jews, foreign workers, and asylum seekers as backward and threatening can be seen as a way for him to find a favourable position within the so-called Western, Ashkenazi, and European echelons of Israeli society. Considering Goldshtein's economic struggles, social marginalization, and linguistic alienation from his host society, it is possible to interpret his unwavering attachment to Russian and world culture as an attempt to regain the social status he lost following his move to Israel. Goldshtein is well aware of Western norms of political correctness and intentionally and provocatively breaks them precisely because he does not identify with the Western mainstream. This allows him to assert his place, undoubtedly marginal, in the imaginary East/West borderland that is Tel Aviv, Israel's cultural centre. For Goldshtein and others associated with the journal *Zerkalo*, particularly Mikhail Grobman, political correctness is linked to the Israeli left-wing cultural establishment. Rejecting political correctness is seen as an attempt to create a new cultural position for themselves within the broader Israeli cultural field. This criticism, however, does not negate Shumsky's findings but rather explains their social and historical context in relation to Israeli society.

Building on the theories by Shumsky and Lerner et al., it becomes evident that post-Soviet Jewish cultural producers in Israel face a dual marginalization. Not only are they positioned as immigrant writers and artists vis-à-vis the state-supported Hebrew cultural scene and institutions,[41] but they also find themselves on the periphery of the global Russophone cultural geography, with Moscow at its centre. During the Soviet era, when the world was sharply divided by the Cold War ideological rivalry between capitalism and communism, the Soviet Union's cultural institutions had abundant resources, yet it was the unofficial literature published in the West (*tamizdat*) or self-produced and circulated in the underground (*samizdat*) that garnered global prestige among Western critics. However, in the post-Soviet era, the situation drastically changed. With decreased Western interest in Russophone cultural production, the right to consecrate and establish cultural hierarchies returned to Moscow's critics and cultural producers.

In this context, Goldshtein's paradoxical pursuit of cosmopolitanism can be seen as a response to Moscow's newfound cultural hegemony, perpetuated by its cultural institutions, critics, and publishing houses. Building on the work of Pascale Casanova, who describes the literary universe as a unified system of circulation and exchange of cultural capital organized around its incontestable centre in Paris, I argue that in the case of Russophone literature in Israel, and elsewhere in the post-Soviet diaspora, we have a more complex system, one that is articulated in multiple stages: first the national and then the global.[42] One may still have to go through Paris to achieve world recognition, as Casanova suggested, but in order for a Russophone writer working in Berlin, Tel Aviv, or New York to get a shot at Paris, they must go through Moscow first – the express train to where the big decisions are made.[43]

From this perspective, Goldshtein's literature and literary theory can be seen as a response to Moscow's cultural hegemony in the post-Soviet period and Israel's peripheral position on the global Russophone literary map, struggling with both structural inequality and symbolic violence from the centre in Moscow. Alongside Soviet-born Israeli poet and writer Alexander Barash, Goldshtein formulated his theory of contemporary post-Soviet writing and the place of Russophone-Israeli diaspora within it, aiming to stake a prominent position for themselves in the global Russophone literary sphere. Goldshtein initially approached this issue at the end of *A Farewell to Narcissus*, in the chapter "Thetis, or Mediterranean Post." In this covert artistic manifesto, Goldshtein calls on fellow Russophone-Israeli writers "to cut a window onto the Mediterranean Sea and the myth of the Levant"[44] and create Mediterranean literature that would incorporate the diverse historical, cultural, and religious specificities of the region they inhabit.[45] "This would be," Goldshtein writes, "the fulfillment of the most sacrosanct and trauma-laden intentions of our culture, for so long yearning for lost Hellenist totality and Alexandrian *ecumene*."[46] This passage reveals the author's intent to embed Russia's imperialism in the realm of culture.

When Goldshtein calls on his fellow Russian-Israeli writers "to cut a window onto the Mediterranean Sea and the myth of the Levant," he deliberately pays homage to the imperial project started by Peter the Great, which aimed to conquer nature in order to fortify the empire politically and militarily in an effort to elevate Russia to the same level as the Western powers – to "cut a window onto Europe," according to Alexander Pushkin's formulation in his canonical *Bronze Horseman*. The function of the Mediterranean Sea in this passage is threefold: it makes Russia into a proper colonial power by securing access to seaports; it provides genealogical ties to Hellenist/Greek culture; and it offers Russia a chance to carve out and dominate a new piece of the Orient. What distinguishes Goldshtein's cultural project from Pushkin's is that the latter did not imagine Russophone authors writing about life in Europe. Goldshtein borrows the metaphor but entirely changes the parameters of the project – not just looking (like Pushkin imagines) but rather jumping through the window into unknown terrain, and then aspiring to cultural mastery of that terrain (while refusing to learn the local language).

The concept of Mediterranean literature is central to Goldshtein and Barash's attempt to offer an alternative to the Russophone literature emerging from Israel. "The point is not to celebrate the break with the tradition of the metropolis,"[47] Goldshtein writes, "the goal is to create a new geo-cultural perspective, one that is more vibrant and appealing than the reality of the Russian-Israeli literary enclave, contemplating in a tongue-tied manner ['kosnoyazychno'] – for lack of other occupations – its own bellybutton."[48] Ultimately, Barash and Goldshtein envision a Mediterranean literary project where Russian-language writers in Israel connect with counterparts in cities like Casablanca, Tangier, Istanbul, and others, forming a multilingual community and a "guild" of like-minded individuals.[49] In the passage, Goldshtein uses the idea of Mediterranean geography to distinguish his work from both Moscow's literary tradition and local Russian-language authors in Israel.

He does so by dismissing post-Soviet literature in Israel as "tongue-tied" (*kosnoyazychnaia*), a term inspired by Osip Mandelstam's description of his father as such. In his autobiography, *The Noise of Time*, Mandelstam contrasts his mother's acculturated and educated speech with his father's "languagelessness." He writes: "My father had absolutely no language; his speech was tongue-tied and languagelessness. The Russian speech of a Polish Jew? No. The speech of a German Jew? No again ... It was anything in the world, but not a language, neither Russian nor German."[50] Drawing on Mandelstam's complex relationship with his father and Jewish identity, Goldshtein rebels against what he perceives as a powerless generation of post-Soviet Israeli writers who, like Mandelstam's tongue-tied father, struggle to produce meaningful literature. In parallel with Mandelstam, who introduced the concept of "world culture" in Russian poetry, Goldshtein and Barash envision a new global cultural project that would break free from the national boundaries of both Russian and Israeli cultures.

The second manifesto – also developed with Alexander Barash – announces the creation of "International Russian Literature" aimed at challenging Moscow's cultural dominance. In the manifesto, Barash passionately argues for a literature without geographic or literary boundaries. "In the same way as French, English, Spanish and German literatures have no geographic or literary boundaries, so can Russian literature abandon the artificial form to which it was subjected, liberate its limbs from the Chinese Lotus Shoes, and start spreading all over the globe," he writes.[51] "This way, Russian imperialism can find a new life in all the former territories and zones of influence of the totalitarian Soviet state, and even beyond these."[52] Once again, the empire and Russia's historical land-gathering (*sobiranie zemel' russkikh*) emerge as cultural models that spark Goldshtein and Barash's imagination both in "Mediterranean Literature" and "International Russian Literature." It is telling that Barash and Goldshtein use the term "imperial" rather than "transnational," "international," "global," or "cosmopolitan." Bracketing the long history of Russian and Soviet domination over peripheral regions, including the imposition of the Russian language, the Cyrillic alphabet, and Moscow's cultural policies on non-Russian republics, Barash and Goldshtein use the unsettling metaphor of Chinese lotus shoes to convey the territorial binding of Russian literature in the Soviet land. Presumably, the writers have much larger territorial ambitions for Russian literature, using the spread of French, English, Spanish, and German literature across the globe through imperialism and colonialism as their model. Ultimately, Barash and Goldshtein maintain that Russophone literature can only earn the respect it deserves by encompassing the entire world and competing in global hierarchies among the "great powers" of culture.

Herein lies the logic of Goldshtein's distinctive cosmopolitanism. It is evident that Barash and Goldshtein's cultural geopolitics are driven by resistance against what Goldshtein refers to as "the unappetizing idea of the unity of Russian literature" under the aegis of Russian nationalism and Moscow's pervasive cultural institutions, both because of Israel's peripheral place in such a formulation and because it might exclude Jews.[53] These projects aim to detach the Russian language from Russian territory, creating space for writers marginalized within Moscow's dominant system to envision a different literary world in terms of aesthetics and ideology – one not controlled or structured by Moscow. From this perspective, Goldshtein's imperial cosmopolitanism offers marginalized writers a roadmap to carve out a space for themselves in a world where literary power and resources are unevenly distributed.

However, in incorporating elements of orientalism and imperialism, both "Mediterranean Note" and "International Russian Literature" somewhat naively attempt to uncouple the empire as a cultural concept associated with high arts, enlightenment, and civilization from the less admirable aspects of imperial exploitation, including political hegemony, resource exploitation, population control, social engineering, and psychological trauma. To put it more forcefully, based on Goldshtein's writings, it appears that he does not seek to uncouple the empire from its less desirable elements – he seems to embrace them, especially the logic of orientalism, racism, xenophobia, Islamophobia, and Eurocentrism. This acceptance of the darker aspects of empire is critical to acknowledge, as it complicates the ostensibly progressive goals of Goldshtein's and Barash's cultural projects. These portrayals reinforce harmful stereotypes and therefore naturalize derision, exploitation, and violence against various "non-western" social groups. Ultimately, the excessive emphasis on notions of "civilization" and "empire" underscores a problematic framework that seeks to reshape the literary world by replacing one form of dominance with another, rather than fostering genuine inclusivity and equality for marginalized voices.

Zoya Cherkassky-Nnadi: The Egalitarian Cosmopolitan

Zoya Cherkassky-Nnadi, like Goldshtein, is a bold and critically acclaimed contemporary Soviet-born Israeli cultural producer known for her provocative and multidisciplinary art. Born in Kyiv in 1976, she attended art schools during her early years in Ukraine. At the age of fifteen, just before the USSR's collapse, she and her family immigrated to Israel. When faced with mandatory army service in Israel, she made a bold decision to enrol in the prestigious Hamidrasha School of Art at Beit Berl College instead, literally and symbolically choosing art over arms. Throughout her career, Cherkassky-Nnadi has earned several esteemed scholarships and grants and participated in artist residency programs across Europe. Her works have garnered recognition and have been acquired by major galleries in Israel and worldwide.

Like the cohort of leftist post-Soviet artists such as Kiril Medvedev, Victoria Lomasko, and the collective Chto Delat, Cherkassky-Nnadi combines her artistic practice with political activism. She advocates for the rights of African asylum seekers and labour migrants in Israel, being married to a Nigerian asylum seeker, Sunny Hyacineth. She also supports the Da'am Workers Party, a Jewish-Arab socialist political party advocating for a one-state solution to the Israeli-Palestinian conflict. Her art serves as a platform for highlighting the experiences of marginalized minorities that are congregated in Israel or hamstrung by the ruthless workings of global capitalism elsewhere. Cherkassky-Nnadi's life journey, artistic endeavours, and political commitments attest to her cosmopolitan set of values – a cosmopolitanism directly opposed to Goldshtein's, yet nevertheless derived from many of the same cultural and social traditions.

Cherkassky-Nnadi's artistic career can be divided into two periods. The first period, from 2002 to 2010, showcases her engagement with the art world in general, and the avant-garde in particular, using irony, violence, shock, and cartoon aesthetics to challenge art as an institution. In her first solo exhibit, *Collectio Judaica*, presented on Christmas Eve at the Rosenfeld Gallery in Tel Aviv in 2002, Cherkassky-Nnadi explored the connections between Jewish and antisemitic imagery. She created provocative pieces, including golden necklaces inspired by the yellow badge, an embroidered pillow depicting a blood-drenched Wandering Jew, and seder plates showing tied-up Christian babies (alluding to the blood libel). She even contemplated using real Christian blood to bake Matza bread but decided against it.

In her second major exhibit, *Action Painting*, held in 2006, Cherkassky-Nnadi continued her institutional critique of the art world. The exhibit featured sculptures of bronze feces (an homage to Piero Manzoni) and large-scale paintings depicting violence against art-goers. It traced the historical trajectory of art, questioning the contemporary artists' strategies to revolutionize social and political realities. Seemingly in agreement with Peter Bürger about the failure of the historical avant-garde to destroy art as an institution, Cherkassky-Nnadi's exhibition demonstrates how, in the contemporary, neo-liberal context, avant-garde strategies like nudity, defecation, and violence have lost their shock value.[54] At best, critics and audiences pinch their noses, like in the painting *Merda d'Artista*, and continue to revere these objects as expressions of the sublime. This presents a defeatist view of art's influence on social and political realities in late capitalism.

In interviews, Cherkassky-Nnadi attributes her decision to leave Israel for a five-year artist residency in Berlin to *Action Painting*'s inability to enact protest of any kind. When she returned in 2010, she was ready to reinvent herself as an artist, marking the beginning of a new phase in her artistic career. She joined forces with four other post-Soviet Israeli artists – Olga Kundina, Anna Lukashevsky, Asia Lukin, and Natalia Zourabova – to form the "New Barbizon" artist group.[55] Inspired by the nineteenth-century Barbizon School of painters in France, the artists chose to leave their isolated studios and paint on the Israeli streets ("the urban jungle"). Their collaboration aimed to move away from the prevalent "art for art's sake" approach in Israeli contemporary art and instead embrace open-air painting, observation, and a "realist" style.

According to Nicolla Trezzi, who wrote the New Barbizon manifesto, the artists' background in traditional art academies in the former USSR have influenced their work.[56] It brought a collective spirit to Israel's art scene, which is mostly individualistic. Moreover, Cherkassky-Nnadi's post-Berlin works challenge the contemporary Israeli art scene by embracing ideologies of social justice, equality, class consciousness, and internationalism, which had lost popularity among artists and politicians in Israel. I will delve deeper and argue that Cherkassky-Nnadi's post-Berlin works are subversive not just because of their unique painting style and collectivist spirit, which Trezzi attributes to her Soviet/Russian background, but also because of their unfamiliar ideological stance, which is informed by the Soviet rhetoric of social justice, social equality, class consciousness, and the discourse of internationalism – ideas that were once central to Israeli (Labor Zionist) rhetoric but have since fallen out of favour among contemporary artists and Israeli politicians.

The group's shift toward "realism" (be it social or socialist) was not merely an aesthetic choice. Unlike the nineteenth-century French Barbizon painters, Cherkassky-Nnadi and her colleagues did not merely abandon their studios to paint landscapes or still life. A much more apt parallel can be drawn from Russian imperial history, where socially oriented members of Russian intelligentsia (*narodniki*) embarked on "going to the people" (*khozhdeniye v narod*) at the end of nineteenth century. They travelled to rural areas of the Russian Empire to educate and revolutionize the peasants, considering their social organization as authentic, untouched by corrupting Western influences, and a model for socialism in the Russian Empire. Cherkassky-Nnadi's socially conscious initiative reflects the *narodniki*'s idealization of the lower classes and belief in culture's power to bring about political change. Therefore, when Cherkassky-Nnadi and her colleagues left their studios, they intentionally selected politically contested spaces and zones of social friction in Israeli society, including the 2011 Israeli Social Justice Protests, the Arab-majority neighbourhood of Ajami in Jaffa, the enclave of African refugees and foreign workers at Neve Sha'anan in South Tel Aviv, and the Palestinian refugee camp Dheisheh in the West Bank which is under Israeli military control.[57]

The lives of African migrants in Israel became a predominant theme in Cherkassky-Nnadi's works as part of the New Barbizon collective, including *Levinsky Park* and *Nigeria- Argentina*. These paintings, in sharp contrast to Goldshtein's abrasive and xenophobic gaze that characterizes his fiction, depict an idyllic representation of African migrants in Israel. In *Nigeria-Argentina*, for instance, we witness a family's private realm, enjoying their time together while watching a soccer match between Argentina and Nigeria. Instead of setting the African family apart from the larger Israeli society, thereby othering them, the painting strongly resonates with Israel's ideological emphasis on the nuclear family and childbearing. Ultimately, the painting emphasizes their happiness despite living in apparent poverty – there is a bed in the living room where the couple sleeps, and windows are sealed up with newspapers to prevent drafts or unwanted scrutiny by the neighbours or the police. Even the presence of the Christian cross does not taint the idyllic representation. Instead, its placement alongside the Israeli flag portrays Israel as a multi-confessional place, fostering a sense of cultural cohabitation among diverse religious and ethnic groups.

Cherkassky-Nnadi's painting *Levinsky Park* takes us to the most abandoned site in Israel's richest and most cosmopolitan city of Tel Aviv, the place Jon Emont rightly described as "a park for those who have nothing."[58]

Figure 3.1
Zoya Cherkassky-Nnadi, *Nigeria-Argentina*, 2015, oil on canvas, 120 × 150 cm.

Levinsky Park is often the second place African refugees encounter upon arriving in Israel – after the detention centre in the Negev.[59] Before they can afford secure housing, many refugees rely on the park for essential needs like sleeping, answering the call of nature, and finding work (waiting for trucks to pick them up as cheap, undocumented labour for construction sites and restaurants). In the last decade, the park has become a symbol of African visibility in Israel, witnessing numerous protests and demonstrations (sometimes violent) related to asylum seekers.[60] Therefore, Cherkassky-Nnadi's choice to paint the park in the most ordinary and bourgeois manner is telling. The painting depicts a leisurely afternoon stroll by a couple with other migrants playing basketball, presenting an idyllic image without signs of hardship. There are no signs of garbage. No sleeping bodies on the grass.

On the contrary, the bright green palette, trimmed palm trees, and orderly lawn accentuate the bucolic quality of this well-maintained park and contribute to its portrayal as part of Israel's middle-class utopia.

Commenting on Cherkassky-Nnadi's artworks portraying African refugees, prominent Israeli art critic Galia Yahav describes the artist's project as a shift from her previous work. "What is the gaze that she directs at the urban sights?" she asks bombastically, and then answers her own question that these "are depictions of a community of blacks that is occupied with itself, seen up close and empathetically."[61] Using sarcasm and irony to hint at her doubts regarding the portrayal's authenticity and depth, Yahav continues: "These are street scrawls according to a "sensitive," "authentic" schema, signifying love of humanity … It is a style of a happy bourgeois template, blue-collar folk portrayed whistling contentedly, happy with their lot, living their lives, court painting draped in humanist sensitivity."[62] The

Figure 3.2
Zoya Cherkassky-Nnadi, *Levinsky Park*, 2014, oil on canvas, 100 × 150 cm.

critic concludes by imagining the artist sitting in the Louvre, wearing a beret and humming a *chanson* as she copies masterpieces, like amateurs not *au courant*. Indeed, Cherkassky-Nnadi's paintings pose significant questions about their content and style. On one hand, her focus on marginalized and excluded members of Israeli society, akin to Goldshtein's literary works, raises concerns about Western appropriation and orientalist fantasies. Furthermore, her chosen style, with expressive bright colours and abstract figuration, situates her art within the long tradition of European colonialism, equivalent to Paul Gauguin's appropriation of subaltern populations as exotic and sexualized objects of fascination for a (largely male) Western audience. Indeed, there are traces of a lost paradise in Cherkassky-Nnadi's paintings, a modernist fascination with folk and naïve art, and an unproblematized commodification and idealization of non-Western people whom Rousseau called "simple souls."

However, what Galia Yahav's criticism overlooks is the political dimension of Cherkassky-Nnadi's art and its relevance to Israel's society and political realities. Over the past decade, approximately 60,000 African asylum seekers, mostly from Eritrea, Darfur, and South Sudan, have sought refuge in Israel. Instead of finding safety, they have faced escalating racism, discrimination, and physical abuse, akin to the backlash against Muslim refugees in Europe. The Israeli government implemented various measures, such as the Anti-Infiltration Bill, detention centres, and border fences, exacerbating the public backlash against asylum seekers, leading to an unprecedented level of open racism in public protests, media, and daily life.[63] Instances of discrimination and racism against African refugees in Israel include frequent anti-refugee rallies demanding deportation, an edict against renting apartments to African "goyim" by prominent rabbis, verbal and physical abuse, property vandalism, and incitement by high-profile politicians, portraying them as a threat and carriers of diseases.[64]

Cherkassky-Nnadi's art, which portrays African migrants as orderly citizens, devoted families, and loving couples, challenges the prevailing stereotypical representation of asylum seekers as criminals and sex workers. Her inclusive vision seeks to counteract the exclusive nature of Zionist ideology that prioritizes Jewish language, religion, and nation-state over others, as exemplified by Israel's controversial "nation-state law," which defines Israel as the nation-state of the Jewish people, thereby marginalizing non-Jewish communities.[65] In contrast to Goldshtein's overt intolerance toward African and Asian non-citizens, Cherkassky-Nnadi offers an egalitarian vision of Israel, accommodating all people regardless of their background. The artist's sympathetic portrayal aims to change the perception of these vulnerable populations as dangerous and barbaric. Ultimately, Yahav's critique of Cherkassky-Nnadi's humanism disregards the potential of cosmopolitan and intersectional solidarity as a tool to combat rising nationalism and xenophobia, not just in Israel but globally.

Goldshtein and Cherkassky-Nnadi's distinct portrayals of foreign people and cultures reveal a notable generational gap between them. Although both arrived around the same time, Goldshtein's mature immigration and exclusive socialization with Russian-speaking émigrés (he never learned Hebrew) contributed to his skepticism toward multiculturalism and political correctness, shaped by his (anti-)Soviet habitus. Having lived through Soviet anti-Jewish persecution and experiencing the violent disintegration of the Soviet cosmopolitan project of "friendship of the peoples," many Russian-speaking Jews of Goldshtein's generation, after immigration to Israel, gladly embraced their newfound status as part of the dominant Jewish majority, aligning themselves with the titular nation and as part of the European/Ashkenazi dominant group.[66]

In contrast, Cherkassky-Nnadi's early arrival in Israel as a teen led to her complete integration into its society – embracing its language, values, and outlook. Describing herself as a "typical Israeli who eats hummus and hates [Avigdor] Lieberman," her political habitus aligns with the left-leaning perspectives of Israel's creative class.[67] Unlike the older generation, influenced by (anti-)Soviet cultural models, Cherkassky-Nnadi draws on dominant Soviet-era cultural and political ideas like socialism and internationalism, shaping her distinctive leftist beliefs. This sets her apart not only from younger contemporary Israeli artists but also from the broader Russian-speaking community, which adores Lieberman much more than hummus. Through leftist political discourse centred on internationalism and class-based critique, Cherkassky-Nnadi seeks to initiate a conversation within Israeli society about ethnic nationalism, inequality, and xenophobia. As she highlights in an interview:

> Here in Israel, it is normal to talk this way [expressing Islamophobia against Palestinians] because of the so-called "Jewish character" of the State of Israel. Even back in Russia, the "other" always interested me;

> it never scared me. The official government propaganda said that we were multicultural. In posters, there was always a Russian person, a Chinese person, and a black person. There was racism in Russian society on an everyday level, and on the institutional level as well, but when I was a kid, I believed what they taught us in school. In school they taught us that all peoples were equal. And that's what I believed when I came here, that differences are interesting.[68]

As she notes in her interview, the Soviet cosmopolitanism and the "friendship of the peoples" depicted in propaganda posters, though not always reflective of lived experiences in the USSR, are nonetheless significant for Cherkassky-Nnadi because these ideas directly challenge Israel's narrative of Jewish exclusivity and the resulting normalization of ethnocentrism and Islamophobia.

In her solo exhibition *Pravda*, Cherkassky-Nnadi continued blending Soviet-Russian cultural models into Israeli art, presenting the history of Russian speakers in Israel as the penultimate story of Israel's attitude toward strangers and different cultures. It was created almost a decade after the artist's return from Berlin in 2010, and ultimately exhibited at the Israel Museum in Jerusalem, the country's most important cultural institution. The exhibition focuses on the struggles of Russian-speaking Jews in Israel during the 1990s. The title, *Pravda*, is ironic. In Russian, *pravda* means truth, but it also coincides with the name of a renowned Soviet newspaper known for its propaganda. To borrow the words of Olga Gershenson, "The title purports to reveal the unadorned truth about Russian immigration to Israel, yet it also alludes to the ideological brainwashing, both Soviet and Zionist, to which immigrants were subjected."[69]

Between 2010 and 2018, the working title for *Pravda* was "Aliyah 91," reflecting its central theme of Soviet-born Jewish immigration to Israel. In Hebrew, *aliyah* carries ideological weight, framing immigration to Israel as a return of the Jewish people to their ancestral homeland. However, Cherkassky-Nnadi seeks to challenge this notion, especially with regard to ex-Soviet Jews. Instead of depicting seamless integration, the series portrays the difficulties the community faced in their early years in the country, including poverty, alcoholism, military service, bullying, and more. These unapologetic depictions confront Hebrew-speaking Israelis with accounts of social suffering that are often excluded from official history.

In *Pravda*, the Russian-speaking community is cast as the unfortunate victim of new circumstances in Israel. One painting, titled *New Victims*, suggests that ex-Soviet immigrants did not find the Promised Land, and their lives in Israel are just as challenging, if not more so, than in the Soviet Union. Each artwork portrays bitter disappointment with Israeli reality, be it professional downgrading, cultural alienation, or unsafe living conditions. On the macro level, the series reveals the hollowness of Israel's ideological discourse of homecoming, highlighting the stark contrast between the ideal of repatriation from its actual reality, eroding the Zionist narrative. Instead of presenting life in Israel through a Zionist angle, Cherkassky-Nnadi portrays a dog-eat-dog world where scenes of poverty, violence, and suffering undermine the idea of Jewish brotherhood and unity. Ultimately, the exhibition does not try to cover up the problem of difference and create a false sense of coherence – on the contrary, she approaches these problems head-on.

The series not only focuses on the harsh social reality in Israel but also explores the pre-migration history of the Jewish community in the Soviet Union. The paintings *1991 in Ukraine* and *Friday in the Projects* form a diptych – an art term for a two-panel work that typically depicts a single scene or theme across two related but separate canvases. With this diptych, Cherkassky-Nnadi underscores the significance of this link for the artist. The diptych comprising *1991 in Ukraine* (oil on linen, 2015) and *Friday in the Projects* (oil on linen, 2015) establishes a stark dialogue between the crumbling realities of post-Soviet Ukraine and contemporary Israeli society. In these Bruegel-inspired works, the artist constructs two harrowing dystopian portraits where law and order are nowhere to be found. The painting *1991 in Ukraine* depicts the political collapse with a chillingly detailed tableau set against a bleak snowy backdrop. The painting is a retelling of Bruegel's *The Massacre of the Innocents*, capturing a similar sense of brutality and disorder through its fragmented composition and stark imagery, evoking the same atmosphere of chaos and moral disintegration. The foreground of *1991 in Ukraine* reveals a series of disturbing details: on the left, a man is being beaten to death; in the centre, a woman lies fallen in a pit, seemingly injured; on the right, a man is exposing his penis to children. The upper sections of the painting show additional scenes of debauchery and violence: a teenager defecating at a construction site, a woman being raped, an intoxicated man vomiting in the snow, and unsupervised preschoolers

Figure 3.3
Zoya Cherkassky-Nnadi, *1991 in Ukraine*, 2015, oil on canvas, 200 × 270 cm.

Figure 3.4
Zoya Cherkassky-Nnadi, *Friday in the Projects*, 2015, oil on canvas, 200 × 270 cm.

huddling around a bonfire for warmth. Dominating the top of the painting, a dramatic confrontation between Ukrainian nationals and pro-Soviet supporters unfolds, illustrating the causes of societal breakdown and moral disintegration in front of the viewer.

Friday in the Projects extends the dystopian theme into the Israeli context, providing a contemporary counterpart to the historical decay depicted in the first painting. The painting frames Israel – or more specifically, the working-class outskirts where many immigrants settled due to affordable rents subsidized by government incentives, and where they crossed paths with Mizrahi Jews, who were forcefully settled in these areas in the 1950s by the state – as a setting for unemployment, violence, and disillusionment. Every detail of this incisive painting – lack of paved roads and basic infrastructure, the knife brawl between pale-skinned "Russians" and dark-skinned Mizrahi men, an old man rummaging through garbage, young men shooting up heroin, Hebrew graffiti reading "Russians Go Home!," the eschatological Chabad poster proclaiming "Prepare for the Coming of the Messiah," and a Kassam rocket about to wipe out this sorry town – reveals the complete disintegration of social and political structures in Israel's periphery. Taken together, these scenes illustrate the breakdown of societal frameworks in both Israel and the Soviet Union, emphasizing the government's failure (or reluctance) to prevent such tragedies. By continuously drawing parallels between Israel and the Soviet Union, Cherkassky-Nnadi underscores the sad reality that for many ex-Soviet Jews, life appears to have been bad both before and after immigration in strikingly similar ways.

Pravda's political and subversive stance is evident – it challenges the Zionist narrative of *aliyah* by questioning Israel's depiction as a safe haven for Jews. Instead, it reveals how antisemitic violence and persecution experienced by Russian-speaking Jews in the Soviet Union persist in Israel, now manifesting as violence against "Russians." Despite this critical edge, many critics have been puzzled and troubled by Cherkassky-Nnadi's portrayal of Mizrahi Jews. For instance, Ortal Ben Dayan, a prominent feminist of Mizrahi background, has particularly criticized two paintings, *Itzik* (2012) and *First Job in Israel* (2010). Sharing these works on Cherkassky-Nnadi's Facebook page, Ben Dayan condemned them with the remark: "Racism disguised as art, and so-called leftist artists can't seem to get enough."

Figure 3.5
Zoya Cherkassky-Nnadi, *Itzik*, 2012,
oil on canvas, 150 × 200 cm.

A few days later, she published a full-length article, "Don't Put Art on the Internet, All the Arsim [offensive slang for Mizrahi men] Will Come." In the article, Ben Dayan contextualizes *Itzik* and *First Job in Israel* within the broader tradition of xenophobic and racist depictions of Mizrahi Jews by the Ashkenazi elites. Ben Dayan concludes her piece with the following: "Cherkassky's paintings operate in a field accessible mainly to Ashkenazi elites, seeking further Westernization. She is aware that Itzik and his family from *First Job in Israel* will not attend her exhibition. Itzik's only chance to be part of a Tel Aviv gallery is as a subject of her paintings. The orientalist dynamic persists. Both Cherkassky's Itzik and the real-life Itzik are confined to a shawarma joint."[70] Both the post and the article ignited a heated debate about Cherkassky-Nnadi's stereotypical and orientalist representation of

Figure 3.6
Zoya Cherkassky-Nnadi, *First Job in Israel*, 2010, acrylic on canvas, 35 × 45 cm.

Mizrahi Jews, dividing Facebook users into two camps. Some, primarily from the former Soviet Union, saw Cherkassky-Nnadi's paintings as a realistic reflection of the traumatic experiences many Russian-speaking women faced during the 1990s and the power imbalances in social and professional relationships between immigrants and locals. Others, mainly Mizrahi Israelis, viewed these representations as abrasive, orientalist, and racist, reflecting the perceived arrogance and racism of Russian speakers toward the less-educated Mizrahi community and all local Israelis.

Indeed, it is possible to find parallels between Cherkassky-Nnadi's artworks and Goldshtein's virulent passages, as both resort to primitivism, exaggeration, stereotypes, and racism in depicting life in Israel. In *Itzik*, there are blatant antisemitic markers of Jewishness, like Itzik's large, hooked nose, swollen lips, wild eyes, hairy body, and aggressive sexual behaviour, as well as the clichéd representation of Mizrahi men (the Star of David necklace, golden rings, protruding stomach, and cheap slippers). The painter contrasts Itzik with a frail, fair-skinned, Slavic-looking waitress, portraying her as a damsel in distress. An approving glance from Rabbi Ovadia Yossef (Mizrahi chief rabbi of Israel) on the wall, like the portraits of Stalin in socialist realist paintings, seemingly endorses the sexual assault in Itzik's falafel store. Similarly, in *First Job in Israel*, the Mizrahi family members are portrayed as grossly overweight, their clothes struggling to contain their protruding stomachs, while the unruly children are roaming, demanding "Bamba," a beloved Israeli snack. In contrast, the slim, beautiful, Slavic-looking cleaning lady is wearing a long skirt in Eastern European folk style and looking down meekly. Like Cinderella, she quietly accepts her fate of cleaning up after them.

Instead of debating the historical accuracy of the represented, focusing on the dynamic interplay between form and content in Cherkassky-Nnadi's art is more productive. Specifically, the formal techniques she employs in her earlier exhibitions, such as stereotypes, shock value, and cartoon aesthetic, reappear in *Pravda*. The comic book style (in *First Job in Israel*, there is even a speech bubble), the flat perspective, and her use of oil and acrylic paint on large canvases, reminiscent of American pop artist Roy Lichtenstein's works, indicate a deliberate disjunction between the medium and the message the artist seeks to convey. When viewed within the broader context of Cherkassky-Nnadi's provocative use of stereotypes and exaggeration for specific artistic and political purposes, *Pravda* can be understood as staged forms of public "happenings" designed to elicit a reaction from the general public – a deliberate provocation challenging established norms ("a slap in the face of public taste," borrowing Mayakovsky's words to describe his futurist aesthetics). In *Collectio Judaica*, for instance, she transformed Holocaust imagery into beautiful art objects; wore a yellow badge to art exhibitions while living in Germany; and created T-shirts with portraits of contemporary Russian artists with the label "shitty artists" in *Olga Sviblova Is Shit, or the End of the Critical Discourse* (presented in Moscow in 2007) with Avdey Ter-Oganian. In the same vein, *Itzik* and *First Job in Israel* can be viewed as forms of "trolling" that strategically provoke reactions, simplify complex issues, and bring hatred into the spotlight. Ultimately, by breaking taboos, social conventions, and political correctness, this series aims to reveal the tensions and mechanisms of stereotypes in the interactions between different groups within Israeli society.

In an interview with the Israeli newspaper *Kal'kal'ist*, Cherkassky-Nnadi clarifies her objectives with paintings such as *Itzik* and *First Job in Israel*. She explains that these artworks represent a specific "Russian" perspective or "gaze" on local Israelis. When asked to elaborate, she replies: "The Russian community believes that local Israelis haven't quite reached the level of Homo sapiens; they consider them dim-witted and unable to absorb all the culture we brought from Russia. And trying to teach them is as useless as teaching a monkey how to smoke … So in my paintings, I bring this hidden Russian perspective to light."[71] By casually performing orientalism and racism, Cherkassky-Nnadi's artworks and media persona ironically reflect the themes present in Goldshtein's fiction. This includes Goldshtein's imperialistic view of Israel's Levantine character, his dissatisfaction with Israel's allegedly "Mizrahi" identity, and his belief in a cultural hierarchy where some hold a monopoly on culture while others are seen as lacking it.[72] In this way, the artist shows how adopting the language of Soviet cosmopolitanism – favouring Western culture as a benchmark for social hierarchy – can be used to marginalize and alienate other groups from crucial social, professional, and economic opportunities. However, an important question remains: to what extent do works that engage in a meta-critique of racism and orientalism differ substantially from those that merely perpetuate racism and stereotypes? After all, irony only works if the recipient can recognize it as such. This is important considering that a great many Russian- and Hebrew-speaking Facebook users failed to grasp Cherkassky-Nnadi's irony and interpreted these artworks as straightforward and accurate portrayals of Mizrahi and Russophone Jews.

In conclusion, both Goldshtein's and Cherkassky-Nnadi's portrayals of Israeli society are deeply unsettling. Instead of depicting Israel as a liberal utopia where different groups harmoniously coexist alongside each other, they reveal the opposite side of cosmopolitanism, highlighting the challenging reality of social discord in contemporary Israel. What distinguishes Goldshtein's and Cherkassky-Nnadi's projects is the underlying cause of their pessimism. While Goldshtein's disappointment with Israeli reality stems from feelings of cultural superiority and the pain associated with the author's arrival to what he sees as a cultural wasteland, Cherkassky-Nnadi's harsh images are motivated by her critique of the exclusionary principles of Zionist ideology and the discrimination against non-Jews. While Goldshtein seeks to break all ties with other social and ethnic groups in Israel,

Cherkassky-Nnadi attempts to construct a broader, cross-sectional alliance that encompasses all marginalized groups that, in one way or another, are excluded from Israel's ideological framework (although her ironic and self-reflective style can sometimes alienate potential allies). One reason Soviet cosmopolitanism remains relevant for such distinct and opposing cultural projects is that it cuts across Israel's celebrated rhetoric of integration and assimilation. Instead of merely paying lip service to an imagined Jewish unity in Israel, Cherkassky-Nnadi's and Goldshtein's works expose the multiplicity of languages, cultures, traditions, and individuals that fight for belonging in Israel. What both artists uncover is that beneath the facade of assimilation, there are always unadulterated pain and violence, abandoned traditions, self-doubt and self-loathing, and fractured communal life. Cherkassky-Nnadi's paintings ultimately serve as a reminder that to truly integrate all the different communities living in Israel, such as asylum seekers from Sudan, Palestinians from the Gaza Strip, Orthodox Jews from Bnei Brak, and Russian speakers from Ashdod, the whole structure of Israeli society must be changed. This is precisely why there is no explicit "friendship of the peoples" in Cherkassky-Nnadi's paintings – this trope is ultimately postponed and projected into the future.

CHAPTER 4

Artists of the 1.5 Generation

From Post-Soviet Nostalgia to the 2022 War in Ukraine

The Roaring Nineties in Israel

Back in Russia, my mother was a math teacher, she was respected. But here in Israel, she had to work double shifts of manual labour just to make ends meet. Unsurprisingly, this led to extreme loneliness and isolation, but I don't blame her. On the contrary, I'm grateful for the sacrifices she made for us, like wearing a pair of worn-out shoes throughout the entire winter to provide for our food and education.

At school, nobody wanted to talk to me, not even other immigrant kids like me. Even our Russian music teacher exclusively screamed at me in Hebrew, even though she knew I didn't understand a word. So, I quickly learned Hebrew. I was determined to keep my name, though. Everything was taken from me, but I wanted to keep my name.

For years, I endured both mental and physical abuse from my peers. I faced daily bullying, with stronger kids targeting me for my small sandwich. No one intervened until my mother, in broken Hebrew, confronted the principal and the girl leading the campaign against me.

After that, the bullying finally stopped.

These words were written in Hebrew on 14 November 2019, by thirty-five-year-old Ira Vaisberg, one of hundreds of ex-Soviet Jewish women (and some men) who openly shared their deeply moving experiences of migrating to Israel during the 1990s in the Hebrew-language Facebook group "Russian Women Without a Sense of Humor." These testimonies, often accompanied by nostalgic family snapshots from their previous lives in the USSR, are full of pain, trauma, and a profound sense of disillusionment. Some narratives are minimalist and poetic, while others, like the above, unfold in substantial length and are rich with intricate details. Yet, what binds them together is the overwhelming degree of suffering that underpins every single testimony of migration.

What prompted this sudden surge of painful memories by Israeli men and women who had immigrated to Israel nearly three decades ago? The year these stories appeared, 2019, might hold a clue. During that year, Israel commemorated the thirtieth anniversary of the massive migration that brought 1.2 million Russian-speaking Jews to the country. Throughout the year, Israeli newspapers were full of accounts of doctors and scientists who had successfully integrated into the local job market, software engineers who had fuelled the meteoric rise of Israel's high-tech industry, accomplished writers and artists who had achieved remarkable acclaim both at home and abroad, and athletes who had proudly earned coveted Olympic medals for Israel. In other words, the media painted an appealing picture of a model minority, often accompanied by the widely echoed phrase-turned-hashtag "ha'aliyah achi tova she-hayta lanu" ("the best migration we ever had"), and many Israelis – particularly those from the USSR – were seduced by its flattering rhetoric.

The one-sided focus on communal success, however, had inadvertently swept all stories that did not fit into the media's adulatory portrayal under the rug. In a way, the rapid eruption of historical narratives by Vaisberg and others could be interpreted as an attempt to present an alternative narrative of the ex-Soviet Israeli community and develop a more nuanced understanding of its initial years in the country. This discord between Israel's official history and personal memories provokes the central question of this chapter. Now, thirty years after the arrival of Russian-speaking Jews to Israel, the question remains: how should this history be recounted? Should it be remembered as a story of a community that had found refuge after years of Soviet persecution and achieved unprecedented success, or, alternatively, should it be remembered as a story of adversity, intolerance, and hostility, much like the stories shared in numerous Facebook posts?

To answer this question, I examine how artists of the 1.5 generation – writers and painters who were born in the Soviet Union but resettled in Israel in their teens, such as Alex Rif, Rita Kogan, and Zoya Cherkassky-Nnadi – engage with the prehistory of the Jewish community in the USSR and the period following their emigration in Israel in the 1990s. The term 1.5 generation was introduced by Cuban-American sociologist Rubén Rumbaut in an attempt to differentiate the immigration experience of children and young adults both from the experiences of their parents (the first generation) and from those of their younger siblings who were born in the destination country (the second generation).[1] The 1.5ers examined in this article arrived in Israel at a young age (between the ages of five and sixteen), lived in low-income neighbourhoods on the edge of Israeli geography, and were socialized in Israeli institutions and in the Hebrew language. In their Hebrew-language artistic works from 2015 to 2019, they challenge Israel's ideological narrative of *aliyah*, which frames immigration to Israel as a triumphant return of Jews to their ancestral homeland. Extending from the 1990s to the new millennium, the poetry by Rif and Kogan and visual art by Cherkassky-Nnadi suggest that for many Russian-speaking Jews in Israel, the desired happy ending was never achieved. Additionally, these poets and artists offer an alternative perspective on the Soviet-Jewish past. Instead of emphasizing antisemitism and discrimination, this generation of artists depicts the last years of the Soviet regime with tenderness, longing, and nostalgia.

Ultimately, these artists – individuals brought to Israel as children and young adults, often against their will – propose a new understanding of the post-Soviet Jewish experience by juxtaposing Soviet nostalgia with Israeli disillusionment. While previous generations of Russophone-Israeli authors also expressed disappointment with Israel and a sense of nostalgia for the Soviet past, their sentiments were much more temperate, short-lived, and less frequent.[2] As Mikhail Weiskopf explains, ex-Soviet Israeli authors' negative attitude toward Israel in the 1970s and 1990s waves "was quickly overcome, either through adaptation to life in Israel or through professional integration to and recognition by the sizable Russian-speaking community."[3] In contrast, idyllic memories of Soviet childhood and lachrymose accounts of post-emigration suffering continue to animate the literary and visual works of ex-Soviet Israeli 1.5ers, even after twenty-five years in the country. After keeping silent about their own and their parents' traumatic experiences in Israel, this generation is finally ready to present their unapologetic, politically engaged, Hebrew-language works to Israeli society in a language they can understand. The change of language is significant. By writing in Hebrew, they not only assert their place within Israeli society but also ensure that their stories, perspectives, and critiques are accessible and resonate more powerfully with the broader Israeli public.

Alex Rif: An Unhappy Childhood

Alex Rif is the leading voice of the poets of the 1.5 generation. She immigrated to Israel from Ukraine in 1991 at the age of five and spent her formative years in the small coastal city of Netanya in Northern Israel where many Russian-speaking Jews settled. Her debut book of Hebrew poetry, *Tipshonet mishtarim* (*Silly Girl of the Regime*), sold nearly 500 copies before its official release in December 2018. The book's funding came from a successful crowd-funding campaign on the popular Israeli platform Headstart. Following its official release, it received the Matanel award for Promising Young Jewish Poet and the Bourgeoning Poets Award from the Ministry of Culture. In addition to writing poetry, Rif is a passionate promoter of Russian/Soviet culture in Israel. Together with activists from the organizations Generation 1.5 and Cultural Brigade, Rif has initiated a number of cultural and social projects aimed at bridging the gap between Hebrew and Russian speakers in Israel. One of these, Israeli Novyi God, seeks to introduce the secular, non-Christian nature of the Soviet holiday of Novyi God (Russian for "new year") to Hebrew-speaking Israelis. Another, Operation Veteran, aims to convey the little-known but heroic stories of Jewish soldiers in the Red Army during World War II and integrate them into the collective Jewish history during the era of the Holocaust. Rif also curates the poetry series Tusovka – Immigration Poetry, offering post-Soviet Israelis a platform to share their immigration stories through art and poetry, in a language accessible to Israeli society (Hebrew). All the poems featured in this chapter were presented during Tusovka readings held in towns across Israel.

Despite these accomplishments, the historical narrative of the "Russian" *aliyah* that Rif portrays in her poetry is deeply pessimistic. This is somewhat unexpected, given her remarkable personal achievements: holding a BA in business and political science and an MA in public policy from the Hebrew

University in Jerusalem, securing a profitable position in the Ministry of Economy, being a successful poet, and currently serving as the founder and CEO of One Million Lobby, advocating for improved social, economic, and cultural conditions for ex-Soviet Israelis. Nevertheless, the narrative of immigrant upward mobility is conspicuously absent from her profoundly personal poetry. Instead, it invokes the experience of her brother's adult circumcision, her parents' downward social mobility, alienation from her grandparents, and sexual obsession with *sabra* (Hebrew for "native-born Israeli Jew") men as a strategy of assimilation. She emphasizes these experiences in order to present a particular picture of communal disenfranchisement, revealing to Israeli society the painful ordeals that Russian speakers faced during the 1990s.

For instance, the poem "Milah" uses the disturbing act of adult circumcision – which is a prominent theme in global post-Soviet Jewish literature, memorably depicted by writers like Gary Shteyngart from the United States and Wladimir Kaminer from Germany – as a metaphor for the painful and often messy transition of young Soviet-born émigrés to life in Israel. The poem draws on the experiences of Rif's brother, Max, who like the poem's speaker had moved to Israel when he was fourteen, experienced adult circumcision, and struggled to find a sense of belonging in the new homeland.

I'm Max
We to immigrate to Israel
I love Ukraine
But mom say there good.

Haifa very beautiful.
Tomorrow I start army boarding school.
I to see teacher and new class,
Maybe I *kapitan.*

At boarding school Alex and Yuri,
We good friends.
People say we not circus-sized.
I understand but not very.

Today father said tomorrow surgery.
There little shot no sleep and big shot sleep.
I scared little.

Dad photos I bed hospital.
In the room *chabadniks* songs dances.
I want quiet.[4]

The poem is divided into a before and after – a happy life in Ukraine prior to immigration and the precarious reality in Israel that followed.[5] In clumsy Hebrew that communicates both incomplete assimilation and incomplete comprehension of his own experiences, Max describes the reason his parents decided to immigrate to Israel – simply because "there good." Their pursuit of a better future, however, does not have a happy ending. Unable to care for Max in a new country, he is sent to a military boarding school, triggering a change from the initial optimistic tone in the first stanza to a notably darker one in the subsequent one.

Like the majority of ex-Soviet Jews, Max was not circumcised.[6] This was largely due to the Soviet Union's anti-religious policies, popular antisemitism, acculturation, and a desire of some Soviet Jews to hide their Jewishness and "pass" as Russians. Max's parents, once again without consulting him, decide to subject the submissive son to this painful procedure to reassert his Israeli/Jewish identity, which was questioned in the military boarding school.[7] Employing a concrete-poetry technique akin to E.E. Cummings, the poem concludes with two "shortened" stanzas, which visually outline Max's circumcision and convey the fear and dejection he feels. Max's preference for general anesthesia that will put him to sleep and the closing line, "I want quiet," can be interpreted as a literal yearning for rest but also as a metaphorical death wish, a wish that directly follows from Max's crushing immigrant experience. The final *tableau vivant* of Max lying in the hospital, yearning for solitude and escape from his circumstances, while his dad "snaps" pictures and Orthodox Jews sing and dance around him, establishes Max as the ultimate victim, deprived of agency and abused by everyone around him.[8] This image emphasizes Max's vulnerability and underscores the profound alienation he experiences within a cultural and religious context that he struggles to reconcile with his own identity.

Continuing the childhood cycle, Rif's poem "Evgenii" opens a window into the early struggles of the members of the 1.5 generation, whose painful encounter with Israeli society started as early as kindergarten:

The day Evgenii arrived in kindergarten,
The sun shone.
He was smaller than me,
Paler than me, and he smelled
Of fear.
This time, it was I
Who explained to him,
In ordered Hebrew words,
That socks and sandals is, how to say, ugly,
That a herring sandwich is, how to tell, stinks,
And that he should speak Hebrew,
This is not Russia!

The day Evgenii arrived in kindergarten –
I was truly happy![9]

Through irony, the poem explores the cyclical nature of violence against ex-Soviet newcomers, this time inflicted by fellow immigrants on their peers. The poem suggests that the only way to assimilate into the Israeli collective is by violently repudiating one's "Russian" identity – supposedly manifested in wearing sandals with socks and eating salted-fish sandwiches – and adopting the prevailing anti-"Russian" stance of the surrounding society. The speaker takes pleasure in tormenting poor Evgenii, meticulously listing everything he should or should not do in his new homeland. The stylization of the imperfect speech of the narrator, amplified by the "how to say" and "how to tell" asides, magnifies the irony of her demand that Evgenii speak Hebrew because "This is not Russia!" – a hegemonic demand most post-Soviet émigrés heard in their first years in the country.[10] By the end of the poem, the speaker becomes "truly happy" because after a long period of suffering and humiliation, this is the first time she has assumed a position of power and agency. The dramatic irony here is that the speaker's innocent tone suggests she may not even be aware of the violence she inflicts on Evgenii. This reflects the tragic fact that experiencing violence against oneself does not necessarily lead to future compassion.

The notion that a personal trauma might lead to re-traumatization of others instead of fostering empathy and compassion echoes a scene from Art Spiegelman's Pulitzer Prize–winning graphic novel *Maus*. In this scene, despite his own harrowing experience at Auschwitz, the grandfather nevertheless refuses to pick up African American hitchhikers, convinced they are all thieves.[11] This contradiction prompts his grandson to question how a Holocaust survivor, who suffered so profoundly from racism, could hold such prejudiced views. Ruth Klüger, a survivor and scholar, can offer insight into this issue. In her memoir, she recounts a conversation in a student cafeteria where a PhD candidate expressed disbelief that a Hungarian Auschwitz survivor would harbour contempt for Arabs.

> I get into the act and argue, perhaps more hotly than need be. What did he expect? Auschwitz was no instructional institution, like the University of Gottingen, which he attends. You learned nothing there, and least of all humanity and tolerance. Absolutely nothing good came out of the concentration camps, I hear myself saying, with my voice rising, and he expects catharsis, purgation, the sort of thing you come to the theater for?[12]

Both Klüger's reflections and Spiegelman's narrative, similar to Rif's poem, illustrate that expecting tolerance and humanity from those who have endured trauma may be unrealistic. Instead, abuse and trauma often form a cycle, with past victims frequently replicating abusive behaviours in their interactions with others. Rif's poem, therefore, underscores the urgent need for a conscious effort to break this cycle of re-traumatization within Israeli society and address its detrimental effects.

In addition to giving voice to the difficult social adjustment of her own generation, Rif's poetry also exposes the historical wounds of her parents' generation – an aspect rarely addressed in Israeli public discourse, especially in Hebrew. Larissa Remennick characterizes the connection between the first and 1.5 generations of post-Soviet Israelis as one between silent parents and articulate children.[13] She further observes that the demand "for visibility, belonging, and at times the political protest of young Russian Israelis

[was] not really typical for their parents, the first immigrant generation."[14] Rif's Hebrew poem "Halom hozer" (2015) ("Recurring Dream") achieves precisely this, giving voice to the painful history that was quietly endured and suppressed by the parents' generation:

My mother tells me
That when we immigrated to Israel,
And the financial situation was tough,
She sold her body to men.
In other words, my mother did not work as a house cleaner,
My mother was a whore.
And I was shocked,
Not by the transaction itself,
Because if you can sell your soul, you can sell your body,
But by her demand
For a fair wage
From someone who fuck her in the ass [tachat].
My mom was not a stinking Russian immigrant.
My mother was a liberal,
With explosive sexuality
And forbidden desire.
She was not a floor rag,
My mother was ready
To go down,
For a chance to rise up again.
My mother was a whore![15]

In this sexually explicit poem, the poet addresses the challenges faced by her parents' generation in adapting to life in Israel. From the daughter's perspective, the poem portrays the mother's precarious situation (metonymic for Russian-speaking women in Israel) by casually suggesting that, during the 1990s, Russian-speaking women had only two options – house cleaning or sex work. The title, "Recurring Dream," subverts Israel's narrative of repatriation and its aspirational nature. Instead of portraying Israel as a Promised Land, Rif describes it as a source of trauma, where Russian speakers are compelled to either mop floors or turn to sex work for survival.[16] Spatially, a vertical movement downwards frames the poem, starting at the heights of *aliyah* (which in Hebrew means both "immigration to Israel" and "ascendance," suggesting a rise to heaven) and culminating in the depths of being "fucked in the ass." The polysemantic Hebrew word "tachat," signifying both "ass" and "lowest point/bottom," captures the mother's path from the peak of repatriation and homecoming to the nadir of prostitution. This trajectory suggests disillusionment and a story of a fall rather than a triumphant arrival in the Promised Land, contrasting with dissident and refusenik writers' portrayals of Israel as the culmination of their spiritual journey from the Soviet underworld to the Holy Land in Israel.

The expectation that the speaker is going to be shocked by her mother's revelation is undermined in the second stanza. Instead, what takes the speaker by surprise is her mother's bold demand for a fair wage. This act of social protest from the vulnerable position of victimhood becomes a source of inspiration for the daughter. As a result, the daughter refuses to pass judgment on her mother and upholds her right to do what she wishes with her body. Instead of repressing this dark past, the speaker takes ownership of the traumatic experience of her parents' generation and proudly uses it as a template for her personal activism and defiance. In so doing, the speaker transforms the entrenched stereotype of the "Russian whore" (*zona rusia*), ubiquitously hurled at Russian-speaking women in Israel during the 1990s, into an alternative liberal narrative of agency, uninhibited sexuality, and forbidden desire.[17] However, this portrayal of agency somewhat contradicts the poem's initial assertion that financial difficulties forced her mother into sex work. The cathartic last line, "My mother was a whore!," is ambiguous and can be read both as a way to reclaim and redeem the pejorative term and as a cry of desperation.

The intergenerational relationship between a mother and daughter is also a topic of Rif's poem "Agiley ha'yaalom shel ima" ("Mother's Diamond Earrings"). This time, the poem explores how Soviet-Jewish history and memory shapes the identity of 1.5ers:

Mother,
At thirty,
I put on
Your diamond earrings,
And I bragged with pride:
"They were purchased back there,
On the black market,
And they cost

A four-month salary."
I made you into a partisan,
A freedom fighter,
A national hero.
You've made *aliyah* because you wanted to,
And you wanted to, of course,
Because you were Zionist.
A light unto the nations
No more diasporic darkness.
What I didn't tell them –
You working as a house cleaner,
Erasing your dreams,
And the never-ending anxiety.
In the evening,
When I stopped serving your life story
In cups of lies,
I wanted to take off the earrings,
But they were not.
The lie literally merged with my body,
Like a successful melting pot.
Like a corpse.[18]

This deeply introspective poem explores the narrator's struggle with self-deception and self-effacement in her life in Israel. The diamond earrings, a symbol for the Soviet-Jewish past, become a mask that the narrator dons for the sake of the Israeli audience. The poem starts as an ode to her mother but quickly transforms into a dialogue with Israeli society. First, the simple act of buying earrings on the black market is hyperbolized, transformed from an everyday matter of life in the USSR into an act of heroism that makes the mother an exemplar of Zionism and dissent. The lie snowballs: the speaker wants to take pride in her mother, even if this means misrepresenting her life. She knows that the past she describes is false, but nonetheless describes it in the dissident key because that narrative amends a fractured collective identity and brings pride to places where there was only shame. The lines "A light unto the nations / No more diasporic darkness" utilize the biblical words of Isaiah to frame her mom as a moral guide of the Jewish people and humanity.

In the second half, the speaker realizes with bitterness that by shaping herself according to the historical narrative that Israeli society wants to hear – the hardships endured under the Soviet regime, the determined efforts of her mother to reach Zion, and the ultimate bliss to live among one's people in Israel – to fit in, she and other ex-Soviet Jews inadvertently project themselves into a false past, erasing a significant part of their post-emigration struggles that have shaped their identities. The suppressed memory that the speaker ultimately shares is that of occupational downgrading. When one million post-Soviet Jews arrived in Israel in 1990s, jobs were scarce, and many newcomers were forced to accept any form of employment in order to survive. Women experienced particularly harsh professional downgrading, as patriarchal pressures often compelled them to make sacrifices and take jobs below their educational qualifications and professional expertise. Not all newcomers succeeded in climbing the professional ladder in Israel, including Rif's mother, who continued working as a school janitor all her life. Recent studies support the anecdotal evidence of Ira Vaisberg and the bleakness expressed in Rif's poems: they reveal and highlight the exploitation, housing difficulties, and conflicts endured by Russian-speaking women in the Israeli workforce.[19] These experiences, integral to the immigrant journey, profoundly influence the literature and art of post-Soviet Israeli artists.

The poem's speaker is aware of her mother's considerable personal and professional sacrifices but struggles to articulate them because of their incompatibility with the Zionist master narrative. Both "Recurring Dream" and "Mother's Diamond Earrings" present complex accounts of speakers attempting to project themselves into someone else's historical and ideological narratives, but with no success. In "Recurring Dream," the speaker adopts an empowering narrative of sex work that does not entirely mirror her mother's precarious experiences, while in "Mother's Diamond Earrings," the speaker endeavours to embody a narrative of dissent that similarly falls short. Indeed, in the last two stanzas, there is an uncanny merger of the earrings – a material object – with the speaker's own body. The syntax breakdown in the line "But they were not" (in Hebrew, *ve lo hayu*) mirrors the narrator's emotional turmoil. In the final stanza, literal mortification is the price paid for historical hyperopia and rapid assimilation via the melting pot. In this complex interplay between the past and present, Rif demonstrates that simplifying or erasing the Soviet past for the sake of assimilation is a Faustian pact struck by Russian speakers in Israel. The speaker dies at the poem's end, reduced to a corpse without a soul. By employing anaphora to liken the "melting pot" to "death" in the final lines, the poem concludes with a powerful image of the destructive impact of cultural assimilation.

Rif's poems shed light on the childhood deprivations of her generation, the fractured professional biographies of the parent generation, and the tension between official and personal memory. While Rif's poetry hints at the gendered experiences of the 1.5 generation, other cultural producers, such as Rita Kogan, make them front and centre in their work.

Rita Kogan: The Intersection of Gender, Sexuality, and Immigration

Rita Kogan, another critically acclaimed poet of the 1.5 generation, was born in 1967 in Leningrad (today, St Petersburg) and migrated to Israel in 1990. To date, she has published three full-length books of poetry and one book of prose, all in Hebrew. Her poetry collections include *Rishayon li-shegiot ketiv* (*License to Misspell*, 2015), *Sus bahatzait* (*Horse in a Skirt*, 2018), a runner-up for the prestigious Gardner Simon prize for Hebrew poetry, and *Mahalat yabasha* (*Land Sickness*, 2022). She also authored *Eretz-sela* (*Stoneland*, 2021), a collection of short stories. Beyond her original verse, Kogan's noteworthy achievements include translating Russian-language poets like Anna Akhmatova, Marina Tsvetaeva, Osip Mandelstam, Joseph Brodsky, and a complete rendition of Alexander Pushkin's *The Tale of the Dead Princess and the Seven Knights* into Hebrew.

Because Kogan arrived in Israel at a later age than Rif, her poetry is less concerned with childhood and more with the challenges faced by women during immigration. For instance, her debut poetry collection, *License to Misspell*, focuses on the trials of Russian-speaking women in Israel, mirroring the poet's own journey in a new country. In *Horse in a Skirt*, Kogan continues her exploration of the challenges encountered by Russian-speaking women in their daily lives in Israel, including ethnic discrimination, verbal and sexual abuse, confrontations with toxic masculinity, and the complexity of expressing sexuality in a patriarchal society. As an example, Rita Kogan's minimalist poem "[Hagdara-atzmit]" ("[Self-

Definition]") powerfully captures the verbal abuse and pernicious stereotypes that Russian-speaking women experience in their lives in Israel:

– You don't look like you're from here.
– You don't look like you're from there.
– Why are you cold? Aren't you Russian?!
– Why are you hot? Aren't you Israeli?!
– Wow! You don't have an accent.
– Actually, you do have an accent.
– Are you Jewish? From both sides?
– How long have you been in Israel?
– Twenty years and you still haven't got used to it?
– Where are you from?
– (I mean, from here)
– (I mean, from there)
– You're leftist? Weird. You're Russian!
– Do you have a boyfriend? No? Weird. You're Russian!
– You won't fuck me? No? But you're Russian.
– You fucked him? Already? Sure, you're Russian.[20]

The poem, structured as a series of intrusive questions that are hurled at Russian-speaking women in Israel, presents an intersectional critique of oppressive societal expectations for immigrant women who, even after twenty years in Israel, are judged to be unable to fit the established Israeli "norms" and are cast as sexual and ethnic "others." The escalating intensity of these questions reveals the arbitrary, yet pervasive nature of the verbal and sexual abuse endured by Russian-speaking women, as well as the unwarranted scrutiny to which their sexuality, Jewishness, cultural identity, and even bodily reaction to temperature are subjected. Regardless of the addressee's actions – whether she speaks with or without an accent, feels hot or cold, sleeps with her boyfriend or not – she remains an eternal outsider and is perceived through the lens of "Russian" difference.

Written in 2015, the poem sheds light on the largely muted history of sexual abuse of Russian-speaking women in Israel. As Israeli sociologist Larissa Remennick explains, after their arrival in the 1990s, "many former Soviet women experienced culture shock in their encounters with the patriarchal and sexist everyday culture of Israeli men … who construed them mainly as available sex object."[21] Remennick continues: "This atmosphere of negative sex stereotyping and ubiquitous harassment at work, in public transport and in leisure venues poisoned the atmosphere around all Russian-accented women."[22] Kogan's poem confirms that ethnic stereotypes and sexual violence remain a serious issue for ex-Soviet women in Israel, even after twenty-five years in the country.[23] Research by six feminist groups in Israel shows that Russian-speaking women experience sexual harassment and violence at two to three times higher rates than *sabra* women (40 per cent versus 16 per cent).[24] In this particular context, the poem's question "Are you Jewish? From both sides?" gains additional significance. It not only questions the female immigrants' Jewish identity but also sets a correlation between loose morality and non-Jewishness. In essence, the objectifying questions in Kogan's poem, depicting East European women as inherently different and foreign, are used as a strategy to justify their sexual harassment.[25] As Edna Lomsky-Feder and Tamar Rapoport explain: "The aim of the objectifying gaze … is to devalue Russian women by cheapening their bodies. Marking a body as immoral legitimizes the harassment and leads to a physical and verbal infringement of its boundaries."[26]

However, instead of simply reflecting this harassment, the poem disrupts the traditional power dynamics between Israeli men and Russian-speaking women by turning the objectifying Israeli male gaze – instead of a woman's body – into the subject of interrogation. In this self-reflexive approach, the poem unveils the degrading way patriarchal Israeli society regards Russian-speaking women while articulating an urgent call for social change. Poetry becomes Kogan's means to navigate the complexity of her immigrant identity and experiences, highlighting the challenging circumstances that she and many other ex-Soviet women unfortunately continue to confront. The recent arrival of women from Russia and Ukraine, driven by Russia's 2022 invasion and war in Ukraine, maintains the relevance of this poetry even today.

The work of Soviet-born, Israeli visual artist from the 1.5 generation, Tamara Brodinsky's *What Makes a Russian* (2006) resonates closely with Kogan's poem.[27] In this powerful feminist artwork, Brodinsky uses her own body to deconstruct the prevalent stereotypes and biases about "Russian" women in Israel. The artwork strategically labels different parts of her body to challenge these stereotypes. "Not blonde" references her hair, "Doesn't drink vodka" and "Doesn't curse" point to her throat, "Doesn't

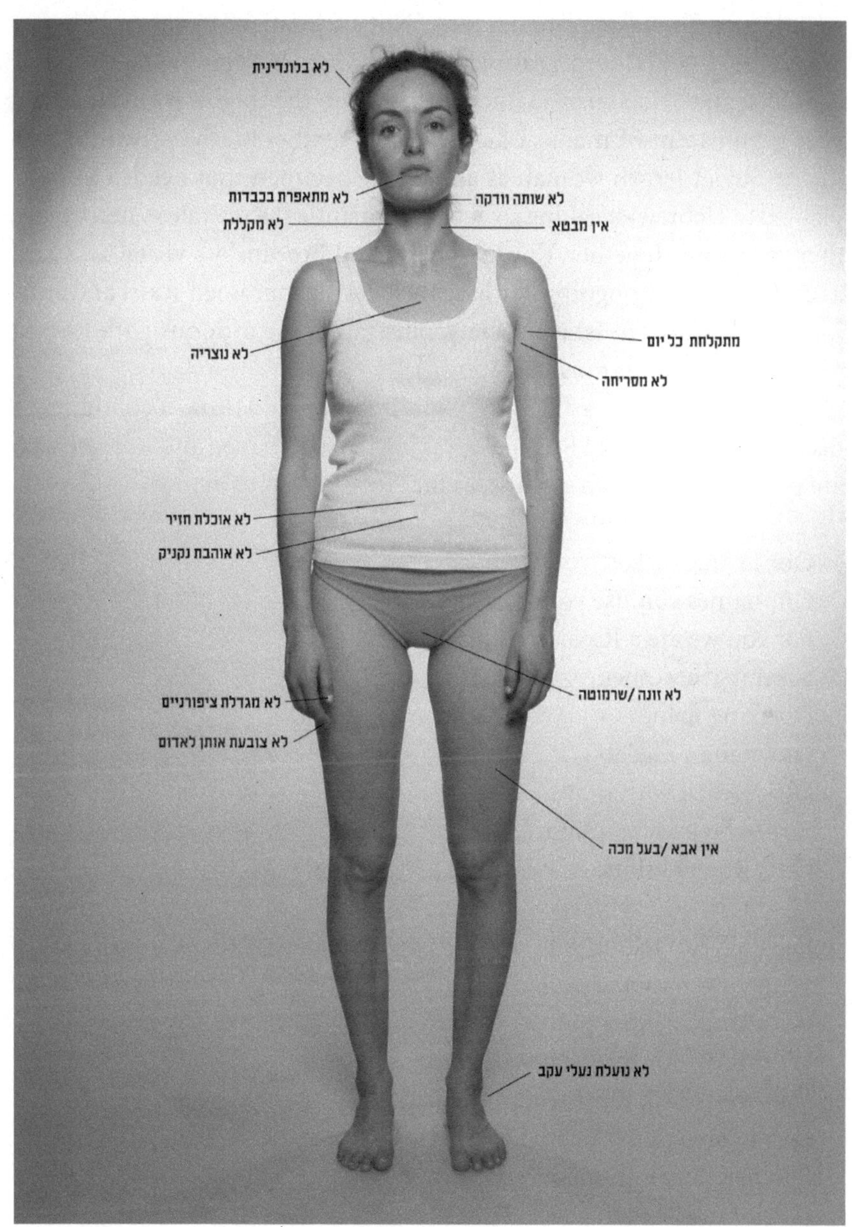

Figure 4.1
Tamara Brodinsky, *What Makes a Russian*, 2006, digitally manipulated colour photograph.

wear too much makeup" to her face, "Not a Christian" to an area where a cross would be, "Doesn't eat pig" to her stomach, "Not a whore" to her genitalia, and "No abusive father/husband" to the thighs. By using visual cues reminiscent of medical diagrams and textbooks, the artwork treats the ex-Soviet Israeli woman as a distinct specimen that needs to be explained to Hebrew-speaking society to dismantle the prevalent stereotypes they may hold. Together, Kogan's poetry and Brodinsky's visual art stand as evidence of the ongoing battle against deeply ingrained sexist and anti-immigrant biases in Israeli society, illustrating the arduous path toward empowerment and transformation.

In the poem "Atzei ashuah lo" ("Fir Trees Aren't"), Kogan continues to decry the stereotypes of Russian-speaking Jews, both men and women, who are perceived, in Kogan's words, as the "Russian circus":

Our fir trees accost your eyes,
Our names confuse your tongues,
For you we are a Russian circus:
Submissive women,
Drinking men,
Old men in medals,
Old women with mops,
Boys who excel in physics,
Girls who are sluts.

Fuck off, I'm telling you,
With your national project,
With your melting pot,
With your "normal" names,
With your Arik Einshtein nostalgia,
Don't come to my Russian circus,
Because I'm a submissive man,
A drinking woman,
An old man in a parking lot,
An old woman on a swing,
A boy in a tutu skirt,
A girl who codes in Python.

We all dance Horah
To the sound of Pussy Riot.[28]

Written in perfect Hebrew and addressed to Hebrew-speaking Israelis, the poem confronts and challenges the ongoing marginalization post-Soviet immigrants still face in Israel, even after twenty-five years in the country. The fir trees in the title – decidedly not Christmas trees – symbolize the beloved Soviet holiday of Novyi God (New Year's Eve), which became a point of contention between Russian-speaking and Hebrew-speaking Israelis.[29] In Israel, Novyi God is criticized in religious (and to some extent, secular) Hebrew-speaking circles as a taboo Christian tradition unfit for the Jewish state. Yet, for Soviet-born Jews, Novyi God represents a secular, family-oriented holiday cherished by the majority of the Soviet population, including Jews, and unrelated to Christmas, a religious observance banned in the atheist Soviet Union. Through this metaphor, the first stanza suggests that even after a quarter-century, post-Soviet "oldcomers" remain the ultimate "other" within Israeli society: seen as drunkards, hypersexualized women, science prodigies, street cleaners, decorated World War II veterans with medals, and Christmas-celebrating gentiles.

However, the poem demonstrates that it is possible to fight back and resist these stereotypes and the social conditions that made the reality of post-Soviet immigrants in Israel so difficult. Full of anger and rebellion, the second stanza begins with a strong denunciation of Israel's mainstream Ashkenazi culture and society, dramatized by the explicit "Fuck off." As in Rif's poetry, the speaker rejects Israel's national and nationalizing project, which compels immigrants to renounce their culture, identity, and historical legacy. The reference to "Arik Einstein," the beloved Israeli rock star of Ashkenazi lineage, offers a poignant critique of nostalgia for Ashkenazi hegemony and a longing for a past era when being "Israeli" meant discarding one's previous culture, past, and identity upon arrival. The speaker in Kogan's poem has grown weary of apologizing for her purported difference. Instead, she reclaims the label "Russian circus" – much like Rif does with the term "Russian whore" – by embracing the collective identity of Soviet-born Israelis that was othered at the start of the poem.

From a stereotypical portrayal of ex-Soviet émigrés, the "Russian circus" metaphor evolves into a collective portrait of difference that proudly resists assimilation. The shift from an individual perspective ("I") to a communal one ("we") dramatizes the speaker's sense of expanding unity with the whole community, particularly the emerging generation of post-Soviet Israelis who defy gender stereotypes in their clothing and occupation. The poem's concluding stanza, "We all dance Horah / To the sound of Pussy Riot," succinctly expresses that whereas in the past, Russian-speaking Jews attempted to fully assimilate as Israelis/Ashkenazim (i.e., attempt to dance the traditional Eastern European folk dance "Horah," a marker of Zionist identity in Palestine at the start of the twentieth century), the new generation of newcomers yearns for rebellion, as symbolized by Pussy Riot, the nonconformist, feminist punk band that courageously challenged the Russian government, church, and patriarchy. The reference to Pussy Riot reveals the revolutionary spirit brewing within these immigrants, even as they seemingly conform to the dominant culture around them and follow the assimilationist paradigms.

The historical accounts of the 1.5 generation are unique in their reluctance to celebrate Israel and forget the Soviet past. Seen from the hindsight of the Israeli present, marked by abuse, economic uncertainty, and a violent demand to assimilate, the Soviet-Jewish past is remembered by some 1.5ers as an idyll where life was good and devoid of contradictions. In a certain sense, the historical "work" of the art by the 1.5 generation corresponds to Svetlana Boym's definition of nostalgia as "a longing for a home that no longer exists or has never existed."[30] In her formative study *The Future of Nostalgia*, Boym distinguishes between two types of nostalgia: restorative and reflective. Restorative nostalgia is associated with nationalism and its stubborn attempt "to rebuild the lost home and patch up the memory gaps,"[31] while reflective nostalgia is more introspective and "cherishes shattered fragments of memory,"[32] delaying the longing for home with a mixture of wistfulness, irony, and desperation. In this framework, Rif's and Kogan's Hebrew-language poetry employs reflective yearning for the time before immigration as a way to disrupt Israel's (restorative) nationalist orientation and to counteract the communal challenges experienced after immigration. Their poetry, therefore, is not about the Soviet past per se or about Russia's nationalist ambitions – instead, it is about finding a space for post-Soviet culture and people in Israel's culturally-aggressive national space, with clear boundaries of cultural and social inclusion and exclusion.[33]

Soviet Childhood: Nostalgia for Communism

Zoya Cherkassky-Nnadi is perhaps the most well-known and critically acclaimed post-Soviet Israeli artist of the 1.5 generation. As seen in the previous chapter, the central themes of her exhibition *Pravda* – sex work, homelessness, alcoholism, bullying, drug addiction, sexual harassment, and adult circumcision – echo the themes of much of Rif's and Kogan's poetry and can function as accompanying images.[34] The painting series I focus on here, *Soviet Childhood*, illustrates Boym's notion of reflective nostalgia as a creative vehicle for artistic expression. The series, which was initially uploaded to Facebook from 2014 to 2018, was later showcased at Tel Aviv's trendy Rosenfeld Gallery in 2018 and then at New York's Fort Gansevoort Gallery in 2019. Featuring over a hundred drawings and paintings, the series aptly captures childhood memories from Cherkassky-Nnadi's time in the Soviet Union.

As defined by Boym, reflective nostalgia involves a contemplative and introspective longing for the past, often marked by fragmentation and ambivalence. Cherkassky-Nnadi's exhibition resonates with this idea as it contemplates on the artist's personal and collective memories of growing up in the Soviet empire, and presents them as a complicated, ambivalent, and multi-layered experience. Some artworks seem to cherish and even celebrate certain aspects of her Soviet past, capturing a sense of nostalgia beyond a simple desire to recreate or restore the past. Reflective nostalgia, according to Boym, values the fragmented and conflicting nature of memories, avoiding a complete return to the past. In Cherkassky-Nnadi's works, her portrayal of everyday Soviet life captures moments that are both tender and unsettling, mundane and enigmatic.

Despite this complexity, the series received mixed reviews in Israel. Some critics argued that the paintings gloss over the harsh realities of the Soviet system and its mistreatment of Jews. Others argued that the works, in a manner reminiscent of Cold War propaganda, exaggerated the poverty, despair, and lack of private space in the USSR, neglecting to depict the material abundance that existed under state socialism. I propose a different interpretation. In dialectical fashion, the series stages moments of a happy childhood in the late Soviet period as a counterpoint to prevailing narratives in Israel that depict the Soviet past solely in negative terms. By embracing reflective nostalgia, Cherkassky-Nnadi's works invite viewers to engage with a nuanced and multifaceted perspective on the past.

Even the style with which Cherkassky-Nnadi chooses to render this period is tailored to the subject matter: each painting is executed in a child-like manner, using markers on paper (and sometimes acrylic paint), and is drawn in bright, warm colours. These warm hues and idealized subject matter convey the sense of love and yearning enshrined in many of these works. Collectively, they depict harmonious scenes of family life and innocent coming-of-age in a seemingly stable and uniform empire. These drawings and paintings seem frozen in time, evoking a sense of stillness and nostalgia. Instead of highlighting antisemitism, discrimination, repression, and the Soviet Union's decline – the "push" factors that precipitated the mass migration of 1.6 million Soviet Jews to Israel, North America, and Europe in the 1990s – *Soviet Childhood* affectionately captures the last years of the Soviet regime with longing, wistfulness, and tenderness.

The series presents snapshots of happy childhood in the USSR. For instance, *The Grandmother* (figure 4.2) portrays a family idyll. At the centre of the painting, a grandmother is embraced by her grandchildren, illustrating a warm, affectionate bond. This warmth contrasts with the external cold, indicated by the winter jacket, *valenki* (felt winter boots), and winter hat. Inside, the children's attire suggests a cozy atmosphere, further emphasized by their body language and the intergenerational hug. The use of warm colours – reds, oranges, purples, and browns – enhances this sense of comfort. The joy is palpable: the grandson, eagerly anticipating his grandmother's return from the store, has already plunged his hand into her red, white, and blue bag (*klechetaia sumka*), eager to discover the treats she has brought for him.

Teenage Rebellion (figure 4.3) presents an affectionate account of the split between the younger and older generations. It depicts a nuclear family sharing a single room due to the space constraints common in Soviet households, contrasting sharply with the more privatized living arrangements typical in capitalist societies. Despite being confined to one space, the separation between the generations is evident. On the right, the older generation – traditional Soviet parents – are shown in their home attire and *tapochki* (slippers), eating in front of the TV and framed by a carpet on the wall. They inhabit their own domestic world, which stands in stark contrast to their son's lifestyle. The boy, by contrast, epitomizes

Figure 4.2
Zoya Cherkassky-Nnadi, *The Grandmother*, 2015, markers on paper, 19 × 26.5 cm.

the countercultural movement of the young generation we have seen in the analysis of Balsky's novel. Clad in army boots, a studded leather jacket, skinny jeans, and a studded leather choker, he rejects Soviet conformism. His side of the room is adorned with posters of Western rock bands like KISS and AC/DC on his closet, positioned in front of his bed, along with a *magnetophon* (tape recorder), capable of playing forbidden rock music. This visual setup highlights his rejection of the older generation's values and his embrace of individualism. Despite these differences, there is an underlying warmth and harmony in the scene. The colour scheme – the prominence of red on the rock band posters and the carpet, or the dominance of white on the boy's undershirt and the parents' clothes – creates a visual rhyme, suggesting a subtle cohesion rather than conflict. The family appears to accept each other's quirks and preferences without surprise or

Figure 4.3
Zoya Cherkassky-Nnadi, *Teenage Rebellion*, 2016, markers and acrylic on paper, 19 × 26.5 cm.

hostility. The cat, remaining neutral in this generational clash, adds a touch of humour to the portrayal, symbolizing the household's overall sense of balance and acceptance.

Cherkassky-Nnadi's meticulous attention to detail enhances the nostalgic quality of these paintings. In these paintings, she painstakingly recreates elements such as the traditional Soviet wallpaper and the lace doily beneath the telephone in *The Grandmother*, as well as the distinctive diamond-cut pattern of Soviet-era blanket covers, the bright wall carpets (*kovry*) used for decoration and insulation, and the herringbone-patterned parquet flooring in *Teenage Rebellion*. This historical precision, evocative of family snapshots, makes the series resonate even more strongly with the 300 million former Soviet citizens, many of whom possessed identical household items due to the centralized nature of Soviet production and the uniformity of Soviet taste and aesthetics.

At the same time, Cherkassky-Nnadi employs a style that prevents a straightforward identification with the depicted scenes. Indeed, her use of polychromic representation, warm colour palette, and distinctive naiveté aligns the artist with the tradition of Russian and European neo-primitivism. Like avant-garde artists Natalya Goncharova and Mikhail Larionov a century earlier, Cherkassky-Nnadi uses crude lines, flattened perspective, expressive colours, and a focus on "simple folks" to portray the late Soviet period. This hyper-stylized, neo-primitive approach of depicting the Soviet period deliberately draws attention to itself, creating a gap between the artist and the subject matter. The paintings' exaggerated emotionality and naivety suggest that Cherkassky-Nnadi acknowledges the past's complexity but still portrays it as a cherished golden age in a conscious performance of nostalgia. In so doing, the artist seeks to remedy the trauma of her generation in Israel and to reconstruct the coherent collective identity for post-Soviet émigrés that was shuttered in their encounter with Israeli society in the 1990s.

In contemporary scholarship on post-Soviet nostalgia, Marta Rabikowska suggests that "salvaging the remains of communism is [traditionally] explained either as an ironic nostalgic recall which is often commercially driven … or as an expression of primitive nostalgic attachment to the ruined past, which is incompatible with the period of transition."[35] In this framework, Soviet nostalgia is often negatively perceived as outdated, atavistic, anti-modern, or opportunistic. However, it is vital to stress that one's affective relationship is greatly influenced by one's ability to seize opportunities in the post-Soviet present, whether within the former USSR or elsewhere. The dismissive understanding of nostalgia risks obfuscating the full complexity of the affective responses of underprivileged populations, which are often lumped together in the discourse of nostalgia.[36] Keeping this in mind, Cherkassky-Nnadi's perspective (and to some extent Rif and Kogan's as well) on the Soviet past demonstrates the potential of post-Soviet nostalgia as a mobilizing force and a tool for shaping collective identity for a community that struggled with its transition to Israel, but also as a means to glean symbolic and economic capital, judging by the success of Kogan, Rif, and Cherkassky-Nnadi in Israel.

Post-Soviet Nostalgia After the War in Ukraine

The reluctance of the 1.5 generation to depict the Soviet era in a minor key might stem from the fact that, as children, they were largely shielded from the forces that shaped their parents' painful narrative of the past. Moreover, life in Israel – particularly in the peripheral towns where many émigrés settled – was extremely challenging, especially when considered (in the abstract, at least) in comparison to Soviet social welfare: extended and funded maternity leaves, centralized housing, annual paid vacations, and free higher education.[37] It is unsurprising that discontent with Israel's neoliberalism and the rapid downward social mobility of the older generation animate the poems and paintings by Rif, Kogan, and Cherkassky-Nnadi. It is telling that Rif and Kogan choose images of sex work, house cleaning, and the circus to capture the marginalized position of Russian speakers in Israel. In each instance, class-inflected categories are mobilized to articulate the profound pain and shared hardship of post-Soviet migrants, describing in stark detail their overnight loss of social and economic status. Intentionally, Rif and Kogan select historical moments that directly challenge Israel's ideologically sanctioned historical narrative, while Cherkassky-Nnadi invokes her childhood in the USSR as an idyll worthy of yearning and nostalgia.

Ultimately, post-Soviet Israeli literature and visual art of the 1.5 generation are deeply influenced by their Israeli social experiences and personal histories of exclusion and marginality, even when exploring the Soviet past. This is evident in a Hebrew-language interview with *Haaretz* reporter Liza Rozovsky, where Cherkassky-Nnadi reflects on her generational perspective. "My generation did not experience all the horrors of the Soviet system firsthand. For us, the Soviet Union represents childhood, and that childhood was very good," she explains.[38] She further clarifies: "Our memories differ from those of the older generations. They are not necessarily tied to the Soviet system but to childhood itself. Our attitude toward the Soviet Union is calmer and less critical."[39] In contrast to their parents' generation, whose thorny relationship with the USSR resulted in a profound mistrust and animosity toward the Soviet Union and left-wing politics in general, the younger generation is not interested in beating the dead Soviet horse. Despite their backward gaze into the 1980s and 1990s, their projects are not interested in the past; rather, they are using the past to talk about the present of the post-Soviet community in Israel. As evidenced by the quote, Cherkassky-Nnadi's idealized depiction of the Soviet past should be read in the nexus of her generation's drama of resettlement and painful adjustment in Israel. As Rif's and Kogan's poetry demonstrates, after years of having to downplay, renounce, and feel ashamed of their Russianness, the artistic projects of 1.5ers signal a new readiness to celebrate their history, culture, identity, and fight for inclusion. Therefore, Cherkassky-Nnadi's focus on the positive aspects of the Soviet experience enables fellow 1.5ers to articulate a shared collective identity, while the assault on Israel's melting pot policy by Rif and Kogan allows them to construct their hyphenated post-Soviet Israeli identity in defiance of monocultural conceptions of Israeli society. In so doing, all three artists contribute to a different configuration of Israeli culture and society, fostering an environment that can accommodate diverse historical narratives, political legacies, and cultural nuances.

However, the ongoing tragic events in Ukraine, driven by Russia's unprovoked invasion and war in 2022, have destroyed, at least for the time being, any possibility of finding refuge in nostalgia or communism, both for Cherkassky-Nnadi and for others. The artist, who spent her formative years in Kyiv and remained in Ukraine until the age of fifteen, responded to the distressing news of bombings and Russian tanks entering Ukraine with the following: "I was really feeling like they're coming into my childhood landscapes and ruining them."[40] This comment, while somewhat overlooking the direct suffering of people affected by the war, still conveys an important insight into the challenge faced by post-Soviet writers in Israel who attempt to hold onto the idealized Soviet past – an era rife with imperial violence – as the foundation of their identity.

Recognizing the complexities of her affective subject position, Cherkassky-Nnadi embarked on a new series just a week after the war's onset, entitled "Before and After." Through this series, she reimagined the nostalgic landscapes of her childhood in the aftermath of Russia's brutal invasion in the contemporary context. Two aftermath paintings can be seen in figures 4.4 and 4.5. It is significant that Cherkassky-Nnadi did not simply produce new paintings depicting the harrowing scenes from Ukraine but superimposed the war and violence onto the existing scenes of childhood from her exhibition *Soviet Childhood*. This artistic process is an act of revision or reevaluation of her own original assumptions about the Soviet reality, where

Figure 4.4
Zoya Cherkassky-Nnadi, *Public Shelter at the Khreshchatyk Subway Station*, 2022, mixed media on paper, 17 × 21 cm.

Cherkassky-Nnadi appears to finally give in to critical voices who asserted that her exhibition had omitted the darker aspects of Soviet history. In these chilling anti-nostalgic paintings, Cherkassky-Nnadi shows the savage truths of the war, revealing its violence and suffering. In the context of Russia's war in Ukraine, the original paintings undergo revision as schools become targets of bombardment, a metalhead son enlists in the Ukrainian army, the grandmother and her grandchildren seek refuge from aerial attacks in the subway, Russian tanks intrude on the Ukrainian landscape, and people standing in a breadline are reduced to disintegrated remnants of flesh, blood, and bone. This endeavour serves a dual purpose: it both acts as a cultural testament to the war's atrocities and prompts a reconsideration of her earlier stance on Soviet history and its aftermath. Appropriately,

Figure 4.5
Zoya Cherkassky-Nnadi, *Teenage Rebellion (After)*, 2022, mixed media on paper, 17.5 × 20.5 cm.

Cherkassky-Nnadi decided to auction her war paintings, directing the proceeds toward various non-governmental organizations operating in Ukraine. And yet, when asked by *Vogue* magazine a year after the start of the war whether there is still a narrative of growing up in the Soviet Union that she wants to complicate in her work, Cherkassky-Nnadi replied: "There is no truth; it's all personal experience. I'm not pretending to tell the truth. I'm just trying to evoke my memories as a teenager."[41] Clearly, the artist remains unable to detach her personal memories from her artistic expression. Rather than engaging with broader historical contexts, her art remains trapped in subjective nostalgia, offering an individualized perspective on the past that struggles to address the complex realities of the present.

CONCLUSION

The Future of Russophone Culture in Israel?

Let me conclude this book with a question: "What is the future of post-Soviet literature and culture in Israel?" Frequently, when this question has been raised in Russophone intellectual circles in Israel – in the 1970s, the 1990s, and through to the 2020s – the answer has been categorical: "There is none!" Grigorii Kanovich, for instance, a highly successful Soviet-born Jewish writer who immigrated to Israel in 1993, casts a pessimistic outlook on the future of Russophone literature in Israel, declaring: "Literature cannot survive without its national soil."[1] To argue his position, he draws upon the historical parallel of Russian-language émigré literature in the 1920s and 1930s in Berlin and Paris as an example of a once-thriving Russophone literary field that eventually faded away, concluding (incorrectly) that "today there are no Russian readers left in both France and Germany."[2] Literary critic Svetlana Blomberg-Jatskina shares Kanovich's pessimism but attributes her predictions of downfall to socio-cultural factors. In her view, Russophone literature and culture are disappearing because of the widening linguistic and cultural divide between the elder and younger generations of ex-Soviet Israelis. As she points out: "The descendants [of post-Soviet Israeli authors] are not familiar with their works – they are foreign to them in both content and language. Indeed, they can't even read Russian."[3] Dina Rubina offers yet another explanation for the decline of Russian-language writing in Israel. In *Messiah*, she humorously likens Israel's official Hebrew-language culture to Bluebeard, portraying it as having already starved to death several other cultures that settled in Israel, adding that there is still "room for Bluebeard's new wives" in his crypt.[4] In other words, she attributes the end of Russophone culture in Israel to Israel's aggressive monolingualism and to a lack of government support – a uniquely Soviet way of viewing the relationship between culture and society.

However, a narrative about the disappearance of Russophone literature and culture in Israel does not adequately capture what has unfolded in Israel over the past four decades. As illustrated in this book, we are witnessing a notable – and ongoing – transformation of post-Soviet culture and cultural identity in Israel. In the realm of history, there is a shift in the way Soviet-born Jews think about their history, transitioning from narratives shaped by Soviet discrimination, where Israel functions as a Promised Land, to narratives that retrospectively engage with the Soviet-Jewish past through the sentiment of nostalgia and view the Israeli experience as a source of trauma. Moreover, a notable transformation in ex-Soviet Jewish religiosity is evident, with the community moving from widespread atheism to robust religious commitment. The enthusiastic "self-proselytism" of some post-Soviet Jews, the book argues, is linked to three factors – the alignment of organized religion with right-wing politics in Israel, the desire to refute the negative perception of Soviet-born Jews as "non-kosher," and the residence pattern of the community on the outskirts of Israel's geography and in illegal settlements, populated largely by religious Zionists and Orthodox Jews. Finally, we observe how the transplantation of the Soviet imperial-cosmopolitan discourse to Israel activates biases and cultural superiority that already existed within Israeli society, especially between Ashkenazi and Mizrahi Jews. Ultimately, it is safe to say that post-Soviet culture did not dissolve or disappear within Israeli society; rather, it adapted to the new local context and gave rise to new cultural hybrids and expressions.

Indeed, the trajectory of post-Soviet Israeli literature and culture over the past four decades contradicts the defeatist predictions of its demise. Instead of disappearing, it has integrated itself into the mainstream of Israeli society and has been successfully transmitted to future generations. Decades ago, Mikhail Weiskopf used the metaphor of a "wall" to describe the relationship between Israeli and Russophone cultures and people. Today, a new generation of ex-Soviet Israeli artists and activists is actively working to break down that wall.[5] Consider the transformation of the celebration of

Novyi God (New Year) within the Israeli social fabric. What was once perceived as Soviet immigrants embracing a taboo Christian observance in the 1990s now stands as a trendy holiday that Hebrew speakers aspire to be part of. Similarly, Soviet Victory Day over Nazi Germany, celebrated on 9 May, has been formally incorporated into the Israeli calendar. After years of advocacy by Jewish Red Army veterans and their families in Israel, the holiday has become a significant aspect of Israel's shared historical memory, commemorating Jews not only as victims of the Holocaust but also as victors over Nazism. In the cultural arena, the situation is even more impressive. Countless poetry readings, theatrical performances, concerts, and painting workshops by post-Soviet artists take place in Tel Aviv, Jerusalem, and Haifa on a regular basis. A crowning achievement comes from artist Zoya Cherkassky-Nnadi, who recently showcased her solo exhibition at the Israel Museum in Jerusalem, arguably the most prestigious art institution in the country. This exhibition is a testament to the resounding success of ex-Soviet Jews within Israel's cultural landscape.

The discrepancy between predictions of death and the actual vibrancy of post-Soviet Israeli literature and culture relates, at base, to the fundamental instability of the category of "Russian culture," often employed by cultural producers to mean "post-Soviet." Kanovich, Blomberg-Jatskina, and Rubina – who settled in Israel in their forties to sixties and have continued their cultural activities mainly within a monolingual Russophone cultural field – primarily imagine "Russian" culture exclusively within the realm of literary and artistic works produced in the Russian language. For them, Soviet-born writers who write in Hebrew, such as Alex Rif and Rita Kogan, fall outside the scope of Russophone literature – regardless of whether they address their immigration experiences or translate Akhmatova or Tsvetaeva into Hebrew. Especially during Russia's ruthless war on Ukraine, it is crucial to emphasize that cultural identities should not be claimed beyond their respective national borders. For this reason, I am careful to use terms like Russophone or post-Soviet as a way to discuss the literary, cinematic and artistic works that emerged from the ex-Soviet Jewish diaspora, taking into account their social, political, and historical contexts. In other words, the terms "Russophone" and "post-Soviet" do not solely refer to cultural works produced in the Russian language; they also encompass works created within the broader post-Soviet diaspora, which may incorporate various linguistic influences and address different local and global issues. What makes Rif and Cherkassky-Nnadi post-Soviet Israeli writers and artists is not their language of choice but how they draw on their cultural and historical heritage as Soviet-born Jews residing in Israel.

It is important to emphasize that the inscription of the borders of Russian culture is not only a literary or cultural question, but also a political one that relates to the exercise of power. As Kevin M.F. Platt notes, "'Russian culture' projects may claim to be singular, correct in their constructions of geography, and authentic."[6] This includes, he notes, Putin's speech on Crimea, which framed the annexation as a legitimate extension of national culture; the cosmopolitan image of "global Russian culture" promoted by the glossy journal *Snob*, targeting wealthy Russians in global cities; and the patriotic organizations backed by the Russian World Foundation, which aim to secure the loyalty of Russians in neighbouring countries. Yet such claims, Platt explains, are not just cultural assertions but also strategic moves – power grabs that may coincide with territorial or financial ambitions.[7] Kanovich, Rubina, and Blomberg-Jatskina are probably correct in predicting that their conception of Russian literature – one exclusively created in the Russian language – might gradually fade in Israel. Nevertheless, as demonstrated above, Russophone culture in Israel can be defined in multiple ways, and in a certain sense one can argue that there has been Russophone culture in Israel/Palestine for over a century – as early as the first pioneers from the Russian Empire settled in Palestine in the nineteenth century. Furthermore, while many readers claim Rubina as a "Russian writer," some nationalists and anti-Semites might dispute this classification. Indeed, it is crucial to recall the not-so-distant past when Russian literature authored by Jews was termed "Russophone" ("russkoyazyichnaya") but not considered truly "Russian" within antisemitic circles. Lastly, Mikhail Gendelev's designation of Russian-language literature in Israel as "*nerusskaya* literature" (non-Russian literature) introduces another dimension to this intricate phenomenon.[8]

Regardless of definitions, the ongoing clashes between various cultural producers and factions illustrate the evolution of the post-Soviet Israeli artistic and social landscape. This evolution reflects the continuing processes of cultural development that began in the 1970s and persist to this day. In particular, the evolving contours of Russophone culture hold significant and shifting political meaning within Israel. One major arena of contention has been the conflicts between older and younger generations of cultural producers. For instance, Alex Goldshtein (not the author of the same name discussed in chapter 3), a prominent figure in the Israeli Russian-language media, has emerged as a vocal critic of the 1.5 generation artists, including Alex Rif. In a recent interview, Goldshtein accused these artists of promoting Russian cultural symbols that, in his view, do not resonate with "most Olim who identify as Jews, not Russians."[9] He further argues that, despite their integration into Israeli society and their fluency in Hebrew, these artists misrepresent the Russophone-Jewish experience and lack genuine commitment to Israel. According to Goldshtein, their emotional attachment to the country is superficial compared to the deeper bond he attributes to the Zionist ex-Soviet community.

In this interview, Goldshtein positions himself as a champion of traditional Zionist values, while simultaneously contrasting himself with the 1.5ers whom he sees as inauthentic, disloyal, and politically unreliable. He asserts, "They [1.5ers] are not really connected to Israel, despite their perfect Hebrew – tomorrow, if opportunity comes by, they'd leave for Canada or the US without looking back." This stance highlights an ironic twist: despite their impeccable Hebrew, Rif and other members of the 1.5 Generation are said to lack a genuine emotional attachment to Israel – a bond that, according to Goldshtein, is preserved within Israel's Zionist ex-Soviet collective (but lost among Israel's post-Zionist cultural elites). Ultimately, Goldshtein's critique of the 1.5ers for their alleged disloyalty, compromised patriotism, and political unreliability echoes historical accusations against Jews for their purported "rootless cosmopolitanism," implying that their integration into Soviet culture was incompatible with true loyalty.

Goldshtein's pronouncements upend the previous predictions about the decline of Russophone culture in Israel. In many ways, they signal the entrenchment of Soviet-Russian political culture within Israeli society, reinforcing ultra-nationalist and far-right stances, and even evoking Stalinist rhetoric. Curiously, Goldshtein contends that three decades after the fall of the USSR, Soviet-born newcomers, though they may not yet speak perfect Hebrew or still operate within the so-called Russian ghetto in Israel, have become more committed Zionists than the left-leaning Hebrew cultural establishment, with which the 1.5ers have assimilated. Goldshtein's rhetoric calls for a return to Zionist roots, leveraging figures like Jabotinsky, Ahad Ha'am, and Pinsker to connect contemporary post-Soviet Jewish immigrants with the foundational Zionist pioneers of Israeli society. In fact, he uses these figures to make the claim that Zionism is indigenous to Russian-Soviet culture, a birthplace of the movement. Ultimately, Goldshtein's assault on the identity politics of the 1.5ers is his attempt to assert his vision of authentic Jewish nationalism and secure a dominant position within the Russophone-Israeli cultural sphere.

Zoya Cherkassky-Nnadi's exhibition in the Israel Museum sparked another round of intense generational conflict within the Russophone-Israeli cultural sphere. This clash was ignited by Yacov Shaus, a member of the editorial board of the Russophone journal *Zerkalo*, who shared his exhibition review on his Facebook page. The exhibition was described as "ideological prostitution, funded by Meretz and Avoda" (referring to left-wing political parties in Israel), a case of "Stockholm syndrome," "pure self-hatred," "shitpainting" (*govnozhivopis'*), "chernukha" (a slang term denoting a tendency to focus on dark aspects of late Soviet reality), and "nasty Soviet scribbles."[10] The reviewer's anger was triggered by the artist's one-sided portrayal of the Russian-speaking community as "alcoholics, ignoramuses, prostitutes, and consumers of non-kosher food."[11] The critic asks, using Cherkassky-Nnadi's first name in a patronizing and condescending manner: "Is this everything that Zoya managed to discern and understand about the million-strong *aliyah* from the Soviet Union?"[12]

The author concludes his review by questioning what drives such a negative portrayal of the Russian-speaking community. Instead of leaving this as a rhetorical question, Shaus offers his own explanation: "Unfortunately, the reason is quite simple and clear. The artistic establishment wants to portray 'Russians' in this manner!" He goes on to clarify that museum and gallery leaders, like other cultural influencers, do not have personal ethnic prejudices against "Russians." Rather, their bias is a byproduct of their leftist politics. Their disenchantment with the "Russian" immigration began in the mid-1990s, when it became evident that the new arrivals did not support Rabin's "peace process" and were unlikely to vote for the leftist parties. Consequently, the intellectual elite of the nation lost interest in the newcomers, who had climbed up the social ladder and become professors, engineers, doctors, programmers, philosophers, and journalists. This success and high level of intellectual achievement among Russian speakers, concludes Shaus, "upsets the leftists – it intimidates them.[13]

In Shaus's opinion, Cherkassky-Nnadi misconstrues the post-Soviet community in Israel by portraying it in an overly negative light to pander to Israel's leftist cultural establishment. Like Goldshtein, Shaus wants to see depictions of ex-Soviet *olim* that can inspire the Russian-speaking audience – mathematicians, physicists, philosophers, and doctors – and not as broken victims of the Israeli absorption process, reduced to the roles of drunkards and sex workers. His criticism is twofold: first, he calls for more inspiring representations of Russian-speaking Israelis; second, he believes that post-Soviet Jews have a clearer-eyed understanding of political reality in Israel – one that is superior to that of the craven, leftist cultural establishment and the younger "Russians" who cater to it.

In response, Cherkassky-Nnadi shared Shaus's article on her Facebook page and playfully mocked the review's shortcomings: "Since my commission from the enemies of the state, I've been incredibly busy these days!" she wrote in a comment.[14] The painter's Facebook friends contributed to the merry atmosphere by poking fun at "Comrade Shaus's" outdated Soviet rhetoric and writing style. One commentator even labelled the review as "a Soviet-style denunciation" (*sovetskii gazetnyii donos*).[15] MP Ksenia Svetlova chimed in, adding a touch of sarcasm to the debate: "That's right, Zoya! Where's your patriotism? Where's your love for Itzik, the Jewish Agency, and Netanyahu? Why not create installations about the Star of David and the mezuzah? Did the country support you for free? Shame on you!"[16] These reactions, in various ways, criticized the author's antiquated Soviet rhetoric and mindset, which likely rubbed against Shaus's anti-communist/Zionist political inclinations. Furthermore, they highlighted Shaus's Soviet expectations for art – that it should be accessible, dignified, and patriotic. However, instead of dismissing Shaus's post as a relic of the Soviet past, I contend that this expectation aligns with the current trajectory of Israel's cultural policy, especially in the aftermath of the Israel-Hamas war. In the cultural policy advocated since Miri Regev, it is expected that Israeli artists display loyalty and respect for Israel; otherwise, they risk losing their national funding. In a twisted way, Israel is becoming more and more like the Soviet Union/Russia.

If this chapter began with uncertain Russian-speaking cultural producers who fear that their culture is at risk of assimilating and disappearing, thirty-five years down the line we have an entirely different situation. Instead of a deracinated immigrant community, we have a politically powerful bloc of ex-Soviets who believe that they have become more Israeli than the extant Hebrew-speaking Israelis – more Catholic than the pope, one might say. Emboldened by their significant numbers, this community – who constituted about one million of the country's 6,000,000 citizens in the 1990s – did not merely abandon their culture and identity in the Israeli environment. Rather, they fundamentally transformed all walks of life in Israel, setting down roots and transforming themselves in the process. As a result, they not only became "Israelis" but also reclaimed their heritage and identity as post-Soviet Jews, demonstrating that the processes of acculturation and assimilation are a two-way street.

Arik Eber's performance poem "Mi ani ma?" ("Who Am I, What?") illustrates the thorny, two-way journey of ex-Soviet Jews as they navigate their place within Israeli society. Eber, a Leningrad-born poet, musician, and spoken-word artist equally at home in both Hebrew and Russian, gives voice to the poet's raw experience of dual diaspora, identity loss, and cultural hybridity:

At eight: cut right out from the Soviet Union
And pasted into Israel. What could I do?
I, a Russian boy, in a religious school
Who was told that God rules
But just as I learned how and when to pray
My parents decided that God was not the way
First they say religious, then they say not. For God's sake!
What am I, who am I, who am I
Who am I, who am I, who am I, what?

In middle school I took another look around
Confused, what can I do if there's no God to be found
I realized that in Jerusalem to be popular and cool
I had to be more like the Moroccan youth
Moroccan is code for all Mizrahi Jews
Moroccan, Iraqi – all the same to stinking Russian tools.
Let's drop that, not relevant right now.
Look at me: a Russian listening to Eyal Golan
Faded jeans, gel in his hair,
Platform shoes, I tried but no one seemed to care
I always stayed a foreigner, strange kind of stranger.
Who am I, who am I, who am I, what?

In high school I tried to get back to my roots
"Belomor" cigarettes and Russian swear words
I hung out with the slackers, smoking out back
Wearing a tracksuit, accent so fake
But I failed to fit in, blend with the masses
My Russian vocab was zilch, what were my chances.

In the army I finally realized what's what
In the beds of elite girls I screwed my way to the top
The canon was revealed to me in all its glory
I swallowed it without gagging, no worry
Two servings of Leah Goldberg, Alterman and Oz
I became an Ashkenazi without any flaws.

I rested on my laurels
Thought I found out who I was
'Til somebody blurted out: Nah,
You are just an Ashki-passing Russian from nowhere.
Who am I, who am I, who am I, what?
I searched far and wide for who I was
Until I finally found a clear response:
I am Russian
I am a Russian Israeli or Israeli Russian or Hebrew-speaking Russian
  or Russophone Israeli or Israeli whose mother tongue is Russian
I mean, whose mother talks to him in Russian and he answers her
  in that language
Unless he wants to make a point and then he switches to Hebrew
  to make that point
Because, for real, Hebrew is his language
He's an Israeli, the case's closed, enough already! The guy's Israeli!
But then again: what is Israeli?
Who am I, who am I, who am I, what?[17]

This piece, a blend of poetry and spoken word, brings the challenges of double diaspora and cultural dislocation to the fore. The poem begins with a striking image of displacement: "At eight: cut right out from the Soviet Union / And pasted into Israel." This metaphor of being "pasted" into a new world underscores the abrupt and artificial nature of the poet's relocation. Displacement abounds as the poem progresses. The speaker faces a crossroads. He can either embrace Israeli society by adopting religious, Mizrahi, or Ashkenazi identities, or, challenging Israel's infamous melting pot, he can preserve his post-Soviet specificity. The speaker soon discovers the impossibility of either route, since the predefined, ready-made identities he tries to adopt (Orthodox, Mizrahi, Ashkenazi, and post-Soviet) do not fit him very well. Instead, the speaker's cultural hybridity makes him an eternal stranger, doubly alienated from himself and his new homeland, evident in the lines "I always stayed a foreigner, strange kind of stranger." The recurring questioning and refrain "Who am I, who am I, who am I?" capture the essence of his identity crisis, emphasizing the poet's deep-seated confusion and sense of alienation after immigration. His identity dissonance is so profound that in the last stanza, he tries but ultimately fails to define himself, presenting a severe case of deculturation and identitarian confusion.

Formally, the situation is more complex. In contrast to the societal alienation that the poem stages, it reflects deep-rooted connections to Hebrew literature and Israeli culture. For instance, it draws upon a rich array of local sources and traditions, including intertextual allusion to Israeli songs and musicians, interlingual puns spanning multiple languages, the use of Hebrew slang and colloquialisms, and references to highly specific Israeli markers of identity that would be incomprehensible to those unfamiliar with the culture. Moreover, the way Eber delivers the poem during performances, with its heightened rhyme schemes, rhythmic patterns, and witty wordplay, firmly situates the poem within the realm of spoken word and performance poetry. This genre of performance establishes an immediate connection with the audience, paradoxically creating a sense of intimacy that runs counter to the poem's predominant theme of alienation. These formal elements stand in direct contradiction to the poem's overarching message, placing a wedge between the poem's form and content.

How do we square this circle, then? On one hand, the poem interrogates the process of cultural and ethnic reconstitution experienced by post-Soviet Jews in Israel. As noted by Larissa Remennick and Anna Prazhisky, "Who Am I, What?" is "full of references to ethnic ambivalence, transitions and passing."[18] These themes are characteristic of local discourse in Israel, the scholars explain, reflecting the deep-seated tension between East and West in Israel's self-identity. In Israel, Mizrahi Jews are viewed as representatives of Arabic-Levantine culture, while Ashkenazi Jews are seen as embodying European-Western culture. This dichotomy is shaped by both physical attributes (such as skin tone) and symbolic markers (such as last names, accents, and cultural tastes).[19] Indeed, the poem underscores the absence of ready-made ethnic categories for the recently arrived cohort of Russian-speaking Jews in Israel. It suggests that they not only struggle to "pass" as Mizrahi or Orthodox Jews but also, despite their lighter skin and ties to Eastern Europe, cannot be considered "Ashkenazim" due to their lack of economic resources and symbolic capital. Just as "whiteness" is not a category that only hinges on skin colour and ethnicity but also describes access to power through cultural, social, and economic resources, "Ashkenazi" also denotes not only one's European heritage but, above all, one's position within the power structure of Israeli society. In this context, the slang term Eber uses in the poem to describe his attempt to be more like Ashkenazi Jews, *rusi mishtaknez* – which Zackary Sholem Berger and I translated as "Ashki-passing Russian" – suggests that post-Soviet immigrants in Israel are not "Ashkenazim" either but form a distinct social group, in many cases devoid of real power.

At the same time, it is possible to understand the poem in a different way. As previously mentioned, this Hebrew-language poem is rich with references to Israeli culture and society. Moreover, its central themes of identity, cultural heritage, language loss, and discrimination strongly resonate with the broader concerns of Israeli literature. For instance, this extends to German-speaking Jews who relocated to Israel and felt reluctant to use German or Yiddish, particularly in the aftermath of the Holocaust. It also encompasses the experiences of Mizrahi, Ethiopian, and Palestinian writers who faced marginalization, inferiority, and exclusion within Israel's Ashkenazi-dominated literary landscape. Finally, it reflects the story of all newcomers to Israel, who were compelled to abandon their native tongues in favour of Hebrew monolingualism. In this context, the poem could be seen as engaging with the major building blocks of Israeli/Hebrew literature, thereby creating the space/legibility for Jews from the USSR and integrating them into the collective narrative of Israeli history.

Ultimately, the poem brings us full circle. While the poem's words describe the speaker's struggle to "pass" as an Israeli, the poem itself – crafted in Hebrew – and the remarkable success Eber achieved in Israel paradoxically contradict this. Instead, it illustrates how Eber draws on the cultural toolkit of Israeli literature and culture to articulate his immigrant experience and encounters with discrimination, ultimately expressing his post-Soviet otherness. The performance of estrangement at the poem's end highlights, in contradictory ways, the level of integration of post-Soviet Jews in Israel. After years of having to downplay, renounce, and feel ashamed of their supposed "otherness," Eber's performance poetry signals a new willingness among artists of his generation to celebrate their history, culture, and identity in defiance of monocultural, melting-pot conceptions of Israeli society.

Yet, amid this celebration, the poem reveals a palpable confusion:

> I am Russian
> I am a Russian Israeli or Israeli Russian or Hebrew-speaking Russian
>   or Russophone Israeli or Israeli whose mother tongue is Russian
> I mean, whose mother talks to him in Russian and he answers her
>   in that language
> Unless he wants to make a point and then he switches to Hebrew
>   to make that point
> Because, for real, Hebrew is his language
> He's an Israeli, the case's closed, enough already! The guy's Israeli!
> But then again: what is Israeli?
> Who am I, who am I, who am I, what?[20]

With this final stanza, the poem suggests that the identity of ex-Soviet Jews in Israel is complex, often defying easy definition and categorization. It is marked by duality, both linguistic and cultural. Furthermore, Eber implies that the category of "Israeli" is just as fluid as "Russian" or "post-Soviet," suggesting that there may not be a universally accepted, clear-cut definition. This ambiguity is underscored by the recurring question, "Who am I, what?" The stanza ultimately reflects a personal identity conflict: on the one hand, the speaker identifies as an Israeli, and that should be sufficient. On the other hand, his post-Soviet heritage and language continue to influence his identity. The poem does not necessarily resolve this conflict but rather highlights its existence and dual nature.

I want to conclude the book by noting the glaring absence of the Arabic language and Palestinians in the poem. This absence is particularly striking, given the significance and presence of Arab culture, society, and identity in Israel-Palestine. In this sense, "Who Am I, What?" highlights Israel's peculiar cultural and social situation, described by the renowned Israeli sociologist Baruch Kimmerling as "a plurality of cultures without multiculturalism." This description encapsulates a situation where different ethnic, religious, and cultural groups simultaneously seek institutional autonomy while, and at the same time, emphasizing their shared Jewish identity to exclude the Palestinian minority, effectively preventing the emergence of genuine multiculturalism.[21] To be sure, Eber's poetry does challenge Israel's monolithic national identity by valorizing post-Soviet identity. However, the notable absence of Palestinians from the various identity categories that the speaker adopts throughout the poem suggests that post-Soviet Jews are primarily seeking acceptance and integration into the Jewish-Israeli collective, rather than advocating for a fundamental reconfiguration of Jewish dominance in Israel. It remains to be seen whether a new generation of post-Soviet writers and cultural producers will champion the cause of a truly egalitarian Israeli society and real equality – a struggle best fought with empathy, words, and culture, rather than with guns and bombs.

Notes

INTRODUCTION

1 *Aliyah* is a Hebrew term, referring to the act of immigration to Israel by a Jewish person. Etymologically, *aliyah* means "to rise up" or "ascent," thus lending spiritual connotation to the worldly act of migration. It is an ideologically loaded term that frames immigration to Israel as a homecoming of Jews to the historical or divinely ordained homeland.

2 Interpellation, a concept introduced by Althusser, describes how individuals are hailed by ideological state apparatuses (ISAs) and thus become subjects of the ruling ideology. It illustrates how civil institutions like schools, families, and media subtly indoctrinate individuals. Seemingly innocent directives from teachers and parents, Althusser argues, actually condition us to become obedient subjects, maintaining the socioeconomic and political status quo, a process epitomized by interpellation, where we instantly recognize a policeman's "Hey, you!" as an address to us. Althusser, "Ideology and Ideological State Apparatuses."

3 Nabokov, *Strong Opinions*, 15.

4 Brodsky, "The Condition We Call Exile," 7.

5 Ibid., 7.

6 These writers include Boris Poplavsky, Lev Lior, Icchokas Meras, Yulia Shmukler, Mark Zaichik, and others.

7 On lachrymose conception of Jewish history, see Baron, "Ghetto and Emancipation."

8 Gendelev, "Russkoiazychnaia literatura Izrailia."

9 A common antisemitic piece of Russian folk wisdom states that you can tell a Jew according to their physical characteristics. See Mondry, *Exemplary Bodies*, 11.

10 Gomel, *The Pilgrim Soul*, 5. The term *sabra* is used to describe Jews born in Israel. The word *sabra* comes from the Hebrew name for the prickly pear cactus, known for its tough, thorny exterior and sweet, tender interior.

11 Ibid., 5.

12 Remennick, *Russian Jews on Three Continents*, 68.

13 Remennick, "Two Waves of Russian-Jewish Migration."

14 On push factors that motivated Soviet Jews to emigrate, see Fialkova and Yelenevskaya, *Ex-Soviets in Israel*, 39–87.

15 In Israel, the religious authorities, specifically the Israeli Rabbinate, hold significant control over certain state functions, particularly in matters pertaining to personal status such as marriage, divorce, and conversion, interpreting and applying *halakha*, Jewish religious law, in these areas. The Law of Return grants Jews and their descendants the right to immigrate to Israel and gain Israeli citizenship. However, the Israeli Rabbinate may determine that some individuals who qualify under this law are not halakhically Jewish according to its criteria, which can include requirements for matrilineal descent or conversion according to Orthodox Jewish standards. Due to high rates of intermarriage between different ethnic groups in the USSR, and the difference between the Law of Return and Jewish recognition in Israel, many ex-Soviet Jews discovered after immigration to Israel that they are not officially considered Jewish in Israel.

16 This phenomenon was largely due to the centrality of the fir tree, chubby bearded man, gift-giving, and Novyi God's temporal proximity to Christmas, which is celebrated on the last day of December.

17 Fialkova and Yelenevskaya, *Ex-Soviets in Israel*, 36.

18 For recent scholarship on global Russophone culture, see Byford and Hutchings, *Transnational Russian Studies*; Platt, *Global Russian Cultures*; Rubins, *Redefining Russian Literary Diaspora*; Platt, *Border Conditions*; Strukov and Hudspith, *Russian Culture in the Age of Globalization*; Michlin-Shapir, *Fluid Russia*.

19 Gitelman, *The New Jewish Diaspora*.

20 Brubaker, "The 'Diaspora' Diaspora."

21 Levy, "A Community That Is Both a Center and a Diaspora," 69.

22 This book is at odds with the iterations of the Jewish and Russian diasporas that are utilized for specific political leverage by the State of Israel and the Russian Federation, respectively, to forcefully impose a ready-made Russian or Jewish identity on the "departing" or "returning" population. Israel uses this discourse to secure a demographic majority over Palestinians, while Russia employs the discourse of protecting Russian compatriots abroad, either to extend Russia's cultural, political, and social influence in neighbouring countries or, at times, even to justify military interventions and war, as illustrated by Russia's 2022 full-scale war on Ukraine. On Russia's use of soft power strategies to extend its cultural and political influence in the former Soviet states, see Gorham, "When Soft Power Hardens."

23 Radhakrishnan, *A Said Dictionary*, 39.

24 Kalik, *I vozvraschaetsia veter*, 1991.

25 Gitelman, "The Decline of the Jewish Nation," 112.

26 Kornblatt, *Doubly Chosen*.

27 Ibid., 96.

28 Ro'i, "The Move from Russia/The Soviet Union."

29 Ibid., 150.

30 The reference to "Jewish themes" appears over a dozen times in Shrayer, *An Anthology of Jewish-Russian Literature*.

31 Grinberg, "Reading Between the Lines," 393.

32 Katz, *Drawing the Iron Curtain*.

33 Senderovich, *How the Soviet Jews Was Made*, 12.

34 Shumsky, "Mi-historiografiyah le-sociologiyah u-vakhzarah."

35 Nathans, *Beyond the Pale*; Slezkine, *The Jewish Century*.

36 Slezkine, *The Jewish Century*, 129; Lerner, Rapoport and Lomsky-Feder, "The Ethnic Script in Action."

37 "Intelligentsia" in the Russian Empire and the Soviet Union refers to a social class or group of intellectuals who historically played a significant role in cultural, political, and social spheres, particularly from the nineteenth century onward. Members of the intelligentsia were often writers, artists, philosophers, scientists, and educators who promoted cultural, social, and political change within their society.

38 Galili and Bronfman, *Hamilion sheshina et hamizrach hatikhon* (*The Million That Changed the Middle East*).

39 Smooha, "The Mass Immigrations to Israel." Anita Shapira explains this phenomenon through the change of immigration policy in Israel from the

"melting pot" ideology to the pluralist "direct absorption" one, which permitted immigrants to retain their cultural specificity and group identity. See Shapira, *Israel: A History*.

40 Gutina, *Israel Goes Russian*, 35.

41 Platt, "The Benefits of Distance," 228.

42 Rubina's residence in Ma'aleh Adumim, a West Bank settlement which she often refers to in interviews as Jerusalem, despite it not being considered part of Israel according to international law, is significant in multiple dimensions. It demonstrates Rubina's Zionist aspirations, discursively annexing Ma'aleh Adumim as part of Israeli territory and heritage while erasing competing claims. Simultaneously, it illustrates the economic history of ex-Soviet immigration to Israel. Many immigrants from the Soviet Union in the 1990s moved to West Bank settlements due to their affordability and availability, based on Israeli government subsidies. Rubina's rootedness in the West Bank and her advocacy for hardline political positions regarding the Israel-Palestinian conflict raise important questions about the geopolitical and cultural contexts shaping her literary identity, which I explore in chapter 2.

43 Gershenson and Shneer, "Soviet Jewishness and Cultural Studies."

44 Shrayer, *Anthology of Jewish-Russian Literature*, 932.

45 Mendelson-Maoz, *Multiculturalism in Israel*, 168.

46 Leshem, "The Israeli Population's Attitude to Immigrants of the 1990s."

47 A tiny minority of ex-Soviet newcomers identify with Christianity and even fewer, those who married Palestinians and moved to West Bank or Gaza, have converted to Islam. On this topic, see Remennick and Prashizky, "Russian Israelis and Religion; Elias and Lerner, "Post-Soviet Immigrant Religiosity."

CHAPTER ONE

1 For methodological analysis of the Soviet Jewish Movement, see Zisserman-Brodsky, "The 'Jews of Silence.'"

2 Sharasnky, "Introduction," 2.

3 Ibid.

4 Senderovich, "Soviet Jews, Re-Imagined: Anglophone Émigré Jewish Writers," 96.

5 Senderovich, "Scenes of Encounter," 103.

6 Senderovich, "Between Literature and Politics"; Senderovich, "Soviet Jews, Re-Imagined: Russian American Jewish Writers."

7 This is partially due to his nationally circumscribed focus on American fiction.

8 Bolton, *World of Dissent*, 2.

9 On memoirs by Jewish refuseniks, see Hoffman, "Voices from the Inside." For analysis of ego documents by Soviet dissidents, see Nathans, "Talking Fish."

10 The decision to publish this memoir in English before Hebrew or Russian was driven not only by market considerations or target audiences. Sharansky's primary aim was to establish his presence on the international stage rather than confining it solely to the national one. As a result of his exposure to the West, his story became synonymous with the plight of Soviet dissidents, writ large.

11 Sharansky, *Fear No Evil*, 224.

12 The "inner freedom" refers to a sense of personal liberation achieved through defiance against an oppressive regime, marking the author's transition from living under fear and repression to asserting his right to self-determination and aligning his actions with his true values and desires. For further discussion of "inner freedom" in late Soviet dissident memoirs, see Nathans, "Talking Fish," 584–5 and 604–5.

13 For more on the intersection of Zionism and anti-Soviet attitudes in the writing and identity of Soviet refuseniks, see Hazanov, "From Confucius to Zion," unpublished.

14 Sharansky, *Fear No Evil*, 222.

15 It is important to note that "Leshana haba'a b'Yerushalayim" is a quote from the Passover Haggadah that directly references the Exodus story. The origins of this phrase are religious, not Zionist, even though it was later adopted as a Zionist touchstone. While it expresses a desire to be in Jerusalem, Zionists interpreted it as a wish to be a Jew in the reconstituted Jewish state, embodying a nationalistic longing. Others have seen it as a longing for the Messianic reconstitution of Temple worship, the ability to perform the pilgrimage to Jerusalem during Pesach, or other traditional feelings predating modern Zionism. For more on this topic, see Ochs, *The Passover Haggadah*, 92–3.

16 This is illustrated, for instance, by the fact that in this passage Sharansky

calls his spouse Avital, not Natasha, even though this is not the name he knew her by at this point.

17 A very similar description of the celebration of Hanukkah in a Soviet Gulag by the Soviet refusenik Yosef Begun can be found in Begun, "Hanukkah in a Soviet Prison," 155–60.

18 Sharansky, *Fear No Evil*, 305.

19 Ibid., 308.

20 Ibid.

21 Ibid.

22 Ibid.

23 Ibid.

24 Tsvetayeva, "Poem of the End," 89.

25 On the lachrymose conception of Jewish history, see Baron, "Ghetto and Emancipation."

26 Slezkine, *The Jewish Century*.

27 While there was a significant divide between the motivations of the State of Israel (seeking the immigration of Soviet Jews exclusively to Israel) and those of the American government and human rights organizations (focused on the freedom of emigration and resettlement), in retrospect, the Soviet Jewish Movement is often remembered as a movement for the right of Soviet Jews to resettle in Israel. A case in point is the 2009 documentary film *Refusenik* by American filmmaker Laura Bialis, which depicts the struggle of Soviet Jews to relocate to Israel without mentioning the quarter of a million Soviet Jews who chose a different destination, such as the United States. It seems that, in terms of the memory of American advocacy for Soviet Jews, American Jews primarily campaigned for Soviet Jews' right to emigrate to Israel rather than for their right to resettle in the United States.

28 Shternshis, "The Ambivalent Emigres."

29 Samoilov, "Kogda nibud.'"

30 Ibid.

31 Ibid.

32 Ibid.

33 Remennick, "The Two Waves of Russian-Jewish Migration."

34 Remennick, *Russian Jews on Three Continents*, 54.

35 A good example is Eduard Kuznetsov's daughter, Anat Zalmanson-Kuznetsov, who recently directed and produced a documentary film, *Operation Wedding* (2016), that focuses on her parents' involvement in an at-

tempted plane hijacking in Leningrad in 1970 to escape from the USSR. The dialogue in the film between the daughter and her parents is entirely in Hebrew – even though her parents' command of Hebrew is rather poor. When I asked her during the Q&A why she chose to communicate with her parents in Hebrew and not in Russian – their native language – she replied that she does not speak Russian. Harbouring animosity towards the Soviet regime, her parents decided to only teach her Hebrew. This is all the more incredible if we bear in mind that when Anat Zalmanson-Kuznetsov was born, her parents spoke virtually no Hebrew and that to this day their Hebrew is far from perfect.

36 Yurchak, *Everything Was Forever*.

37 Ibid., 288.

38 Ibid., 32.

39 Grebenshchikov, "Pokolenie dvornikov."

40 For an analysis of the last Soviet-Jewish generation outside of Russia, see Krutikov, "Four Voices."

41 Bialsky, *Legkaia korona*.

42 Bialsky, *Rainu laila*.

43 Barash, *Schastlivoe detstvo*.

44 Barash, *Svoe vremia*.

45 Bialsky, *Rainu Laila*, 17.

46 Ibid., 42.

47 Barash, *Svoe vremia*, 121.

48 Ibid., 121.

49 Ibid., 115.

50 Nathans and Platt, "Socialist in Form, Indeterminate in Content," 315.

51 Barash, *Svoe vremia*, 115.

52 Or, in a more sinister reading, it is also possible to read this as acceptance of existing structures as long as they do not encroach on him too much.

53 Yurchak, *Everything Was Forever*, 250.

54 Bialsky, *Rainu Laila*, 9–10.

55 Ibid.

56 Ibid., 13.

57 Ibid., 10.

58 For more details, see Nadkarni and Shevchenko, "The Politics of Nostalgia"; Oushakine, "'We're Nostalgic But We're Not Crazy'"; Platt, "Affektivnaya poetika 1991-go goda."

59 Paperno, *Stories of the Soviet Experience*, xi.

60 Nadkarni and Shevchenko, "The Politics of Nostalgia."
61 German *Ostalgie* is a similar phenomenon of former East Germany.
62 Bialsky, *Rainu Layla*, 342.

CHAPTER TWO

1 Mendelsohn, *Zoya Cherkassky: Pravda*, 160.
2 Gitelman, "The Decline of the Diaspora Jewish Nation," 112.
3 Gitelman, *A Century of Ambivalence*, 269.
4 Markowitz, "Jewish in the USSR, Russian in the USA," 81.
5 Ibid., 107–8.
6 Kornblatt, *Doubly Chosen*, 86.
7 Luehrmann, *Secularism Soviet Style*.
8 Remennick and Prashizky, "Russian Israelis and Religion."
9 Leshem, "The Israeli Population's Attitude to Immigrants of the 1990s"; Remennick and Prashizky, "Russian Israelis and Religion."
10 Remennick and Prashizky, "Russian Israelis and Religion," 73.
11 On the interaction of religion, nationalism and conversion in Israel, see Neiterman and Rapoport, "Converting to Belong"; Kravel-Tovi, *When the State Winks*.
12 Brown, "Director Pini Tavger."
13 Idzinsky, "Becoming Israeli, Becoming Mizrahi?"
14 Moshkin, "The Poetics of Marginality in Israel."
15 Shenhav, *The Arab Jews*.
16 Ibid., 77.
17 On the displacement of cultural heritage and the internalized racism of Mizrahi Jews, see Shohat, "Sephardim in Israel"; Khazzoom, "The Great Chain of Orientalism."
18 The song – as well as the title of the novel – is a direct quote from a Chabad slogan: "ot ot kumt Moshiah," or in Hebrew "Hine hine mashiah ba." These words were also imprinted on giant posters all over Israel, featuring Rebbe Schneerson's portrait of the Lubavich movement, stipulating that he was the Messiah.
19 Resurrection of the dead is a sign of the coming of the Messiah.
20 Rubina, *Messiah*, 316.
21 Krutikov, "Constructing Jewish Identity," 260.
22 Levantovskaya, "Rootless Cosmopolitans."
23 Rubina, *Messiah*, 3.
24 Ibid.

25 Krutikov, "Constructing Jewish Identity," 260.
26 Platt, "Benefits of Distance."
27 Levantovskaya, "Rootless Cosmopolitans," 63–4.
28 Rubina, *Messiah*, 129.
29 Ibid., 131.
30 Ibid., 14.
31 Ibid.
32 Ibid.
33 Ibid., 15.
34 Ibid., 103.
35 Derrida, *Specters of Marx*, 102–3.
36 Rubina, *Messiah*, 14–15.
37 Ibid., 15.
38 Ibid., 20.
39 Ibid.
40 Remnick, "The Party Faithful."
41 Viorst, *Zionism*, 186.
42 Aldrovandi, *Apocalyptic Movements in Contemporary Politics*, 89.
43 Persico, "The Movement."
44 Kook, "That All People," 212.
45 Ibid.
46 Ibid.
47 Ibid., 213.
48 Rubina, *Messiah*, 310.
49 Ibid., 77.
50 On the intrinsic connection between (sacrifice of) bodies and nationalism, see Anderson, *Imagined Communities*, 50–1; Hardt and Negri, *Commonwealth*, 33–4.
51 While the novel glosses over Rubina's decision to root her characters in the illegal settlements, it is important to remember that when the Soviet-Jewish exodus intensified in 1989, there was extensive outcry about settling new arrivals in the occupied territories from American, Soviet, British and Palestinian leaders, who were extremely concerned about the destabilization of the political situation and hindering of the peace process that might result from the massive influx of Soviet Jews to the occupied territories. For more, see Gulf Center for Strategic Studies, "The Effect of Soviet Jewish Immigration," 9–29.
52 Rubina, *Messiah*, 102–3.

53 Viorst, *Zionism*, 211–12.
54 Shapira, *Israel: A History*.
55 Viorst, *Zionism*, 262.
56 Rubina, *Messiah*, 218.
57 Ibid., 219.
58 Ibid.
59 Ibid.
60 Ibid.
61 Ibid., 211.
62 George, "'Making the Desert Bloom.'"
63 Rubina, *Messiah*, 211.
64 Yavin, *The Land of the Settlers*.
65 On messianism in Rubina's novels, see Katsman, *Nostalgia for a Foreign Land*, 38–54; Shafranskaya, *Sindrom Golubki*, 109–35.
66 Rubina, *Messiah*, 262.
67 Ibid., 281.
68 Rubina, "Beli osel v ozhidanii spasitela."
69 Ibid.
70 Ibid.
71 Rubina, *Messiah*, 323.
72 Ibid.
73 Ibid.
74 Ibid.
75 Ibid.
76 Ibid., 334.
77 Ibid.
78 Ibid.
79 Ibid., 344.
80 Ibid.
81 Ibid.
82 Ibid., 345.
83 Ibid., 346
84 Katsman, *Nostalgia for a Foreign Land*, 40.
85 Isaiah 52:1–2 (New American Standard Bible).
86 Isaiah 52:9.
87 Rubina, *Messiah*, 346.
88 Rubina, *Vot idot messia!*, 391.

89 Ibid.
90 Rubina, *Messiah*, 347.
91 Ibid., 129.

CHAPTER THREE

1 For instance, some of the groundbreaking studies on cosmopolitanism have never been translated into Russian, including Kwame Anthony Appiah's *Cosmopolitanism*. Paul Gilroy does not even have a Russian Wikipedia entry.
2 Pinkus, *The Soviet Government and the Jews*; Levantovskaya, "Rootless Cosmopolitans," 1–6; Clark, *Moscow, The Fourth Rome.*
3 Slezkine, *The Jewish Century*; Rapoport and Lomsky-Feder, "'Intelligentsia' as an Ethnic Habitus," 233; Lissak and Leshem, "Russian Intelligentsia in Israel."
4 Khomitsky, "World Literature, Soviet Style."
5 Djagalov, *From Internationalism to Postcolonialism.*
6 Komaromi, *Soviet Samizdat.*
7 Vergara, *All Future Plunges to the Past.*
8 Nathans, *Beyond the Pale.*
9 Slezkine, *The Jewish Century*, 129; Lerner, Rapoport, and Lomsky-Feder, "The Ethnic Script in Action."
10 Gitelman, *A Century of Ambivalence.*
11 Krutikov, "Memory Is Inseparable from Imagination," 16.
12 Efimov, "Alexander Goldshtein: Ten Years Later."
13 Kharitonov, "Pravda vnutrenej suti."
14 Goldshtein, *A Farewell to Narcissus*, 8.
15 Ibid., 8.
16 On the need to sum up the Soviet history of the twentieth century, see Paperno, *Stories of the Soviet Experience.*
17 Goldshtein, *A Farewell to Narcissus*, 77.
18 Goldshtein, *Aspects of Spiritual Matrimony*, especially the essay "Nashestvie"; Shavit, "This Is Culture?"
19 In one, he attempted to sell himself as an artist at Ben Yehuda market in Jerusalem to prove that no one is interested in culture in Israel; in another he carried an enormous hand-made zero on his back down the path of Via Dolorosa in the old city of Jerusalem, recreating Jesus's fatal path; in the last one, he went to clean up the grave of the Jewish extremist Baruch

Goldshtein, who perpetrated the mass murder in the Cave of Patriarchs in Hebron, killing 29 Palestinians and injuring 125 more.

20 "Narod" is a term in the Russian language and culture that refers to the common people, the masses, or the working class. It can have both positive and negative connotations: positively, it describes the organic populace of a national group; negatively, it can be used in a classist manner to refer to the uneducated rural or peasant population.

21 Shavit, "This Is Culture?"

22 Yevgeny Yevtushenko was a prominent Soviet poet acclaimed for his outspoken poetry that challenged Soviet norms and ideologies, earning international recognition for addressing social and political issues like antisemitism, the Holocaust, and human rights.

23 Lomsky-Feder and Rapoport, "Mizrahiyut be'einay rusim."

24 Krutikov, "Memory Is Inseparable from Imagination."

25 Goldshtein, *Remember Famagusta*, 20.

26 Ibid., 25.

27 Goldshtein, *Aspects*, 37.

28 Ibid. On the connection between food and body in Goldshtein's writings, see Mondry, "The Jewish Patient."

29 Goldshtein, *Aspects*, 37.

30 Kukulin, "Internal Post-Colonization."

31 Shumsky, "Orientalism and Islamophobia."

32 For more on the topic, see Sadowski-Smith, *The New Immigrant Whiteness*; Finkelstein, "A Common Place."

33 See also Finkelstein, "Die Anderen der Anderen."

34 This practice is not limited to Alexander Goldshtein but can be extended to many other post-Soviet Israeli writers and thinkers, including Dina Rubina, Maya Kaganskaya, Alex Tarn, Aleksander Voronel, Nelly Gutina, Yaakov Shechter, and others.

35 Goldshtein, *Aspects*, 17.

36 Ibid., 19.

37 Ibid., 20.

38 Ibid., 25–6.

39 Latour, "Whose Cosmos, Which Cosmopolitics?," 453.

40 Lomsky-Feder, Rapoport, and Lerner, "The Modification of Orientalism."

41 Because most of them are publishing their works in the Russian language, Russophone writers in Israel are unable to sell their books in major Israeli

bookstores, and they are not nominated for Israel's book prizes that are given solely to authors writing in Hebrew.

42 Casanova, *The World Republic of Letters*. On the connection between post-Soviet and world literatures, see Gorski, *Cultural Capitalism*.

43 This analysis is partly complicated by the new stage in the relationship between the Russian Federation and "the West" and what critics call the new Cold War. In this context, Svetlana Alexievich's Nobel Prize for Literature signals a return to the Cold War phase of the relationship and a total disregard of Moscow, both official (Kremlin sanctioned) and unofficial (the opposition). Instead, by selecting Svetlana Alexievich (a Belorussian writer who writes in Russian) the academy succeeded both in vexing Russia's imperial mentality (much in the spirit of the Cold War) by selecting a non-Russian writer and in hinting at a resumed insignificance of Moscow's cultural institutions in consecrating Russophone writers.

44 Goldshtein, *A Farewell*, 161.

45 This movement was interchangeably referred to as "Mediterranean Note" and "The Kavafis Variant." For more on these movements, see Rubins, "A Century of Russian Culture(s)."

46 Goldshtein, *A Farewell*, 164.

47 Ibid., 176.

48 Ibid.

49 Ibid.

50 Mandelstam, *The Prose of Osip Mandelstam*, 90.

51 Barash, "International Russian Literature."

52 Ibid.

53 Goldshtein, "Tri darovaniia."

54 Peter Bürger is a German philosopher and literary theorist known for his work *Theory of the Avant-Garde* (1974). In his book, Bürger examines how avant-garde movements from the late nineteenth and early twentieth centuries aimed to challenge established artistic conventions and norms. He argues that while these movements sought to break away from traditional art forms and institutions, they ultimately failed to completely abolish or replace them.

55 For detailed analysis of the New Barbizon group, see Dashevsky, "The Phenomenon of the New Barbizon."

56 Trezzi, "New Barbizon Manifesto."

57 Bartos, "New Barbizon Group."

58 Emont, "In Tel Aviv, a Park."

59 For refugees arriving in Israel, the process typically begins with entry through border crossings or, more often, through irregular means such as crossing from Egypt. Upon arrival, many refugees are taken to detention centres, such as the one in the Negev desert. These centres serve as initial holding facilities where refugees undergo security screenings and legal status evaluations. After being released from the detention centre, refugees face numerous challenges, including obtaining work permits, accessing social services, securing housing, and integrating into Israeli society.

60 Sherwood, "Levinsky Park Migrants."

61 Yahav, "African Migrants in Tel Aviv."

62 Ibid.

63 African Refugee Development Center, "Israel's Violation of the Convention."

64 Friedman, "MK Apologizes."

65 On Israel's newly adopted nation-state law, see Sommer, "Basic Law or Basically a Disaster?"

66 For more on this topic, see Shumsky, "Ethnicity and Citizenship."

67 Marmari, "Zoya Cherkassky."

68 Sheen, "Israel's True Colors."

69 Gershenson, "A Dancing Russian Bear," 72.

70 Dayan, "Don't Put Up Art."

71 Gilerman, "Thank You Yitzhak Shamir."

72 On this topic, see Waysband, "Alexander Goldstein's 'Tethys or Mediterranean Mail.'"

CHAPTER FOUR

1 Rumbaut, "Ages, Life Stages, and Generational Cohort."

2 Smola, "Israel and the Concept of Homeland"; Rubins, "A Century of Russian Culture(s)," 37–45; Weiskopf, "Myi byli kak vo sne."

3 Weiskopf, "Myi byli kak vo sne," 249.

4 Rif, "Milah," 49. All translations of poetry are those of the author, unless otherwise indicated.

5 The contrast between idealized representations of life in the Soviet Union and those of a precarious reality in Israel runs through much of Rif's poetry. For instance, the poem "Zionism" undermines Israel's ideological narrative that perceives Jewish life in the diaspora as dangerous and advo-

cates a national rebirth in Israel. Instead, like "Milah," the poem subverts this metanarrative by describing the opposite – the speaker's deteriorating psychological state that results from immigration to Israel. It concludes with the ominous line: "One day I wanted to be, the other I did not."

6 Remennick and Prashizky, "Russian Israelis and Religion," 64–5.

7 Circumcision is an important topic in literary and visual art by Russian Jews. Zoya Cherkassky-Nnadi has created several gory paintings that deal with adult circumcision such as *The Circumcision of Uncle Yasha* (2013). In addition, Soviet-born American writer Gary Shteyngart describes his own adult circumcision in his biography *Little Failure* (2014) and also touches on this topic in his novel *Absurdistan* (2006).

8 On Chabad's outreach activities that target Russian-speaking Jews, see Aviv and Shneer, *New Jews*, 26–50; Zelenina, "'Our Community Is the Coolest in the World.'"

9 Rif, "Evgeni," 12.

10 On Israel's language politics, "Hebrew only," and the role of Hebrew in the state-building project, see Safran, "Language and Nation-Building in Israel," 43–64.

11 Spiegelman, *Maus II: A Survivor's Tale*, 98–9.

12 Klüger, *Still Alive*, 65.

13 Remennick, "Silent Mothers, Articulate Daughters," 58–76.

14 Prashizky and Remennick, "Subversive Identity."

15 Alex Rif, "Halom hozer," 34.

16 Sex work is a common theme that runs through literature and visual art by former post-Soviet Israeli women. On this topic, see Dekel, *Transnational Identities*, 17–58.

17 Lemish, "The Whore and the Other," 333–49.

18 Rif, "Agiley ha'yaalom shel ima," 36.

19 Dekel, *Transnational Identities*, 41.

20 Kogan, "[Hagdara-atzmit]."

21 Remennick, "Silent Mothers, Articulate Daughters," 62.

22 Ibid.

23 On the longevity of discrimination and harassment of Russian-speaking women in Israel, see Remennick, "Silent Mothers, Articulate Daughters."

24 Istoshina and Zamir, *Women's Security Reports 2012 and 2013*. The survey was also analyzed in Remennick, "Silent Mothers, Articulate Daughters," 62, and Dekel, *Transnational Identities*, 36.

25 Golden, "A National Cautionary Tale"; Lemish, "The Whore and the Other."

26 Lomsky-Feder and Rapoport, *Visibility in Immigration*, 79 (Hebrew). Quoted in English in Dekel, *Transnational Identities*, 37.

27 Tamara Brodinsky, *What Makes a Russian*, 2006. Digitally manipulated colour photograph.

28 Rita Kogan, "Etzei ashuah lo" ("Fir Trees Aren't"), 82.

29 On the celebration of Soviet holidays in Israel, read: Prashizky and Remennick, "Celebrating Memory and Belonging," 76–82; Fialkova and Yelenevskaya, "Holidays as Border Crossing," in *In Search of the Self*, 147–82.

30 Boym, *The Future of Nostalgia*, 19.

31 Ibid., 132.

32 Ibid., 30.

33 Sasha Senderovich describes the State of Israel as a "restorative nostalgia" nation par excellence in Senderovich, "In Memoriam."

34 For close analysis of Cherkassky-Nnadi's painting series that focuses on the experiences of ex-Soviet Jews in Israel, see *Zoya Cherkassky: Pravda*.

35 Rabikowska, "The Memory of the Communist Past," 15–16.

36 On the ideological complexity of the post-Soviet nostalgia, see Nadkarni and Shevchenko, "The Politics of Nostalgia"; Platt, "Russian Empire of Pop."

37 In the last years of the Soviet Union, the government expanded paid maternity leave to eighteen months, and unpaid leave was given for an additional eighteen months. On this topic, see Malkova, "Can Maternity Benefits," 692–3.

38 Rozovsky, "Missing Communism."

39 Ibid.

40 Marius, "'It Is Also an Invasion.'"

41 Ibid.

CONCLUSION

1 Kanovich, "Schitaiu sebya russkim pisatelem."

2 Ibid.

3 Blomberg-Jatskina, "Kratkaia istoria rosskoiazichnoi literaturyi v Izraiele."

4 Rubina, *Messiah*, 32.

5 Weiskopf, "Hachoma."

6 Platt, "Putting Russian Cultures in Place," 9.

7 Ibid., 9.

8 Gendelev, "Literaturnyi pas'yans russkogo izrail'ia."

9 Prashizky and Remennick, "Ethnic Awakening," 14.

10 Yacov Shaus, "Bol'shoi stiob kak bol'shoi sotsial'nii zakaz," Facebook post, 11 July 2018, https://www.facebook.com/yacov.shaus/posts/2263654457199299.

11 Ibid.

12 Ibid.

13 Ibid.

14 Zoya Cherkassky-Nnadi, Facebook post, 14 July 2018, https://www.facebook.com/zoya.cherkassky/posts/10157480176787542.

15 Ibid.

16 Ibid.

17 Eber, "1991/Who Am I, What" (translated by Alex Moshkin and Zackary Sholem Berger).

18 Remennick and Prashizky, "Subversive Identity and Cultural Production," 13.

19 Ibid.

20 Eber, "Who Am I, What."

21 See Shumsky, "Ethnicity and Citizenship," 154–6; Kimmerling, "The New Israelis."

Bibliography

African Refugee Development Center. "Israel's Violation of the Convention on the Elimination of All Forms of Racial Discrimination with Regard to Asylum Seekers and Refugees in Israel." 30 January 2012. http://ardc-israel.org/sites/default/files/cerd_ardc_final_0.pdf.

Aldrovandi, Carlo. *Apocalyptic Movements in Contemporary Politics: Christian and Jewish Zionism*. New York: Palgrave Macmillan, 2014.

Althusser, Louis. "Ideology and Ideological State Apparatuses." In *Lenin and Philosophy and Other Essays*, translated by Ben Brewster, 127–86. New York: Monthly Review Press, 1971.

Anderson, Benedict. *Imagined Communities: Reflections on the Origin and Spread of Nationalism*. Revised edition. London: Verso, 1983.

Aviv, Caryn, and David Shneer. *New Jews: The End of Jewish Diaspora*. New York: New York University Press, 2005.

Barash, Alexander. "International Russian Literature." Paper presented at the seminar *Geopolitics of Culture and Our Literary Condition*, Tel Aviv, 25–6 December 2008.

Barash, Alexander. *Schastlivoe detstvo*. Moscow: Novoe literaturnoe obozrenie, 2006.

– *Svoe vremia*. Moscow: Novoe literaturnoe obozrenie, 2014.

Baron, Salo W. "Ghetto and Emancipation." *Menorah Journal* 14, no. 6 (1928). Reprinted in *The Menorah Treasury*, edited by Leo W. Schwartz, Philadelphia: Jewish Publication Society, 1964.

Bartos, Ron. "New Barbizon Group: Social-Realism Today." *Erev Rav*, 2 December 2014. http://www.erev-rav.com/archives/34013#_ftn4.

Begun, Yosef. "Hanukkah in a Soviet Prison." In *Chicken Soup for the Jewish Soul: Stories to Open the Heart and Rekindle the Spirit*, edited by Jack Canfield, Mark Victor Hansen, and Karen Solomon, 155–60. New York: Health Communications, 2002.

Bialsky, Alice. *Legkaia korona*. Moscow: Eksmo, 2011.

– *Rainu Laila*. Tel Aviv: Afik, 2014.

Blomberg-Jatskina, Svetlana. "Kratkaia istoria rosskoiazichnoi literaturyi v Izraiele." *Gostinaya*. Accessed 23 July 2024. http://gostinaya.net/?p=11678.

Bolton, Jonathan. *World of Dissent: Charter 77, The Plastic People of the Universe, and Czech Culture under Communism*. Cambridge, MA: Harvard University Press, 2012.

Boym, Svetlana. *The Future of Nostalgia*. New York: Basic Books, 2001.

Brodinsky, Tamara. *What Makes a Russian*. Digitally manipulated colour photograph, 2006.

Brodsky, Joseph. "The Condition We Call Exile." *Culture, Theory and Critique* 34, no. 1 (1991): 7.

Brown, Hannah. "Director Pini Tavger on the Life Behind Israeli Film *More Than I Deserve*." *The Jerusalem Post*, 11 February 2023. https://www.jpost.com/israel-news/culture/article-731159.

Brubaker, Rogers. "The 'Diaspora' Diaspora." *Ethnic and Racial Studies* 28, no. 1 (2005): 1–19.

Byford, Andy, and Stephen Hutchings. *Transnational Russian Studies*. Liverpool: Liverpool University Press, 2020.

Casanova, Pascale. *The World Republic of Letters*. Cambridge, MA: Harvard University Press, 2004.

Cherkassky-Nnadi, Zoya. *Zoya Cherkassky: Pravda*. Edited by Amitai Mendelsohn. Jerusalem: The Israel Museum, 2018.

Clark, Katerina. *Moscow, The Fourth Rome: Stalinism, Cosmopolitanism, and the Evolution of Soviet Culture, 1931–1941*. Cambridge, MA: Harvard University Press, 2011.

Dashevsky, Lilia. "The Phenomenon of the New Barbizon in Israeli Art." In *Contemporary Israel: Languages, Society, Culture*, edited by Elena Nosenko-Stein and Dennis Sobolev, 333–64. Moscow: IOS RAS, 2020.

Dayan, Ben. "Don't Put Up Art on the Internet, All the Arsim Will Come." *Erev Rav*, 25 July 2012. http://erev-rav.com/archives/19259. [Hebrew].

Dekel, Tal. *Transnational Identities: Women, Art, and Migration in Contemporary Israel.* Detroit: Wayne State University Press, 2016.

Derrida, Jacques. *Specters of Marx: The State of the Debt, the Work of Mourning, and the New International.* Translated by Peggy Kamuf. New York: Routledge, 1994.

Djagalov, Rossen. *From Internationalism to Postcolonialism: Literature and Cinema between the Second and the Third Worlds.* Montreal: McGill-Queen's University Press, 2020.

Eber, Arik. "1991/Who Am I, What." Translated by Alex Moshkin and Zackary Sholem Berger. *Tel Aviv Review of Books*, Winter 2021.

Efimov, Mikhail. "Alexander Goldshtein: Ten Years Later." *Znamia* 1 (2017).

Elias, Nelly, and Julia Lerner. "Post-Soviet Immigrant Religiosity: Beyond Israeli National Religion." In *The New Jewish Diaspora: Russian-Speaking Immigrants in the United States, Israel, and Germany*, edited by Zvi Gitelman, 87–104. New Brunswick: Rutgers University Press, 2016.

Emont, Jon. "In Tel Aviv, a Park for Those Who Have Nothing." *Roads & Kingdoms*, 30 June 2014. http://roadsandkingdoms.com/2014/in-tel-aviv-a-park-for-those-who-have-nothing/.

Fialkova, Larisa, and Maria N. Yelenevskaya. *Ex-Soviets in Israel: From Personal Narratives to a Group Portrait.* Detroit: Wayne State University Press, 2007.

Fialkova, Larisa, and Maria Yelenevskaya. *In Search of the Self: Reconciling the Past and the Present in Immigrants' Experience.* Tartu: ELM Scholarly Press, 2013.

Finkelstein, Miriam. "A Common Place, a Contested Space: Reciprocal Representations of Russian and Eastern European Migrants in Their Berlin Narratives." *Zeitschrift für Slavische Philologie* 70, no. 2 (2014): 365–400.

– "Die Anderen der Anderen. Rassistische und anti-rassistische Diskurse in der russisch-amerikanischen und russisch-deutschen Gegenwartsliteratur." In *Kulturen verbinden. Connecting Cultures: Festband anlässlich des 50-jährigen Bestehens der Slawistik an der Universität Innsbruck*, edited by Jürgen Fuchsbauer, Wolfgang Stadler, and Andrea Zink, 285–302. Innsbruck: Innsbruck University Press, 2021.

Friedman, Ron. "MK Apologizes for Comparing Migrants to Cancer." *The Times of Israel.* 27 May 2012. http://www.timesofisrael.com/mk-apologizes-for-comparing-migrants-to-cancer/.

Galili, Lili, and Roman Bronfman. *Hamilion sheshina et hamizrach hatikhon* (*The Million That Changed the Middle East*). Tel Aviv: Matar, 2013.

Gendelev, Mikhail. "Literaturnyi pas'yans russkogo izrail'ia." *Literaturnyi Vestnik* 22 (1986). http://gendelev.org/proza/index.php?option=com_content&view=article&id=132:literaturnyj-pasyans-russkogo-izrailya&catid=18:o-literature&Itemid=155.

– "Russkoiazychnaia literatura Izrailia." *Obitaemyi ostrov* 1 (1991). Translated in Vitaly Chernetsky, "Russophone Writing in Ukraine: Historical Contexts and Post-Euromaidan Changes." In *Global Russian Cultures*, edited by Kevin M.F. Platt. Madison: University of Wisconsin Press, 2019.

George, Alan. "'Making the Desert Bloom': A Myth Examined." *Journal of Palestine Studies* 8, no. 2 (Winter 1979): 88–100.

Gershenson, Olga, and David Shneer. "Soviet Jewishness and Cultural Studies." *Journal of Jewish Identities* 4, no. 1 (2011): 129–47.

Gershenson, Olga. "A Dancing Russian Bear." *Shofar* 37, no. 2 (Summer 2019): 71–80.

– *The Phantom Holocaust: Soviet Cinema and Jewish Catastrophe*. New Brunswick: Rutgers University Press, 2013.

Gilerman, Dana. "Thank You Yitzhak Shamir and the State of Israel for Bringing Me Here." *Kal'kal'ist*, 8 December 2010. http://www.calcalist.co.il/consumer/articles/0,7340,L-3440724,00.html. [Hebrew].

Gitelman, Zvi. *A Century of Ambivalence: The Jews of Russia and the Soviet Union, 1881 to the Present*. 2nd ed. Bloomington: Indiana University Press, 2001.

– "The Decline of the Jewish Nation: Boundaries, Content, and Jewish Identity." *Jewish Social Studies* 4, no. 2 (1998): 112.

– *The New Jewish Diaspora: Russian-Speaking Immigrants in the United States, Israel, and Germany*. New Brunswick: Rutgers University Press, 2016.

Golden, Deborah. "A National Cautionary Tale: Russian Women Newcomers to Israel Portrayed." *Nations and Nationalism* 9, no. 1 (2003): 83–104.

Goldshtein, Alexander. *Aspects of Spiritual Matrimony* (*Aspekty dukhovnogo braka*). Moscow: Novoe Literaturnoe Obozrenie, 2001.

– *A Farewell to Narcissus* (*Proshchanie s Nartsissom*). Moscow: Novoe Literaturnoe Obozrenie, 1997.

– *Remember Famagusta (Pomni o Famaguste)*. Moscow: Novoe Literaturnoe Obozrenie, 2004.

– "Tri darovaniia." In *Vid na zhitel'stvo*, by Aleksandra Petrova. Moscow: NLO, 2000. http://www.vavilon.ru/texts/prim/goldstein1.html.

Gomel, Elana. *The Pilgrim Soul: Being Russian in Israel*. New York: Cambria Press, 2009.

Gorham, Michael S. "When Soft Power Hardens: The Formation and Fracturing of Putin's 'Russian World.'" In *Global Russian Cultures*, edited by Kevin M.F. Platt, 185–206. University of Wisconsin Press, 2019.

Gorski, Bradley A. *Cultural Capitalism: Literature and the Market after Socialism*. Ithaca, NY: Cornell University Press, 2025.

Grinberg, Marat. "Reading Between the Lines: The Soviet Jewish Bookshelf and Post-Holocaust Soviet Jewish Identity." *East European Jewish Affairs* 48, no. 3 (2019): 393.

Gulf Centre for Strategic Studies. "The Effect of Soviet Jewish Immigration on the Arab-Israeli Peace Process and the Settlement of Soviet Jews in the Occupied Territories." In *The Emigration of Soviet Jews to Israel: An Interpretation of British Press Coverage and a Statistical Brief*, 9–29. London: Gulf Centre for Strategic Studies, 1990.

Gutina, Nelly. *Israel Goes Russian*. Tel Aviv: Mercur Publications, 2011.

Hardt, Michael, and Antonio Negri. *Commonwealth*. Cambridge, MA: Belknap Press of Harvard University Press, 2009.

Hazanov, Alex. "From Confucius to Zion: Vitalii Rubin and the Making of an (Anti-) Soviet Zionist." Unpublished manuscript.

Hoffman, Stefani. "Voices from the Inside: Jewish Activists' Memoirs, 1967–1989." In *The Jewish Movement in the Soviet Union*, edited by Yaacov Ro'i, 227–49. Washington, DC: Woodrow Wilson Center, 2012.

Holy Bible: New American Standard Bible. Isaiah 52.

Idzinsky, Vicki. "Becoming Israeli, Becoming Mizrahi?" Master's thesis, Tel Aviv University, 2014. [Hebrew].

Istoshina, Assia, and Iris Zamir. *Women's Security Reports 2012 and 2013*. Haifa: Women's Security Coalition, 2013. http://isha2isha.com/תחומי-פעילות/מדד-הביטחון/.

Kalik, Mikhail, dir. *I vozvraschaetsia veter* (And the wind returns). Feature film. Moscow: Mosfilm, 1991.

Kanovich, Grigorii. "Schitaiu sebya russkim pisatelem." *Voprosi literatury* 4 (2003). http://magazines.russ.ru/voplit/2003/4/kanov-pr.html.

Katsman, Roman. *Nostalgia for a Foreign Land: Studies in Russian-Language Literature in Israel*. Boston: Academic Studies Press, 2016.

Katz, Maya Balakirsky. *Drawing the Iron Curtain: Jews and the Golden Age of Soviet Animation*. New Brunswick: Rutgers University Press, 2016.

Kharitonov, Mark. "Pravda vnutrenej suti." *Lechaim*, 6 June 2009. http://www.lechaim.ru/ARHIV/206/haritonov.htm.

Khazzoom, Aziza. "The Great Chain of Orientalism: Jewish Identity, Stigma Management, and Ethnic Exclusion in Israel." *American Sociological Review* 68 (2003): 481–511.

Khomitsky, Maria. "World Literature, Soviet Style: A Forgotten Episode in the History of the Idea." *Ab Imperio* 3 (2013): 119–54.

Kimmerling, Baruch. "The New Israelis: Plurality of Cultures without Multiculturalism." *Alpayim* 16 (2001): 264–308. [Hebrew].

Klüger, Ruth. *Still Alive: A Holocaust Girlhood Remembered.* New York: Feminist Press at the City University of New York, 2003.

Kogan, Rita. *Rishayon li-shegiot ketiv.* Tel Aviv: Elrom, 2015.

Kogan, Rita. "Sus bahatzait (Horse in Skirt)." Tel Aviv: Esh Ktana 77, 2018.

Komaromi, Ann. *Soviet Samizdat: Imagining a New Society*. Ithaca, NY: Cornell University Press, 2022.

Kook, Rav Zvi Yehuda. "That All People of the Earth May Know." In *Lords of the Land: The War Over Israel's Settlements in the Occupied Territories*, edited by Idith Zertal. New York: Nation Books, 2009.

Kornblatt, Judith. *Doubly Chosen: Jewish Identity, the Soviet Intelligentsia, and the Russian Orthodox Church*. Madison: University of Wisconsin Press, 2004.

Kosharovsky, Yuli, and Stefani Hoffman. *"We Are Jews Again": Jewish Activism in the Soviet Union*. Edited by Ann Komaromi. Syracuse University Press, 2017.

Krasuska, Karolina. *Soviet-Born: The Afterlives of Migration in Jewish American Fiction*. New Brunswick: Rutgers University Press, 2024.

Kravel-Tovi, Michal. *When the State Winks: The Performance of Jewish Conversion in Israel*. New York: Columbia University Press, 2017.

Krutikov, Mikhail. "Constructing Jewish Identity in Contemporary Russian Fiction." In *Jewish Life After the USSR*, edited by Zvi Gitelman et al., 260. Bloomington: Indiana University Press, 2003.

– "Four Voices of the Last Soviet Generation: Evgeny Steiner, Alexander Goldshtein, Oleg Yuryev, and Alexander Ilichevsky." In *The New Jewish Diaspora: Russian-Speaking Immigrants in the United States, Israel and Germany*, edited by Zvi Gitelman. New Brunswick: Rutgers University Press, 2016.

– "Memory Is Inseparable from Imagination." *Sh'ma* 41 (2010): 16–17.

Kukulin, Ilya. "Internal Post-Colonization: Formation of Postcolonial Subjectivity in Russian Literature in 1970s to 2000s." *Gefter*, 19 March 2014. http://gefter.ru/archive/11708.

Latour, Bruno. "Whose Cosmos, Which Cosmopolitics? Comments on the Peace Terms of Ulrich Beck." *Common Knowledge* 10, no. 3 (2004): 450–62.

Lemish, Dafna. "The Whore and the Other: Israeli Images of Female Immigrants from the Former USSR." *Gender and Society* 4, no. 2 (2000): 333–49.

Lerner, Julia, Tamar Rapoport, and Edna Lomsky-Feder. "The Ethnic Script in Action: The Regrounding of Russian Jewish Immigrants in Israel." *Ethos* 35, no. 2 (2007): 168–95.

Leshem, Elazar. "The Israeli Population's Attitude to Immigrants of the 1990s." *Social Security* 40 (1993): 54–73.

Levantovskaya, Margarita (Maggie). "Rootless Cosmopolitans: Literature of the Soviet-Jewish Diaspora." PhD diss., University of California, San Diego, 2013.

Levy, André. "A Community That Is Both a Center and a Diaspora: Jews in Late Twentieth Century Morocco." In *Homelands and Diasporas: Holy Lands and Other Places*, edited by André Levy and Alex Weingrod, 68–96. Stanford: Stanford University Press, 2005.

Lissak, Moshe, and Eliezer Leshem. "Russian Intelligentsia in Israel: Between Ghettoization and Integration." *Israel Affairs* 2, no. 2 (1995): 20–37.

Lomsky-Feder, Edna, and Tamar Rapoport. "Mizrahiyut be'einay rusim." *Haoketz*, 29 June 2013.

– *Visibility in Immigration: Body, Gaze, Representation.* Jerusalem: Van Leer Institute, 2010. [Hebrew].

Lomsky-Feder, Edna, Tamar Rapoport, and Julia Lerner. "The Modification of Orientalism in Migration: 'Russian' Students Read Mizrahim." *Theory and Criticism* 26 (Spring 2005): 119–47. [Hebrew].

Luehrmann, Sonja. *Secularism Soviet Style: Teaching Atheism and Religion in a Volga Republic.* Bloomington: Indiana University Press, 2011.

Malkova, Olga. "Can Maternity Benefits Have Long-Term Effects on Childbearing? Evidence from Soviet Russia." *Review of Economics and Statistics* 100, no. 4 (2018): 691–703.

Mandelstam, Osip. *The Prose of Osip Mandelstam.* Translated by Clarence Brown. Princeton: Princeton University Press, 1965.

Markowitz, Fran. "Jewish in the USSR, Russian in the USA: Social Context and Ethnic Identity." In *Persistence and Flexibility: Anthropological Perspectives on the American Jewish Experience*, edited by Walter P. Zenner, 79–95. Albany: State University of New York Press, 1988.

Marius, Marley. "'It Is Also an Invasion of Our Childhoods': A Ukrainian Artist Reflects on How the War Has Changed Her Memories." *Vogue Daily*, 4 March 2023. https://www.vogue.co.uk/arts-and-lifestyle/article/zoya-cherkassky-nnadi-interview.

Marmari, Sonia. "Zoya Cherkassky: 'I Did a Provocation for the Bourgeoisie, and They Fell in Love with It.'" *Globes*, 4 May 2012. http://www.globes.co.il/news/article.aspx?did=1000738258.

Mendelson-Maoz, Adia. *Multiculturalism in Israel: Literary Perspectives*. West Lafayette, IN: Purdue University Press, 2014.

Mondry, Henrietta. *Exemplary Bodies: Constructing the Jew in Russian Culture, 1880s to 2008*. Brighton: Academic Studies Press, 2017.

Moshkin, Alex. "The Poetics of Marginality in Israel: Ars Poetika and the Russophone Poets of the 1.5 Generation." *Shofar: An Interdisciplinary Journal of Jewish Studies* 42, no. 1 (2024): 175–99.

Nabokov, Vladimir. *Strong Opinions*. New York: Vintage Books, 1990.

Nadkarni, Maya, and Olga Shevchenko. "The Politics of Nostalgia: A Cultural Analysis." *Ab Imperio* 2004, no. 2: 487–519.

Nathans, Benjamin. *Beyond the Pale: The Jewish Encounter with Late Imperial Russia*. Berkeley: University of California Press, 2002.

– "Talking Fish: On Soviet Dissident Memoirs." *Journal of Modern History* 87, no. 3 (2015): 579–614.

– *To the Success of Our Hopeless Cause: The Many Lives of the Soviet Dissident Movement*. Princeton: Princeton University Press, 2024.

Nathans, Benjamin, and Kevin M.F. Platt. "Socialist in Form, Indeterminate in Content: The Ins and Outs of Late Soviet Culture." *Ab Imperio* 2011, no. 2: 301–24.

Neiterman, Elena, and Tamar Rapoport. "Converting to Belong: Immigration, Education and Nationalisation among Young 'Russian' Immigrant Women." *Gender and Education* 21, no. 2 (2009): 173–89.

Ochs, Vanessa L. *The Passover Haggadah: A Biography*. Princeton University Press, 2020.

Oushakine, Serguei. "'We're Nostalgic But We're Not Crazy': Retrofitting the Past in Russia." *Russian Review* 66, no. 3 (2007): 451–82.

Paperno, Irina. *Stories of the Soviet Experience: Memoirs, Diaries, Dreams*. Ithaca, NY: Cornell University Press, 2009.

Persico, Tomer. "The Movement That Saw Israeli Settlements as Redemption for Jews and the World: The Rise and Fall of Zionism as a Religion." *Haaretz*, 22 June 2017. https://www.haaretz.com/israel-news/.premium.MAGAZINE-the-rise-and-fall-of-zionism-as-a-religion-1.5486927.

Pinkus, Benjamin. *The Soviet Government and the Jews, 1948–1967: A Documented Study*. Cambridge: Cambridge University Press, 1984.

Platt, Kevin M.F. "'Affektivnaya poetika 1991-go goda: nostalgiya i travma na Lubyanskoy ploshchadi.'" *Novoye literaturnoye obozreniye* 116 (2012).

– "The Benefits of Distance: Extraterritoriality as Cultural Capital in the Literary Marketplace." In *Redefining Russian Literary Diaspora, 1920–2020*, edited by Maria Rubins, 228. London: UCL Press, 2021.

– *Border Conditions: Russian-Speaking Latvians Between World Orders*. Ithaca, NY: Cornell University Press, 2024.

– *Global Russian Cultures*. Madison: University of Wisconsin Press, 2019.

– "Russian Empire of Pop: Post-Socialist Nostalgia and Soviet Retro at the 'New Wave' Competition." *Russian Review* 72, no. 3 (2013): 447–69.

Prashizky, Anna, and Larissa Remennick. "Celebrating Memory and Belonging: Young Russian Israelis Claim Their Unique Place in Tel-Aviv's Urban Space." *Journal of Contemporary Ethnography* 47, no. 3 (2018): 336–66.

– "Ethnic Awakening among Russian Israelis of the 1.5 Generation: Physical and Symbolic Dimensions of Their Belonging and Protest." *Sociological Papers* 18 (2015): 1–17.

Rabikowska, Marta. "The Memory of the Communist Past – An Alternative Present?" In *Everyday of Memory: Between Communism and Postcommunism*, edited by Marta Rabikowska, 147–82. Bern: Peter Lang, 2013.

Radhakrishnan, R. *A Said Dictionary*. Oxford: Wiley-Blackwell, 2012.

Rapoport, Tamar, and Edna Lomsky-Feder. "'Intelligentsia' as an Ethnic Habitus: The Inculcation and Restructuring of Intelligentsia among Russian Jews." *British Journal of Sociology of Education* 23, no. 2 (June 2002): 233–48.

Remennick, Larissa. *Russian Jews on Three Continents: Identity, Integration, and Conflict*. New York: Transaction Publishing, 2007.

– "Silent Mothers, Articulate Daughters: Two Generations of Russian Israeli Women Doing Jewishness and Gender." *Nashim: A Journal of Jewish Women's Studies & Gender Issues* 32 (2018): 58–76.

– "The Two Waves of Russian-Jewish Migration from the USSR/FSU to Israel: Dissidents of the 1970s and Pragmatics of the 1990s." *Diaspora: A Journal of Transnational Studies* 18, no. 1–2 (2009): 44–66.

Remennick, Larissa, and Anna Prashizky. "Russian Israelis and Religion: What Has Changed after Twenty Years in Israel." *Israel Studies Review* 27, no. 1 (2012): 55–77.

– "Subversive Identity and Cultural Production by the Russian-Israeli Generation 1.5." *European Journal of Cultural Studies* 22, no. 5–6 (2019): 925–41.

Remnick, David. "The Party Faithful." *New Yorker*, 13 January 2013. https://www.newyorker.com/magazine/2013/01/21/the-party-faithful.

Rif, Alex. *Tipshonet mishtarim*. Haifa: Pardes Publishing, 2018.

Ro'i, Yaacov, ed. *The Jewish Movement in the Soviet Union*. Washington, DC: Woodrow Wilson Center, 2012.

– "The Move from Russia/The Soviet Union to Israel: A Transformation of Jewish Culture and Identity?" In *The New Jewish Diaspora: Russian-Speaking Immigrants in the United States, Israel, and Germany*, edited by Zvi Gitelman, 139–55. New Brunswick: Rutgers University Press, 2016.

Ro'i, Yaacov, and Avi Beker. *Jewish Culture and Identity in the Soviet Union*. New York: New York University Press, 1991.

Rozovsky, Liza. "Missing Communism: The Painter Zoya Cherkassky Once Again Breaks Taboos." *Haaretz*, 24 August 2015. http://www.haaretz.co.il/gallery/art/.premium-1.2713887.

Rubina, Dina. "Beli osel v ozhidanii spasitela." In *Tsiganka*. Moscow: Eksmo, 2007.

– *Here Comes the Messiah!*, translated by Daniel M. Jaffe. Brookline, MA: Zephyr Press, 2000.

– *Vot idot messia!* In *Mif sokrovennii*. Moscow: Eksmo, 2010.

Rubins, Maria. *Redefining Russian Literary Diaspora, 1920–2020*. London: UCL Press, 2021.

– "A Century of Russian Culture(s) 'Abroad': The Unfolding of Literary Geography." In *Global Russian Cultures*, edited by Kevin M.F. Platt, 21–47. Madison: University of Wisconsin Press, 2018.

Rumbaut, Rubén G. "Ages, Life Stages, and Generational Cohorts: Decomposing the Immigrant First and Second Generations in the United States." *The International Migration Review* 38, no. 3 (2004): 1160–205.

Sadowski-Smith, Claudia. *The New Immigrant Whiteness: Race, Neoliberalism, and Post-Soviet Migration to the United States*. New York: New York University Press, 2018.

Safran, William. "Diasporas in Modern Societies: Myths of Homeland and Return." *Diaspora: A Journal of Transnational Studies* 1, no. 1 (1991): 83–99.

– "Language and Nation-Building in Israel: Hebrew and Its Rivals." *Nations and Nationalism* 11, no. 1 (2005): 43–64.

Samoilov, David. "Kogda nibud'." *Chto Est' Istina?* 22, no. 9 (2010). www.istina.russian-albion.com/ru/chto-est-istina—022-sentyabr-2010-g/d-samoylov.

Senderovich, Sasha. "Between Literature and Politics: The Refusenik in the 21st Century." Presentation at *In Search of Common Places: Dialogue with the Past in Translingual Post-Soviet Jewish Literature* at the Association for Slavic, East

European, and Eurasian Studies (ASEEES) Conference, Washington, DC, 17–20 November 2016.

– "In Memoriam: Svetlana Boym." *Tablet*, 7 August 2015. http://www.tabletmag.com/scroll/192730/in-memoriam-svetlana-boym.

– "Scenes of Encounter: The 'Soviet Jew' in Fiction by Russian Jewish Writers in America." *Prooftexts: A Journal of Jewish Literary History* 35, no. 1 (2016): 103–27.

– "Soviet Jews, Re-Imagined: Anglophone Émigré Jewish Writers from the USSR." In *The Edinburgh Companion to Modern Jewish Fiction*, edited by David Brauner and Axel Stähler, 87–100. Edinburgh: Edinburgh University Press, 2015.

– "Soviet Jews, Re-Imagined: Russian American Jewish Writers and the Critique of Self-Orientalization." Presentation at The New Wave of Russian-Jewish (Trans-national and Trans-generic) Cultural Production, Columbia University, New York, NY, 5 December 2014.

– *How the Soviet Jew Was Made*. Cambridge, MA: Harvard University Press, 2022.

Shafranskaya, Eleonora. *Sindrom Golubki*. St Petersburg: Svoyo Izdatelstvo, 2012.

Shapira, Anita. *Israel: A History*. Waltham, MA: Brandeis University Press, 2012.

Sharansky, Natan. *Fear No Evil: A Political Prisoner in the Soviet Union*. New York: Random House, 1988.

– "Introduction." In *Jews of Struggle: The Jewish National Movement in the USSR, 1967–1989*, edited by Rachel Schond, 9–14. Tel Aviv: Beit Hatfutsot, 2007.

Shavit, Uriya. "This Is Culture? An Interview with Alexander Goldshtein." *Haaretz*, 26 February 2002. https://www.haaretz.co.il/misc/1.775461.

Sheen, David. "Israel's True Colors: An Interview with Israeli Artist Zoya Cherkassky." *The Daily Beast*, 9 February 2013. http://www.thedailybeast.com/articles/2013/09/02/israel-s-true-colors-an-interview-with-israeli-artist-zoya-cherkassky.html.

Shenhav, Yehouda. *The Arab Jews: A Postcolonial Reading of Nationalism, Religion, and Ethnicity*. Stanford: Stanford University Press, 2006.

Sherwood, Harriet. "Levinsky Park Migrants Live in Fear after Tel Aviv Race Riot." *The Guardian*. 29 May 2012. https://www.theguardian.com/world/2012/may/29/levinsky-park-migrants-tel-aviv.

Shohat, Ella. "Sephardim in Israel: Zionism from the Standpoint of Its Jewish Victims." *Social Text* 19–20 (1988): 1–35.

Shrayer, Maxim, ed. *An Anthology of Jewish-Russian Literature: Two Centuries of Dual Identity in Prose and Poetry*. Armonk, NY: M.E. Sharpe, 2007.

Shternshis, Anna. *Soviet and Kosher: Jewish Popular Culture in the Soviet Union, 1923–1939*. Bloomington: Indiana University Press, 2006.

Shternshis, Anna. "The Ambivalent Emigres." *Jewish Currents*, 23 May 2022. https://jewishcurrents.org/the-ambivalent-%C3%A9migr%C3%A9s.

Shteyngart, Gary. *Absurdistan*. New York: Random House, 2006.

– *Little Failure*. New York: Random House, 2014.

Shumsky, Dmitry. "Ethnicity and Citizenship in the Perception of Russian Israelis." In *Challenging Ethnic Citizenship: German and Israeli Perspectives on Immigration*, edited by Daniel Levy and Yfaat Weiss, 154–78. New York and Oxford: Berghahn Books, 2002.

– "Mi-historiografiyah le-sociologiyah u-vakhzarah: yaldei zeitl ba-brit ha-mo'atzot u-v'yisra'el akharei ha-eidan ha-soviyeti." In *"Rusim" beisrael: pragmatika shel hatarbut behagira*, edited by Julia Lerner and Rivka Feldhay, 51–65. Jerusalem: Van Leer Institute; Hakibbutz Hameuchad, 2012.

– "Orientalism and Islamophobia among the Russian-Speaking Intelligentsia in Israel." *Theory and Criticism* 26 (spring 2005): 89–117.

Slezkine, Yuri. *The Jewish Century*. Princeton, NJ: Princeton University Press, 2014.

Smola, Klavdia. "Israel and the Concept of Homeland in Russian Jewish Literature after 1970." *Journal of Jewish Identities* 4, no. 1 (2011): 171–90.

Smooha, Sammy. "The Mass Immigrations to Israel: A Comparison of the Failure of the Mizrahi Immigrants of the 1950s with the Success of the Russian Immigrants of the 1990s." *Journal of Israeli History* 27, no. 1 (2008): 1–27.

Sommer, Allison Kaplan. "Basic Law or Basically a Disaster? Israel's Nation-state Law Controversy Explained." *Haaretz*, 6 August 2018. www.haaretz.com/israel-news/.premium-israel-s-nation-state-law-controversy-explained-1.6344237.

Spiegelman, Art. *Maus II: A Survivor's Tale: And Here My Troubles Began.* New York: Pantheon Books, 1991.

Tavger, Pini. *More Than I Deserve*. 2-Team Productions, Tel Aviv, 2021.

Trezzi, Nicola. "New Barbizon Manifesto." *New Barbizon*. Accessed 23 July 2024. http://newbarbizon.wixsite.com/new-barbizon/about.

Tsvetayeva, Marina. *Selected Poems*. London: Penguin Books, 1994.

Tzfadia, Erez, and Haim Yacobi. "Identity, Migration, and the City: Russian Immigrants in Contested Urban Space in Israel." *Urban Geography* 28, no. 5 (2007): 436–55.

Vergara, Jose. *All Future Plunges to the Past: James Joyce in Russian Literature.* Ithaca, NY: Cornell University Press, 2021.

Viorst, Milton. *Zionism: The Birth and Transformation of an Ideal*. New York: Thomas Dunne Books, 2016.

Waysband, Edward. "Alexander Goldstein's 'Tethys or Mediterranean Mail': A Russian-Israeli Levantine Literary Idea Reconsidered." *Ab Imperio* 2018, no. 4 (2018): 253–80.

Winestock, Brett. *Written for the Drawer: Leonid Tsypkin, Uncensored Literature, and Soviet Jewishness*. Madison: University of Wisconsin Press, 2024.

Weiskopf, Mikhail. "Hachoma." *Eretz Acheret* 19, 31 December 2003. https://eretzacheret.org/%D7%94%D7%97%D7%95%D7%9E%D7%94/.

– "Myi byli kak vo sne: Tema iskhoda v literature russkogo Izraila." *Novoe literaturnoe obozrenie* 47 (2001): 241–52.

Yahav, Galia. "African Migrants in Tel Aviv, with a Touch of Matisse." *Haaretz*, 2 June 2015. http://www.haaretz.com/israel-news/culture/leisure/.premium-1.640971.

Yavin, Chaim. *Land of the Settlers*. Documentary film. Israel, 2006.

Yurchak, Aleksei. *Everything Was Forever, Until It Was No More: The Last Soviet Generation*. Princeton, NJ: Princeton University Press, 2005.

Zisserman-Brodsky, Dina. "The 'Jews of Silence' – the 'Jews of Hope' – the 'Jews of Triumph': Revisiting Methodological Approaches to the Study of the Jewish Movement in the USSR." *Nationalities Papers* 33, no. 1 (2005): 119–39.

Zelenina, Galina. "'Our Community Is the Coolest in the World': Chabad and Jewish Nation-Building in Contemporary Russia." *Contemporary Jewry* 38, no. 2 (2018): 249–79.

Index